The
New
Venture
Handbook

The
New
Venture
Handbook

New
and
Updated Edition

Ronald E. Merrill and
Henry D. Sedgwick

American Management Association

New York • Atlanta • Boston • Chicago • Kansas City • San Francisco • Washington, D.C.
Brussels • Toronto • Mexico City

Library of Congress Cataloging-in-Publication Data

Merrill, Ronald E.
      The new venture handbook / Ronald E. Merrill and
      Henry D. Sedgwick.
      New and updated ed.
      xiii, 304 p., 24 cm.
      Includes bibliographical references and index.
      ISBN 0-8144-5087-3 (hardcover)
      ISBN 0-8144-7892-1 (pbk.)
      1. New business enterprises—United States—
      management.   I. Sedgwick, Henry D.   II. Title.
  658.1'1—dc20   92-27383
                                                                CIP

First AMACOM paperback edition 1995.

Printing number

10   9   8   7   6   5   4   3   2   1

We hear much these days about mentors in business. Well, entrepreneurs have mentors too, and we dedicate this book to Ron's:

Art Parthé
Stan Rich
Jerry Schaufeld

and to Harry's:

Ellery Sedgwick, Sr.

CONTENTS

Preface   *ix*

Acknowledgments   *xiii*

One   Preparing Yourself   1

Two   The Business Concept   24

Three   Building a Team   53

Four   Market Research   84

Five   Finding Your Niche   105

Six   The Marketing Function   125

Seven   Sales Tactics   147

Eight   Production   171

Nine   Research and Development   189

Ten   Financial Planning   207

Eleven   Management Systems   228

Twelve   The Business Plan   247

Thirteen   Finding Capital   259

Appendix: Assorted Unavoidable Topics   *287*

Reading List   *297*

Index   *301*

PREFACE

Go ahead.

Yes, you really should go into business for yourself. You're thinking about it, aren't you? Otherwise you wouldn't have picked up this book. Of course, it's also possible that you are already running a small company.

In either case, this book is written for you. Entrepreneurs are the lifeblood of the economy. They're the ones who create new industries and new jobs; who develop new technology and make it useful; who build new neighborhoods and revitalize old ones.

Of course, we may be a bit prejudiced on the subject. We're entrepreneurs ourselves.

MODERN ENTREPRENEURSHIP

This book is intended as a practical guide for entrepreneurs. Since we wrote the first edition in the mid-1980s, important new trends have emerged in the world of small business.

Starting and running a new venture is significantly more complicated. Government regulation has become far more pervasive and intricate. The U.S. economy has evolved into a much more turbulent and confusing environment. And the growth of international trade has created new opportunities and new competitors.

Entrepreneurs have changed too. The classic entrepreneurial types have by no means disappeared, but the ranks of small business today are flooded with new entrants with new motives and interests. Women and minority members are starting businesses in increasing numbers, often attracted by the possibility of bypassing the "glass ceilings" that block their advancement in larger companies. Meanwhile, the decimation of middle management in the "restructuring" of American business has created a new class of involuntary entrepreneurs.

Entrepreneurs seem more than ever to be driven either by a need for autonomy or by a desire to shape their careers around their own interests and life-styles. New ventures in the 1990s are less likely to aim at fast growth and big monetary payoffs. Many founders prefer to pursue excellence in some small niche. Modern technology, especially the microcomputer, has made it practical to run significant businesses with little or no staff. The line between entrepreneurship and self-employment is increasingly blurred; probably 10 million businesses are now being operated out of homes.

In short, entrepreneurship used to be regarded as a way to get rich, or at least make a living. Today, it is more often seen as a route to personal fulfillment.

WHO CAN BENEFIT FROM THIS BOOK

This is a book for entrepreneurs by entrepreneurs. It was developed out of our years of experience as founders, CEOs, directors, investors, and advisers of a wide variety of small ventures. Our aim is to provide you with the management tools you need to plan and control your business.

The subject of entrepreneurship is so vast that nobody could possibly cover it completely in a single volume. Therefore, we've chosen to focus primarily on the start-up process—planning the business and seeing it through its first few years of operation.

We haven't limited the book, however, to any particular type of business. Whether you're planning a new computer company or a neighborhood drugstore, a pantyhose factory or a vegetable pushcart, basic business principles remain the same. Of course many of our specific tips apply only to certain types of business; we think you'll have no trouble deciding which advice is appropriate to your venture.

We've never encountered a truly well-rounded entrepreneur. There are many subjects to master—sales, marketing, production, finance, R&D. Each budding CEO is strong in some areas, ignorant in others. So in each chapter we've tried to start pretty much at the beginning, then go on to a fairly advanced level. We've also provided a reading list for those who want to pursue some topics further.

Finally, this book is not for CEOs only. Ambitious start-ups need complete management teams. If you expect to fill a slot in such a venture, you can benefit by understanding the business as a whole, including the tasks and problems faced by your cofounders.

WHAT WE COVER

Here are a few of the important topics we take up in the following chapters:

- How to analyze your personal needs and develop a venture that will fit them
- The "Three M's" critical to building a successful venture (money isn't one of them)
- Why the bottom of a recession is the ideal time to start a business
- Six different ways to manage a small business
- How to spot a dishonest employee before you hire
- Why a market survey is *the* make-or-break factor in a new venture—and how to do a good one
- How to understand your market and develop a coherent strategic plan
- The "atomic bomb" of marketing—and why you should avoid using it
- A critical step in the sales process often neglected even by experienced salespersons
- A common mistake in production that can paralyze your start-up's output
- How fast growth and high profitability can lead to bankruptcy
- Classic mistakes that can cause immediate rejection of your business plan by investors
- Money sources that most entrepreneurs ignore—and how to approach them effectively

We focus primarily on how to analyze and *understand* the key aspects of a new venture. To help you put these principles into practice, we provide exercises throughout the book. They are designed to guide you in making critical decisions during the start-up process. In addition, many chapters contain checklists—to give you a handle on the many important details that can affect your success.

The text is interspersed with examples that show how real businesses have handled specific problems. Many of these are taken from companies we've worked with in the MIT Enterprise Forum. Others are from our own personal experience as entrepreneurs.

Finally, to each chapter we've appended a "Cautionary Tale." These are short but complete accounts of start-ups in which one of us was involved. They describe a variety of companies: a biotechnology start-up, a company that sold railroad ties, a baby-wipes venture, a Cold Fusion Institute. Some were great successes, others total failures. Each one had something to teach us, and we think you'll also find them interesting and instructive. Each tale has some connection to the chapter, but don't expect a tight correspondence; these are real-world companies, not made-up textbook examples. They are included not to illustrate some particular point but to give you a feel for the dynamics of new ventures.

HAVE FUN!

We love being entrepreneurs, and we love working with entrepreneurs. They are the world's most interesting, lively, and challenging companions. If you have not done so already—join us!

ACKNOWLEDGMENTS

We have benefited greatly from the experience and shrewd advice of our colleagues in the MIT Enterprise Forum in several cities. This is not to say that they should be held responsible for our views. We also wish to thank the many entrepreneurs we have worked with who have been immortalized—sometimes anonymously—in the examples and Cautionary Tales of this work.

The New Venture Handbook

One

PREPARING YOURSELF

The market, like the Lord, helps those who help themselves. But, unlike the Lord, the market does not forgive those who know not what they do.

Warren Buffet, *Berkshire Hathaway 1983 Annual Report*

Starting a business is like taking an exam. When you take an exam, your grade is determined mostly in advance—by how well you did your homework.

When you start a business, the same is true. The day you open your doors, the clock starts running. If you don't know what you're doing, it's too late to learn. If you haven't made the right preparations, it's too late to go back and do it properly. If you don't have a plan, it's too late to figure one out. Problems, decisions, hassles are coming at you from all directions. There's never enough time to handle even the most urgent priorities, let alone go back and make up earlier omissions. And with every minute, your cash is ticking away.

Entrepreneurs are action-oriented people, eager to skip the preliminaries and get down to work. But the pre–start-up phase is too precious to be wasted. The plans you make during this period will determine whether you succeed or fail. What's more, this is your last chance for a calm, objective look at your business. To be able to think and plan at leisure, without having next month's cash flow to worry about, is a luxury you'll appreciate when it's too late. Do your homework in advance—it pays.

This is a recurring theme throughout the book: Success depends

1

on preparation. Study a subject *before* it comes up; know the answer *before* the question is asked; anticipate problems *before* they occur. You must become a fanatic about planning, precisely because you cannot plan everything. All too often, when the assembly line stops, when an employee makes a demand, when a customer has an objection, you'll be caught unprepared and will have to improvise. These unpleasant occasions can't be eliminated entirely, but they can be minimized—by intelligent preparation and planning.

It's not only your success that's at stake but your peace of mind. At first, the image of the crisis manager may seem attractive: solving problems on the spot, making snap decisions, beating deadlines by a hair. But for any but the most neurotic CEO, this sort of thing gets old quickly. Life is much more pleasant when things go pretty much according to plan. Getting clobbered by an unexpected crisis can be stimulating as an occasional exception, but as a daily diet it's no fun at all.

So don't be in too much of a hurry to get started. Are you worried that a market opportunity will disappear if you don't move quickly? That's the kind of motive that has bought a lot of salted gold mines. In a hurry because you've lost your job? Watch out you don't lose your life savings also. Think you don't know enough to make a good plan so you might as well wing it? Going down in flames *is* very instructive, but it's a rather painful way to learn.

Where do you begin? By preparing yourself, the entrepreneur. Are you ready?

ENTREPRENEURSHIP: THE PROS AND CONS

First, the bad news.

▪ *Starting a business is risky.* Most new businesses fail. If yours becomes one of them, you could lose everything you invest; indeed, you may even face personal bankruptcy. What's more, under certain circumstances, you may be liable for offenses committed by your employees or agents. It gets worse. If you raise money from friends or relatives—many of us do—then failure can become *really* unpleasant.

You risk not only money. You may be giving up a good, secure job to follow your dream. It might not be easy to get another if you fail—or even if you succeed. Many large companies make it a point to avoid hiring people with small-business backgrounds because they are too independent. Once you've been a pickle, some say, you can never be a cucumber again.

How risky *is* it, anyway? Even in our statistics-oriented age, nobody really knows the true failure rate for new or small businesses—or even the formation rate. According to Dun and Bradstreet, over 600,000 businesses are started every year in the United States. The real number may be as high as 1.5 million, depending on definitions.

How about failures? D&B figures that about 60,000 businesses fail every year. Based on this, you might think your chances are pretty good. How can we reconcile this with the widely quoted claim that four out of five new ventures fail? It's mainly a matter of how you define failure.

The number cited above covers obvious failures—liquidations. Many businesses fail in a less conspicuous way. Mostly they get sold for a few cents on the dollar to some other business. D&B can't easily separate these cases from healthy business mergers, so they don't get recognized as failures in the statistics.

We recommend that you not take these statistics too seriously. The odds on failing in business are much like the odds on getting killed in an auto accident. If you drive carefully, your chances are much better than if you regularly go for eighty-mile-an-hour joyrides after having a few highballs. In the same way, the well-prepared entrepreneur has a better chance of beating the odds in the D&B Destruction Derby.

- *You will face a lot of hassles.* The larger and more successful your business, the more time you have to spend on taxes, regulations, and similar annoyances.

- *You will be under a lot of stress.* The buck stops with you. You have to make the hard decisions, deal with the unpleasant problems, take the responsibility and the risks. Running a business involves hard work, heavy risks, and high stakes, in an uncertain environment—a classic recipe for psychological and physiological stress.

- *You will be unpopular.* Politicians and the media do pay lip service to the importance of small business, but don't expect any real sympathy. Government regards small business as a tax resource to be consumed. Your big-business competitors see you as a threat to be crushed. To labor unions, you are an exploiter of the workers; to environmentalists, a ravisher of Mother Nature.

Now, the good news.

- *Your own business gives you freedom. You* decide when to arrive at work, when to go home, how to use your time, what projects to work on. No more playing Mother May I with your boss every time you get a good idea. Whether you succeed or fail, it's your decision, not somebody else's, that makes the difference.

- *Entrepreneurship is one of the few practical routes to wealth.* Tax rules make it impossible to accumulate a fortune from savings, no matter how well you are paid. Your best chance to get filthy rich is to own your own company.

- *You have an opportunity for achievement.* As an employee, especially of a big company, you have little opportunity to accomplish anything really substantial. It wouldn't fit in with company policy. It would interfere with existing projects. And if you succeeded, it would arouse envy and resentment among your less talented colleagues, upsetting the smooth operation of your department. If you are determined to reach a demanding goal, you may find the only route involves shaking free of the corporate bureaucracy.

- *Ultimately, the most important advantage, you can be independent.* In becoming an entrepreneur, you select not just a different job but a different personality. You leave behind the limits that restricted your options. As an employee, you could not change your profession because you were not "qualified" by the appropriate educational certificates. Now you can switch into any field that interests you. As a woman or a minority member, your career involved a constant struggle against prejudice. Now you can start at the top and succeed or fail entirely on your own merits. As the mother of young children, or as a handicapped person, you were a nuisance to your employer. Now you can arrange your schedule, location, and working conditions to suit your needs.

THE STATISTICAL ENTREPRENEUR

But are you the type? Some scholars who have conducted statistical studies of entrepreneurs identify an "entrepreneurial type": male in his early thirties; close relative of someone who owned a business; began to make money in childhood—with a paper route, lawn mowing, or something similar; takes moderate risks and sets goals just at the edge of his abilities. Those lacking the "entrepreneurial personality," they conclude, are unlikely to succeed.

We have been entrepreneurs ourselves for a long time, and we've talked to, counseled, and worked with hundreds of other entrepreneurs. We're not so dogmatic about the entrepreneurial personality.

Let a Hundred Flowers Bloom. The truly striking thing about entrepreneurs is their incredible diversity. Consider some of the people we've met in our odysseys through the world of small business:

> A professional artist started doing pictures on sidewalks—at first for fun, as a stunt. But when he got some publicity, store owners began to hire him to decorate the sidewalk in front of their stores as an advertising gimmick. Soon he had a thriving business.
>
> A married couple, both enthusiastic pilots, wanted to go into business together. After several false starts, they found a lucrative niche making training videos for passing pilot exams.
>
> Three engineers fresh out of school got an idea for a new type of electronic test instrument. Soon their company was grossing a million a year.
>
> A woman who sold cosmetics for Clinique got an idea: a line of cosmetics designed for people recovering from plastic surgery. When her employer declined to pursue the opportunity, she started her own company.
>
> A seventy-seven-year-old man, retired from a successful career in the food industry, owned a small cattle-feed station—and incorporated it into a very shrewd scheme for making gasohol during the second energy crisis.

Some have wanted to own their own business ever since they were children. Others were bitten by the bug later in life. Some were convinced they couldn't run a business or that they'd hate it if they did—until they tried. Some started just one business, and some started one after another. Some wanted to get rich, some had an idea they were compelled to pursue, and some were dragged into entrepreneurship by circumstances.

ENTREPRENEURIAL QUALITIES

Perhaps too subtle for statistical studies to measure are the qualities that are helpful to success in entrepreneurship. Here are some character traits that are typical of the real winners we've known.

- *Industrious.* As an employee, you work hard, usually because your boss sees to it. As an entrepreneur, you don't have a boss. But you have a lot of work to accomplish and, at least in the early days, won't be able to hire much, if any, help. It's common for founders to work sixty- or eighty-hour weeks. In fact, it's become a sort of macho display for entrepreneurs to brag about their long working hours, just as big-business executives boast about how many people they've fired. Although there comes a point where working to exhaustion is counter-productive, there's no question that starting a business involves a lot of very hard work. It helps if you're naturally industrious. Those of us who aren't need a lot of willpower.

- *Rugged.* Working long hours without holiday or vacation under heavy stress puts a severe strain on your health. This is one reason businesses tend to be started by fairly young people. Before you begin, take steps to get into shape, and make plans to stay in shape. No matter how busy you get, be sure you take time to eat properly— regular meals, no junk food—and consider taking vitamin supplements. Another priority not to be neglected is exercise. It's essential for your health. Also, a good, vigorous workout helps clear the mind. It gives you a refreshing break from constant worry and improves your decisions.

- *Stubborn.* From the moment you first express your idea for a business, people are going to start trying to talk you out of it. Family, friends, coworkers, boss, investors, cofounders, employees—any or all of these may try to persuade you to abandon or modify your project. The ability to resist such pressures seems to be an invariable characteristic of the true entrepreneur. If you listen to the pessimists, you'll never get started. If you quit when the going gets tough, you'll never succeed. Are you stubborn enough? Of course, there are disadvantages to being *too* stubborn!

- *Objective.* Being willing to face facts—including unpleasant facts—is an invaluable asset. You may see a contradiction here: How is it possible to be both stubborn *and* objective? The successful entrepreneurs we've met combine both traits. On the one hand, they disdain *opinions,* even the opinions of experts. On the other hand, they have the utmost respect for reality, and the self-discipline to change their own opinions when change is required by the *facts.*

- *Independent.* An obvious qualification for the business founder is the ability to go it alone. It's hard for managers from a big-company background to adjust to the small-business environment. They miss the facilities, the staff, and the resources they had come to take for granted. They may also miss the camaraderie and support. It's lonely at the top, even if it's the top of a very small organization.

• *Resilient*. It's a very rare start-up that doesn't have at least one major crisis during its early growth. You're likely to experience some serious setbacks at one point or another. How do you respond to failure? Can you absorb a heavy blow—or several blows in succession—and bounce back?

• *Creative*. Although starting a business doesn't take a genius, it does seem to require a certain amount of creative spark. A purely me-too or imitative business seldom does well in the market. A good business idea ought to have something innovative about it—a new product, an unusual marketing approach, a unique location. Once you've started, you'll have an ongoing need for original solutions to the many large and small problems that will come up.

• *Responsible*. When small-business CEOs talk among themselves, they often use a put-down that reveals the naked essence of the entrepreneurial character. Be it an academic expert, an expensive management consultant, or a big-company executive, one hears the dismissive phrase: "She's never had to meet a payroll." This really sums it up. The entrepreneur is responsible in an absolute sense, like the captain of a naval vessel. Many people will be counting on you—your investors, your cofounders, your employees, your customers. If you run your company aground, there will be nobody else to blame and no excuses will be accepted. Do you enjoy responsibility?

One more thing: Reluctance to take on the tough jobs, or disdain for menial tasks, is not becoming in an entrepreneur. When there's danger, you lead from in front. When there's unpleasantness, you lead from below.

When I was running Reaction Design Corporation, the company had five employees—three chemists, an administrative assistant, and me, the exalted president. No janitor. Guess who got down on his knees to scrub the toilet?

REM

KNOW THYSELF

Few of us possess all these valuable qualities to perfection. Fortunately, it's not necessary to be a paragon of entrepreneurial virtue to achieve success. Determination makes up for many deficiencies. But most critical of all is fitting the nature of your business to your own needs, desires, and aptitudes. In order to start not just a business but the right business for *you*, you must thoroughly understand your own unique character and potentialities.

You may find this self-analysis awkward; most of us haven't given it much thought since we were teenagers. Yet it's worth the trouble if it prevents you from starting the wrong business. A surprising number of troubled start-ups had nothing wrong with them except mismatch. The founder was a good, skilled entrepreneur. The company was sound and well positioned. But somehow it just didn't work out. When we analyze these cases we find that the entrepreneurs failed to think through their values and objectives. They created companies that did not satisfy their personal needs.

> A small design and consulting company developed a breakthrough that could revolutionize the multibillion-dollar integrated-circuit industry. Yet somehow this major innovation was not making progress. On analysis, it turned out that the founder simply didn't *want* to be the rich and famous CEO of a major growth company. He'd started his own company in order to have complete freedom to putter at the lab bench. That is what he enjoyed doing and what he wanted to go on doing. Very sensibly, he decided to pass up his great "opportunity" and stick to what he enjoyed.

In the conventional wisdom, the entrepreneur is a sort of mild psychopath who has an unusual ability to start new ventures—but who needs to transform himself into a "manager" as his company matures. Somehow he must rid himself of the informal, intuitive, risk-taking style that served him well in founding his company and become systematic, analytic, and conservative. Better yet, he should get out of the way and let a "real" manager take over.

This classic model doesn't always apply. For one thing, "managers" and "entrepreneurs" are by no means such disjoint classes. One can be an entrepreneur and still possess the skills of systematic management—indeed the purpose of this book is to help you do just that. This is fortunate, because the kind of massive personality transformation so glibly prescribed is a rather tall order. Few of us are capable of such a psychological metamorphosis, and not many of us desire it.

The traditional approach, like much big-business management theory, deifies the company. The company "demands" certain talents and "requires" a certain type of CEO. But as an entrepreneur you create the company; the company doesn't create you. As we see in

Chapter Two, companies come in all sizes, shapes, and col
to you to design and create a company that "demands" and
what *you* can provide.

Set Business Goals.   Most of us are reluctant to take goal setting
seriously because of past embarrassments—teenage vows, New Year's
resolutions, and so on. Few of us reach the classic entrepreneurial age
of thirty-one without unpleasant memories of unrealized promises
made to ourselves. But it is possible to set goals—even extremely
ambitious goals—and meet them, if three simple principles are applied.

1. *Be guided by experience rather than speculation.* The important questions for goal setting are: What do I want? What am I good
at? The very young must of necessity rely heavily on fantasy and
guesswork in answering these questions; they have little experience to
guide them. But successful adults choose the right goals by drawing on
their memories of the past to suggest their plans for the future. What
have I enjoyed? What have I done well at? These are the productive
questions with predictive answers.

2. *Choose process goals rather than end-point goals.* Objectives
that are defined in momentary terms will yield only momentary satisfaction when achieved. The kind of goal beloved of inspirational
authors—"Be a millionaire by age 40" or "make vice-president next
year"—is precisely the sort that gives only fleeting pleasure, followed
by a nasty letdown, when accomplished. What's more, end-point goals
have a nasty habit of becoming obsolete before you get there. Process
goals, on the other hand, give continuing satisfaction and are less
subject to the whims of fortune. Nor need process goals be vague:
"Spend 50 percent of my time at the bench" or "run a company with
fifty to one hundred employees" are process goals.

3. *Build on strength.* Far too often we choose goals to eliminate
or reduce our weaknesses. Such objectives turn out to be frightfully
difficult to achieve; if attained, somehow they seem to bring disappoint-
ing results. Of course it may be necessary to correct a serious deficiency; but when you set major goals concentrate on identifying your
strong points and make them even stronger. The well-rounded person
is the mediocre person. There are no well-rounded geniuses.

In designing your business, begin by asking: Why do I want to
start this business? What's in it for me? Considering your own needs
as a starting point does not mean you should ignore the needs of the
market—your customers. It only means you should aim your start-up

at a market that you are best fitted to serve, and that you will enjoy serving.

> Here's a very valuable question to ask yourself: Do I *like* the kind of people who will be my customers? If the answer is no, better pick a different business.

We've designed two exercises to help you define your goals. They're not very elaborate; if you'd like to get into a deeper self-analysis, you may want to refer to some of the books listed in the Reading List.

The first exercise deals with the simple but by no means obvious question of day-to-day enjoyment on the job. What could be more ridiculous than quitting a secure, highly paid position because you don't enjoy your work; starting your own business with great effort, expense, and risk; and finding that you're still not having any fun? Unfortunately, this is the fate that befalls many entrepreneurs. So design your company, and your job within the company, to suit *you*. Maximize activities you enjoy and minimize activities you don't enjoy. This is not only for your sake but for the sake of others. You, the founder, have got to be the spark plug of the company; if you're not 100 percent excited and enthusiastic, success is unlikely. Furthermore, tasks you dislike are probably tasks you are not good at anyway.

EXERCISE
Part One: Your Needs and Strengths

A. Write down five activities that you do well, that you are really good at. They need not be job-related; consider hobbies and other pursuits. However, list only activities you have actually done.

1. _____

2. _____

3. _____

4. _____

5. _____

B. List five activities that you truly enjoy. Again, these need not be strictly business-related. Confine yourself to pleasures you have actually experienced.

1. _____

2. _____

3. _____

4. _____

5. _____

C. Now go back over your whole life. Pick out the five happiest occasions of your life—your peak experiences—and list them.

1. _____

2. _____

3. _____

4. _____

5. _____

D. Finally, pick out the five greatest achievements of your life—the accomplishments of which you are most proud—and list them.

1. _____

2. _____

3. _____

4. _____

5. _____

Part Two: Your Perfect Day

This exercise is a controlled fantasy. Imagine that it is five years from today. You have started a company and it is successful. You are the CEO (or whatever position you like). Now take a few sheets of paper and write down a complete account of a typical day; begin with when you get up and end with when you go to bed. Describe all your activities in detail. What are your business appointments? What meetings (if any) do you attend? Who are your business associates—cofounders, employees, customers—and what are they like? What decisions do you make? How much of your time do you spend in the office, in the plant, in the lab, on the sales floor? How much time do you spend with your family? What are your surroundings like—the building, the office, the furniture? What do you wear to work? Where are you located geographically?

As you work on this, refer back frequently to your answers in Part One. Try to minimize speculative "I think I'd enjoy. . . ." possibilities and maximize activities that you know from past experience you do enjoy.

Set Personal Goals. The next exercise concerns self-development. Where do you want your company to take you?

To wealth? But what do you consider wealth? Most entrepreneurs have a financial *motive*, but it may not be as easy as it seems to set valid monetary *goals*. The key question is: What do you want the money *for*? Ayn Rand puts the principle eloquently: "But money is only a tool. It will take you wherever you wish, but it will not replace you as the driver. It will give you the means for the satisfaction of your desires, but it will not provide you with desires."*

Think about what you want to accomplish with money, then decide how much you want and when. These numbers will be important factors in the planning for your business.

As the saying goes, money isn't everything. What about status? As an entrepreneur you may, if you choose, make a quantum jump in status—go in a single day from assistant supervisor to president and CEO. Of course, to make it stick, you've got to succeed! Still, the opportunity to skip the whole seniority ladder and award yourself whatever title, perks, and privileges you think appropriate can be invaluable if you use it shrewdly and cautiously.

There are other social goals to consider. Are you too isolated in your present job? Or, conversely, would you like to work in a less crowded environment? How do you like to interact with coworkers? If you have your own ideas of what a workplace should be like, you can now implement them.

What about your career progress? What qualifications would you like to acquire or improve? As an entrepreneur, you are free of the arbitrary restrictions placed upon employees that interfere with the development of new skills. In the corporate climate, for instance, a scientist may be confined to the R&D ghetto, automatically ruled out of consideration for any significant role in management. You can bypass these obstructions by starting your own company and unilater-

---

*Atlas Shrugged (New York: Random House, 1957), p. 411.

ally redefining your career. If you later choose to return to the labor pool, you can usually make your new definition stick.

We've considered the goals you're setting for yourself; what about the goals you set for your company? It's a separate but not unrelated question. Your company is a means to accomplish your goals for achievement. It's been said, and truly, that success depends less on what you choose to do than on choosing to do what you do extremely well. In founding Apple Computer, Jobs and Wozniak aimed not at entry into the Fortune 500 but at "bringing computers to the masses." By focusing on the latter, they accomplished the former. Perfecting a new technology or a new product, putting out merchandise of superb quality, developing a company that really cares about its customers— it's goals of this type that make success stories.

EXERCISE
Your Personal Goals

A. *Financial Goals:* How much money do you want to make out of your business? This generally depends on what you want the money for.

☐ Money as score-keeping: "I want to pile up as many chips as possible, go for billionaire status."

☐ Money for luxury: "I want to be able to buy the good things in life without having to worry about the budget."

☐ Money as independence: "I want my drop dead money. When I sell the company and cash in my chips I want enough to ensure I'll never need to ask for a job or worry about pleasing a boss again."

☐ Money as a living: "I'm not that concerned about building a big estate; I just want my company to provide me with a living and support me in the style to which I've become accustomed—or maybe a little better."

☐ To hell with money: "I'm pursuing life-style or idealistic goals; all I need is a subsistence income."

Conclusion: After I get the company on its feet, I want to draw an income of $_____ per year. By the time I retire, or sell the company, I want to end up with a net worth of $_____.

B. *Intangible Goals:* What social or intangible goals are important to you?

☐ High status—to be deferred to and treated with respect
☐ Popularity—to be liked by colleagues and employees
☐ Independence—to be able to make my own decisions
☐ Fame
☐ Benevolence—to be a benefactor of society or the unfortunate
☐ Other (specify) _____

C. *Career Goals:* What skills would you like to develop or improve?

1. _____
2. _____
3. _____

Assume for the moment that your business is unsuccessful and you have to return to the job market. List three items you would like to be able to add to your resumé from your entrepreneurial experience.

1. _____
2. _____
3. _____

D. *Company Goals:* What do you want your company to achieve? To become a large organization? To revolutionize your industry? To be the perfect place for its employees to work? To solve a major social problem? To provide financial security for your family? To introduce a major technological innovation? Perhaps you want several things; but see if you can capture the essence briefly. Can you define the purpose of your company in twenty-five words or less?

_____
_____
_____
_____

CHOOSE A COMPANY THAT FITS

Once you've defined your goals and needs, you're in a position to decide on some of the characteristics of your company.

How big should it be? Do you want its growth to level off at some optimum size? If so, what size? Why? And how will you maintain those limits?

> The owners of Zabar's, the famous New York delicatessen, made a conscious decision to limit its size by the simple expedient of restricting it to one location—and requiring that a family member taste-test every item sold.

Perhaps you want your company to grow indefinitely. If so, will you stick with it, no matter how large it becomes? Or will you step aside at some point and turn it over to new management? How fast do you want your company to grow? It's nice to get rich quickly, but very fast growth presents difficult management problems as well as high risks.

Where do you want to be within the company? What job would you like, and what duties should you perform? No rule says you must be CEO, and you might be happier in a different slot.

In planning Reaction Design, my original intent was to be the R&D vice-president. A friend was set as marketing VP, and we sought a third co-founder to be CEO. After interviewing several candidates we gave up; it was hard to find the right person, and several of our investors felt I should be the CEO since the project was my idea. It turned out that I was neither well-suited nor happy in the job. I, the company, and the investors would have been better off if we'd stuck to the original plan.

REM

What industry do you want to enter? How should you structure your company? What sort of operating style should it have? Where should it be located? These and many other questions cannot be rationally answered without taking into account your personal goals.

COMMITMENT

Knowing what you want—your personal objectives—is crucial because your business is going to require your *commitment.*

Time.   Make a realistic estimate of the amount of time you can devote to your new venture. The operative word here is "realistic." Many entrepreneurs try to spend every waking moment on their companies; some even succeed in doing so. The companies seldom benefit. The prime responsibility of the CEO is to guide the company and give it a coherent strategy. This requires a lot of careful thought and an ability to see the whole company in context; neither is easy for a founder who is wrapped up in details eighty hours a week.

In the first flush of enthusiasm, you may feel ready to slay dragons and nonchalantly sign up for a workweek far longer than any you've experienced in the past. It can turn out to be more difficult than you expect to carry out such a commitment. This also applies, incidentally, to part-time businesses; you may not have as much spare time as you think. Consider too that it is one thing to work a ninety-hour week once, or even for a couple of months; it's another thing to keep it up for years.

Effort.   Related but not identical is the question of how much effort you can sustain. You must consider your physical and mental stamina. Though you have sixty hours per week available for work, there still may be limits on how productive you can make that time. You cannot do push-ups continuously for sixty hours, and neither can you do high-quality creative thinking. These limitations must be taken into account.

Money.   How much money can you commit? Again, be realistic. If you risk an amount that will devastate you if the company fails, you are not going to have a happy time—and can you make good business decisions under this kind of stress?

An important quality for the successful entrepreneur is the ability to live with a very low overhead. I have seen people start businesses at a time when they were supporting a summer house, a boat, and other expensive toys that their salary from the new company couldn't possibly justify. There also may come a time when little or no salary can be taken. If you have a low fixed household overhead, whatever you want in variable expenses is fine; they can be cut back when necessary. But a heavy load of fixed commitments is very dangerous.

When I became involved with Trig-A-Tape, I think I had a salary of $8,000 a year (this was in 1957). I was married and my wife worked, so we got along all right. But when the company got into difficulty and was about to fail, I stopped taking a salary. Happily, we had enough coming in from our meager investments and my wife's salary to ride out this period.

There is something about personal financial control—a control of one's appetite, a willingness to defer satisfactions—that spills over into the way one runs an enterprise. If you don't have money, you tend to save better than if you do.

HDS

What About Your Family? A question by no means minor is: Where does your family stand on this? If you're alone in the world, there's probably no problem. Otherwise, you'd better be careful.

To put it bluntly, the commitments you make to your company come at the expense of your family. Time spent on your start-up is unavailable for your domestic obligations. Effort commitment is similar; you are using up energy that would otherwise be used to maintain your marital relationship or play with your children. The money you invest is not available for buying a new car or filling other familial needs. Don't kid yourself on this issue, and don't try to kid your family.

You need to be sure that they understand what's involved and are sincerely behind you. This is extremely difficult in most cases. Often a loyal wife, though scared to death of the financial risk, pretends to favor her husband's ambitions. Or a husband, embarrassed to admit his old-fashioned notions, conceals his disapproval of his wife's project. Children, afraid to anger their parents, may hide their resentment at being deprived of attention.

The best approach is negotiative. Tell them what you want to do and why. Be very frank about the consequences and how everybody will be affected. Ask for their support explicitly. Be ready to make some deals. Ask members of the family what you can do to help them through the coming rough time. Reassure them. Mother may want your commitment to maintain certain financial reserves, Junior your promise to attend his Little League games. Make the necessary promises— and keep them. It is a good policy to regard appointments with your family as having the same status as business appointments. You wouldn't think of calling a business associate and saying, "Mr. Jones, I'm going to skip our meeting this afternoon because Mr. Smith wants to see me and he's more important than you are." You keep your business commitments even if they're inconvenient—out of courtesy. Why not extend the same courtesy to your family?

A *tip:* If members of your family are willing to pitch in, even occasionally, in working on your start-up, it will make them much more supportive. It gives them a more personal stake in your success, makes them feel like participants rather than spectators, and helps them understand what you're going through. It also helps if you give them credit for their support.

EXERCISE
Your Commitment

A. On a long-term basis, how much time can you spend on your business *without strain?*
Hours/week: _____

B. During critical periods or emergencies, how much time could you spend for a few weeks flat out?
Hours/week: _____

C. How much money can you spare for the expenses involved in the pre–start-up phase of your business?
Dollars per month: _____

D. How much money can you invest at start-up?
Initial dollar amount: _____

E. How long can you stand to go without any vacation?
Years: _____

THE GREAT TRANSITION

There are three ways to enter the entrepreneurial pool. You can dive in; you can ease in an inch at a time; or you can be thrown in.

The most straightforward approach is to quit your job and work on your start-up full time. Few businesses can turn cash from day one, so you have to bridge the gap between your last paycheck and the first income from the business. It can be a long period—longer than you expect—and a difficult and nervous time. On the other hand, you can work without distraction and your venture will benefit from having your full attention.

Gradual entry has great advantages. Developing your business in your spare time gives you a chance to test the market before you commit yourself. Ideally, you develop cash flow from the business before abandoning your paycheck. On the other hand, your employer will not be pleased if word of your activities reaches her ears. If you are going into competition with your old company, there are serious legal pitfalls; in this case we strongly recommend you *not* use the gradual entry strategy.

Most difficult is the situation of the involuntary entrepreneur. You're out on the streets, stunned, feeling helpless, and possibly broke or looking at ruination. What do you do now?

Advice for the Involuntary Entrepreneur.

Take sharp measures to cut expenses *immediately;* you can always spend money later if things work out better than expected. Then calculate your net loss of cash on a monthly basis; that is your personal "burn rate"—a very important number. Divide it into your total liquid assets (and you should liquidate anything you don't absolutely need, at once), and you know how long you have before total disaster strikes. If you have taken the advice to cut expenses to the bone immediately, you may find that the period thus calculated is surprisingly and gratifyingly long.

Then sit down and list every business opportunity you can think of. Get friends and family to help you brainstorm. Pick the most promising ideas and start pursuing them. For other entrepreneurial types we would definitely not recommend this sort of shotgun approach. They should narrow their options and concentrate on one idea. But as an involuntary entrepreneur, you lack many of the advantages of the prepared company founder. You must be an opportunist, willing to try a lot of things. Of course you should try to make every experiment at least a little bit profitable. If you can pick up a few bucks here and there it will decrease your burn rate and give you more time.

With luck—and, we regret to say, there is luck involved—something will click. You'll start to get repeat business as word gets around. Better yet you go out and spread the word yourself. Remember, the one thing you have is your personal time. You can spend all day as a walking advertisement for yourself. You can sit in someone's office and make a polite pest of yourself till she gives you a contract.

Enhance your education by picking the brains of the experts. Call up somebody who knows the business you're thinking of entering (but isn't a competitor), tell him you're planning a venture and would like some advice and would he let you buy him lunch? People love to give advice, and a forty-dollar lunch will often get you several hundred dollars worth of free consulting. He may even grab the lunch check, or surprise you with an unexpected job offer.

As soon as you have something that produces positive cash flow and seems to have an ongoing market, narrow down your operations and try to develop it. Get out there and sell hard. The day will come when your burn rate drops to zero and you're holding your own. You're over the hump.

Making the Break. Making the break with your current employer can be the touchiest part of starting your own company. If you're going into competition with your employer, or using technology you learned on the job, you may face some legal problems. Many technical types are dismayed to find that their ideas really are owned by the company that paid to develop them. See your lawyer at an early stage. If there's the slightest possibility of being sued, have a contingency plan ready. Don't let yourself be taken by surprise.

Try to avoid activities that are apt to draw a violent reaction from your employer. Soliciting its customers for your new business while still employed is a definite no-no, for instance. Even after you depart, raiding—or even possessing—its customer list can get you into trouble. If a customer approaches you with a new opportunity, and in response you decide to start a business without telling your employer, you're playing with fire. Recruiting staff from your coworkers, especially while you're still working there, is another good ticket to the courtroom.

If you're dissatisfied with your present job you probably look forward to the opportunity to tell off your boss. Don't do it. Just don't do it. You're going to have enough troubles, and you don't need any enemies. When you're rich and powerful you can tell the world how terrible your boss was and be listened to. But by that time you probably will be more inclined to thank him for giving you the impetus to leave the nest.

My own entry into entrepreneurship was more or less involuntary. I started as an executive trainee at the Aluminum Company of Canada. The idea was to put me on the fast track to upper management. But after eight years I was still on a siding. And I frankly admit it was my own fault. I was—and am—a person who detests taking orders. I wanted to do things my way, and AlCan had a different idea of the order of things.

Finally my boss called me in for a little talk. He said, "Harry, you are impossible. I suggest you do one of two things. Either make a complete change in your attitude starting, say, tomorrow; or look for a position elsewhere, in which case you are welcome to take your time. You understand, by the way, that this conversation never occurred."

He did me a real favor. A few weeks later I left AlCan to become General Manager of a start-up called Trig-A-Tape, which (after some hair-raising vicissitudes) turned out very successful. Since then I've started or built several other businesses. I have been much happier—and wealthier—than I could ever have been had I stayed with AlCan.

HDS

CHECKLIST
Preparing Yourself

☐ Have you evaluated your capabilities as a prospective entrepreneur?

☐ If you were hiring someone else to be CEO of your business, would you hire someone with your resumé?

☐ Are you willing to do any task, however menial, to make your business a success?

☐ Do you know what you want from life?

☐ Do you know what tasks you are good at?

☐ Have you set goals based on your experience rather than on fantasy?

☐ Are your goals process goals?

☐ Have you chosen goals that aim to improve your strengths, rather than eliminate your weaknesses?

☐ Is your business aimed at some specific achievement, rather than just making money "somehow"?

☐ Have you developed a new family budget, taking into account the financial commitments you are making to your company?

☐ Have you got the sincere backing of your family in entering this venture?

☐ Have you decided when and how to tell your boss you are leaving?

☐ Have you checked out all potential legal problems with your former employer and developed plans to deal with them?

☐ Have you asked your spouse or someone else who knows you well to confirm your concept of your personal character?

☐ Have you asked some objective source to evaluate the basis of your business and your qualifications to run it?

CAUTIONARY TALE
Foto Finished

One of my early ventures was a company called FOTO COMP INC. The idea was to capitalize on phototypesetting technology by offering a high-technology typesetting service to magazine and book publishers in the New York area. For centuries, type had been set by hand and by machines called Linotypes, using metal matrixes or dies and hot lead—a very primitive and cumbersome process even by the standards of the time. The phototypesetting technique had appeared in the early 1950s but somehow did not really take off. There was a manufacturer of these devices that was very interested in getting some of its equipment out into a service-bureau environment so that publishers could become familiar with the machinery and its performance. I was approached by a friend of mine who had put together a business plan to found a company to operate service bureaus with this equipment.

I had just come off an overnight and very substantial success with my first venture. I was flushed with my ability to do things and eager to get going on another one. I had no particular idea how to find another deal, and this one came along and fell into my lap. My first mistake was to look upon it as my only opportunity, instead of exploring a number of alternatives. I didn't look for other deals but grabbed at this one and worked myself into a lather of enthusiasm, meeting constantly—and solely—with other people who were also enthusiastic. There was a great deal of optimism on the part of a technical group at Time, Inc., which had developed methods of using the equipment for setting type for the Time Book Division. Also enthusiastic, of course, was the company that manufactured the phototypesetting equipment. By that time there were also a number of hangers-on who had joined the chorus.

I plunged ahead into the venture. I got financing from members of the board of directors of the manufacturer (acting as individuals) and some of their friends. Two of the technical people from Time came on as partners. We set up shop and got started. Almost immediately we ran into some problems that I simply had not examined in the initial plan.

First, were there enough trained people to operate this equipment—and, if not, how long was it going to take to train neophytes in the use of it? We found that the answers were "no" and "much too long." This issue was completely overlooked in the business plan, and it turned out to be a major problem because nobody in the typesetting community or indeed in any other existing labor force was familiar with the equipment. The time it took to train people was far, far greater than we had anticipated. I had made the mistake of relying on the technicians from Time, Inc., who had a way of answering specific questions with vague generalities.

A second problem also emerged early. The publishers I had interviewed prior to going into this venture—as to whether they would use this service—all said, "Yes, yes, come to us when you're set up, and we'll give you work." Since I was full of ardor and commitment to the venture already, I took this to mean, "Of course we'll give you work, all you can possibly handle, and you will make a fortune on us." What they were really saying—if I had been willing to listen carefully and objectively—was: "We are curious about this new technology. We might or might not at some point in time, one week or three years after you open, give you a small job to test your ability and the equipment's performance."

Another truly major mistake was my choice of partners. These two technicians who had developed the system for Time, Inc., had done well for Time. The system worked very nicely for Time in the dedicated facility where Time produced type for its book series. What I neglected to explore was the cost of its operation.

For Time and its editors, the important thing was to get these books produced as rapidly as possible. Time had an integrated operation: Its people wrote the books, typeset the books, printed the books, and sold the books. This made it possible for Time to absorb a significantly higher cost for typesetting than a conventional publisher could. For Time, the purpose of this facility was to ease the work of its editors, not to reduce its typesetting costs. That little fact blew by me completely. It wasn't until we got heavily into our own operation and the majority of the capital had been spent in buying equipment and setting up shop and training people that I realized that there was a major question: Could we even compete on cost with the existing, though time-worn, technology?

Of course, by the time I realized all this it was too late. We were out of capital, we were butchering what jobs the publishers would give us, we were late, jobs were done badly, type was set incorrectly. You have no idea how upset magazine publishers get when they receive typeset pages three days after the press is supposed to roll. Holding a press can cost them thousands of dollars a day.

The failure on my part to carefully scrutinize this venture before going into it cost me a great deal of money, time, pain, and embarrassment. I think if I had really *looked* at this project in the first place, I wouldn't have gone into it. There was just too much risk, and we, as a group, were simply too inexperienced in this particular activity.

Unfortunately, at that time I had not developed sufficient objectivity. I had to believe that this company was going to work. I was totally unable to accept any negative thoughts about it, so I didn't seek to find anybody who had another point of view—who would say that the market wasn't ready for this kind of service. I consulted only prejudiced parties—people like my partners from Time, Inc., and the directors of the manufacturer, who had a vested interest in being optimistic and pooh-poohing any caveats. I would pose all my questions in such a way as to elicit a positive response. In spite of all this, occasionally I would get a warning. I would be upset about it for a while and then I would just forget it.

If I'd known then what I know now, I would have proceeded very differently. Instead of jumping on the first opportunity that came along and hurrying into the operation, I would sit down and think about my objectives. What, at that stage of my career, was I ready for? What was the logical next step? After thinking over these and some related questions, I could have examined a whole range of alternative ventures and picked one that would have had much better chances of success.

HDS

Two

THE BUSINESS CONCEPT

The vitality of thought is in adventure. Ideas won't keep. *Something must be done about them.*

Alfred North Whitehead, *Dialogues*

Entrepreneurs come at us from all directions. Both of us are frequently approached by venture founders and prospective founders looking for advice or aid. Some already have their idea: "I've got this widget that turns lead into gold. I've finished the prototype and applied for the patent; how do I market it?" Others know that they want to do *something,* but they don't know what: "I hate my job and I want to start my own company. I've got $50,000 saved up; do you have any ideas for what I should do?" Still others are somewhere in between. Broadly speaking, we encounter three types of prospective entrepreneur: idea-driven, idea-given, and idea-seeking.

NEW VENTURE TYPES

Following are three ways in which people embark upon new ventures. All involve an idea.

Idea-Driven Ventures. Sometimes the idea comes first. You get this really neat-o concept for a business, Feline Nightwear, Inc. Your family and friends all think it's the cat's pajamas. The more you think

24

about it, the more you like it, the more you are convinced that it's a winner. You are an idea-*driven* entrepreneur.

Of course the classic idea-driven entrepreneur is the inventor. The invention, usually a new product, is the idea of the business. The lone inventor is the stuff of American legend. Reports of his death are somewhat premature. It's true that basement-workshop types seldom succeed these days—but they never did. The great inventors of the past century operated much as modern ones do—get an idea while working for a big company, go off on your own and get investors to finance a lab for you.

Idea-Given Ventures. The second basic type of venture is what we call the idea-*given* venture—the business that arises simply from what you have or what you know how to do. There have always been employees with valuable skills—from machinists to typists—who go off on their own. Today, we often see service company start-ups in which the founders sell skills they once practiced as in-house staff functions at big companies.

The small-craft business generally arises in the same way. You suddenly realize that your hobby or skill could be made into a profit center.

> Artist Molly Legend was fascinated by Egyptian hiero-
> glyphics and often incorporated them into her paintings.
> Her husband stimulated her to find out their meaning.
> The couple built a business by creating "personal" art.
> Clients request paintings with their names, professions,
> or messages written in hieroglyphics, paying prices from
> forty-five dollars to several thousand dollars.

When the media talk about the entrepreneurial economy they seldom refer to professional firms: lawyers, doctors, dentists, accountants, and so on. The traditional "practice" is, however, very definitely a business, and these "industries" are becoming quite competitive. Many professionals complete their long and expensive training without realizing that they need to master business management skills if they hope to succeed as independents. Having one or two fresh ideas doesn't hurt either.

> One M.D. made a pile of money by cashing in on a simple
> observation: Kennedy Airport is a big place. When you

consider how many people work there, it's like a small city—and then there are the passengers. Lots of people, which means lots of medical emergencies every day— accidents, heart attacks, apoplectic fits when a plane is late. He figured having a clinic right at the airport would be convenient, and he was right.

Another type of idea-given business is what its practitioners fondly refer to as "the consulting racket." In recent years massive layoffs of managers and professionals have flooded the market with consultants. To survive you must emphasize marketing more than your personal expertise. Plan on spending at least half your time selling. So when you set your hourly rates, set them to cover your personal income needs, expenses and overhead, and a safety margin—on the assumption that you will "work" two days a week and sell on the other three.

A simple rule of thumb is to take your annual salary in thousands of dollars, drop three zeroes, and use that as a minimum figure for your basic hourly rate. This is based on the fact that there are 2,000 working hours in a year.

A strong growth area during the last decade has been business services—from putting out company newsletters to interior decoration of offices to database services. You go into the desktop publishing business simply because putting out a newsletter is what you know how to do; that's your marketable skill.

Big companies are slimming down. They realize that high big-company overhead makes it too expensive to do most staff functions in-house; they can get it cheaper outside. Government regulations and union pressure make it very onerous to hire employees; companies can minimize hassles by minimizing employment, another strong argument for jobbing out staff functions. And, in today's competitive and fast-changing economy, even big companies need to have more mobility. If they decide they no longer need a certain function, laying off or reassigning the people involved is a nuisance; on the other hand, it's easy to simply stop buying the service from outside.

Important to any idea-given business is a willingness to sell. Most idea-given entrepreneurs are knowledge workers who are attracted to their professions, among other reasons, because they don't have to dirty their hands with selling. Once you go out on your own, you have to change your attitude. There is danger, particularly if your former employer provides you with a nice piece of business to start out, that you will neglect the need to go out and *peddle your wares*. You must diversify your customer base, and quickly.

Idea-Seeking Ventures.

Finally, there are idea-*seeking* ventures. When there's no light bulb flashing over your head, when your path is not determined by your professional training, you need to come up with an idea for your venture. You must go out and systematically look for opportunities. How? There are two basic approaches: the "me" approach and the "market" approach.

The "Me" Approach.

The "me" approach starts with your talents. Sit down and list everything you can do or want to do with your time. Be comprehensive. Then go down the list and think about economic opportunities for each. Would anybody *pay* you to do this? Don't be afraid to write down a far-out idea. Just generate possibilities; don't rule anything out as yet. When you're done, do *not* go down the list and get rid of the ridiculous ideas. Instead, go out the door and investigate all your ideas, including the ridiculous ones.

Try playing some games, incidentally. See if you can come up with something really crazy.

Here's an example of how it might be done. Years ago I was running a venture that had expertise in the chemical technology of making pheromones. A pheromone is a perfume produced by a female bug so the male can find her (bugs can't see very well at long distances). Pheromones have exciting possibilities in pest control. You can use them to bait traps, catching the males. Or you can flood the entire area, so that *everything* smells like a female and the males can't find the real females to mate with. Either way, no baby bugs next year. The nice thing is that pheromones are safe and nontoxic (most are chemically similar to things like coconut oil or turpentine), unlike traditional pesticides. They are also highly selective; each species has its own, so you can get rid of boll weevils without murdering useful honeybees. The disadvantage is that most pheromones are expensive to make.

At this time, there was fervent interest in consumer applications of pheromones, partly because farmers were proving more conservative about adopting them than expected. On the East Coast, gypsy moth and Japanese beetle traps were being sold.

Unfortunately, the bottom dropped out of the consumer market after a couple of years. The problem, in hindsight, was obvious: Pheromones work on the moths, not on the caterpillars. If the disgusting caterpillars are eating your trees and crawling all over your house, pets, and kids *right now,* there is limited consolation in knowing that your traps will take the moths months later.

Now what? I reasoned like this. Problem: Pheromones attract butterflies and moths, not caterpillars, which are what we want to trap. Solution: Can we find people who *want* butterflies and moths? How about a pheromone kit for gardeners? "Spray this around your garden and you'll have beautiful butterflies around all summer!" (You may also be three inches deep in caterpillars next year, but we needn't mention that.) Or how about kits for collectors and science teachers?

Unfortunately, the company went broke before I could test this idea. Anybody who would like to try it is welcome to it.

REM

The "Market" Approach. The second approach to finding ideas is the "market" approach. Select some segment of the population (retail or industrial) that has money and is not too averse to spending it. Then investigate it thoroughly. What do they buy now? What do they want that they can't get? What frustrates them? What do they *need?* Go out and talk to them in an open-ended manner. Surprisingly often, they'll tell you very explicitly exactly what they would like to be able to buy.

SOME MARKET OPPORTUNITIES

So you want some hints. Okay, here are six broad areas where we expect market opportunities to develop or expand.

1. *Consumer convenience.* Allegedly we now live in a "service economy." Ironically, service is the one thing you can hardly get these days. Everywhere you go—whether it's to a gas station, a grocery store, or a restaurant—it's "self-service," that is, no service. And it couldn't have come at a worse time for the consumer. In our fast-paced age, the average middle-class American has a full day, a full evening, a full weekend, and an ever-lengthening "to-do" list. And retailers expect us to do all the work ourselves.

For the modern American consumer, "time" is a four-letter word.

Selling convenience and service to affluent or even not-so-affluent consumers can pay off for you. Consider the possibilities. For instance, try selling things to people who are trapped, waiting in line.

Note that "service" is not synonymous with "friendliness." It certainly doesn't hurt for a business to have pleasant relations with its customers—but that isn't service. Service is satisfying the customer's needs, promptly and effectively.

2. *Illiteracy.* About thirty-five years ago American schools abandoned the traditional phonics method of teaching reading and adopted "look-say." As a result, most Americans under forty or so have considerable difficulty with reading. A long memo is a daunting challenge; a "serious" novel, an embarrassing impossibility. The cultural dominance of television may be due not so much to its inherent attractions as to the fact that it is an alternative to (horrors!) reading. Yet—make no mistake—these people are not stupid. Dealing with the printed word may be an unpleasant ordeal, but they have intelligence and widespread interests. You can make money by making it possible for them to indulge their interests without reading. Already there is a substantial and growing market for audio- and videotapes on all sorts of subjects that once appeared only in books.

3. *End of the Advertising Age.* As customers become increasingly sophisticated—not to say jaded—traditional advertising methods lose their effectiveness and new tricks must constantly be invented. The trend indicates the end of advertising as we know it. People simply don't have time to look at ads any more. If a business wishes to get its message to customers, it must do so while providing a real value. The advertising message must be slipped into something that entertains or informs the customer. If you can develop a way to combine advertising matter with useful reference information, or with entertainment, you have the germ of a business concept. Remember that as the economy becomes more competitive, companies require intensive advertising and promotion. If you can find a way to get businesses' messages across to the customer in sugar-coated form, you've got something.

4. *By-products of quality.* The traditional repair business seems to be disappearing from the U.S. economy. The cost of mass-produced goods has dropped, whereas the cost of skilled repair technicians has risen. So nowadays, when an appliance goes on the blink, we often don't get it fixed; it's more cost effective to throw it away and buy a new one. But the economics of repair might change if the repair process were reorganized, as it has been in the auto parts industry. Imagine picking up a television set for the cost of hauling it away, replacing a burned-out resistor, and selling it—perhaps for export to the Third World. What about applying computer-aided diagnostics? Could the repair process be automated? How about introducing economies of scale? Already profitable businesses exist that salvage gold and other valuable materials from scrapped computers. What other opportunities can you think of?

5. *International competition.* American businesses have been slow to understand that we are now part of a global economy. This "sea change" has created dangers—but also opportunities. There are significant markets for all sorts of American goods and services overseas. Because U.S. business traditionally is not export-oriented, many opportunities are simply ignored. The legal and financial hassles involved in an export business are substantial—but so are the profit possibilities.

6. *Health paranoia.* As Americans become more affluent, life becomes very sweet. Disease, death, getting dirty, bad odors, and other unpleasant occurrences now are regarded not as unavoidable parts of human existence but as intolerable outrages. People wish to live in a totally risk-free environment. Philosophers may argue over the validity of this attitude; entrepreneurs exploit it. New wrinkles in health care continue to power a growth industry. Interest in vitamins and nutrition shows no signs of subsiding, though new fads of course come and go. Safety is an increasingly effective selling point for all sorts of products, new and traditional. Many Americans live in abject terror of AIDS, toxic chemicals, and radioactivity and will pay for protection.

BUYING A BUSINESS

Although our primary focus is on the business start-up, creating a new venture from scratch is not the only path to entrepreneurship. One obvious alternative is to buy an existing business. You may also wish to consider the franchising route, which is a sort of hybrid between starting and buying a business. We talk about the franchise option in the next section.

A few tips on how to buy a business follow. But first, we'd like to emphasize an extremely important principle: *Don't buy any business unless you really, truly, like it.*

It's funny. Most people, when applying for a job, are very interested in whether they will like working for the company—even when they have to take it, like it or not. Buying a business is a far more serious decision than accepting a job offer. You have to put up your own money—often a very large sum—and the risks and responsibilities are much greater. Yet unlike job applicants, people who buy businesses often fail to investigate what is involved in running them, and don't think about whether they will really enjoy it.

Probably your odds of success and enjoyment are best if you are buying a business you are already running. Suppose your employer wants to spin off your division or department. You are a logical buyer. You know how to run it, and presumably you like doing so.

Next best is buying a company in an industry in which you are experienced. You won't be familiar with the specifics of the company, but at least you know the ropes.

Most dangerous is buying a company the operations of which you do not understand. Every industry has its idiosyncracies. Many modern middle managers suffer from the delusion that they can manage anything. This "generic-manager" fallacy can get you into big trouble. And note that this applies even to what seem to be very "simple" businesses. The attitude that "anybody can run a dry cleaner" can lead to a nasty shock. Maybe anybody can run one, but not everybody can make a success of it.

Whatever kind of business you buy, see if you can keep, at least for the first year or two, the key people in its management—the ones who know where the bodies are buried. No matter what is on the balance sheet, the real value of a business is in its people, and if you don't retain the important personnel your new purchase may depreciate to nothing very quickly.

Of course, finding a business to buy, like finding an idea, is not always easy. If you are looking in your own industry, you probably have some good ideas about the prospects. Otherwise, you'll have to rely on networking. Lawyers, accountants, consultants, and bankers are often aware of businesses that are for sale. Another good source is salespeople; they visit a lot of companies and often have a very shrewd idea of their status.

What about business brokers? Certainly. They are most useful if you want to find a routine retail business—a bar or a deli or a small boutique. But if you want to buy a computer manufacturer, better plan on doing some legwork yourself.

Once you find an enticing business you need to negotiate the sale. Keep in mind that the asking price will be very inflated. As in any sale, the seller wants to get the maximum possible. But if you go in thinking that this is merely a bargaining position, you may be surprised. The owner (especially if he's the founder) commonly has a strong emotional attachment to the business and sincerely believes it is much more valuable than it really is.

I was once involved in an attempt to purchase a Massachusetts company that sold knickknacks (more politely referred to as "Americana") by mail order. At that time they'd been losing about $125,000 a year for the past four years. They had a terrible inventory problem; the founder bought things he liked, which often were not what the customers liked, so the warehouse was full of redundant

goods. It looked like a nice turnaround opportunity—pick the company up cheap, clear out the useless inventory, start listening to customers, and shape up the business. Unfortunately, the owner was asking $5 million—a price totally out of reason—and wouldn't budge. The purchase fell through. The company went into bankruptcy recently.

HDS

There's a rule in business buying and selling: "The future belongs to the buyer." Be sure you evaluate the company's price based on what it is worth right now. Sellers typically say (and often sincerely believe) that the business will take off soon and become much more valuable. Don't let your enthusiasm run away with you. Remember you're buying the acorn, not the oak, and pay accordingly.

Be sure you look at the books very carefully. Stock market analysts go mad trying to interpret the financial statements of big, public companies. The statements of small, private companies are a hundred times worse. Nobody audits them carefully, so the accounting is often incredibly sloppy. The owner may have three sets of books— one to show the IRS, one to show you, and one for himself. Generally it is wise to call in a professional accountant (yours, not his!) and have the books "reconstructed."

Let's say you're considering buying Ed's Erotic Manuscript Shoppe and the books (financial, that is) are in a mess. You know sales are $2 million, but that's about it. The statements put out by Joe Squink, CPA, show that essentially the shop is breaking even. However, Squink has never done an audit; he's just compiled the statements from data provided by management. When you start talking price, Ed pulls you aside and says, "Psst! Actually, the place makes about $500,000 per year profit."

What's happening is this: Ed doesn't want to show any profits, because profits get taxed. So he has a lot of heavy expenses which are actually perks. There is, for instance, the company car—a Maserati. Naturally Ed has to belong to an expensive country club where he makes useful business contacts. Ed's Aunt Tillie is on the payroll at $30,000; she actually shows up one day a year. Several other relatives are doing the same thing. Ed himself draws a magnificent salary. It all adds up. Your question is, does it really add up to $500,000?

If you bring in your own accountant and go over the place with a fine-tooth comb, you can in fact generally estimate the profits within 5 percent of the true figure. Here's what you must do.

1. *Track down all the perks*. Insist on seeing a paper trail of receipts and so on to prove that the cash really was taken out of the company.

2. *Take a physical count of the inventory.* Fiddling with inventory figures is an excellent way to conceal profits, and the only way to be sure how much inventory is there is to count it yourself. Note that when the true inventory position comes out, it will result in a taxable windfall and the IRS will insist on getting its belated cut. Ed will want you to pay it; you should insist that he do so.

3. *Look into the depreciation figures carefully.* Ed probably depreciated everything to scrap value as fast as he legally could in an attempt to show zero net worth on the books for the IRS. Chances are the real value is much higher.

Your accountant will put all these new data into a realistic "reconstructed" set of financials. Then you have to negotiate. Quite often a private company will be very profitable in reality. You should still be careful. If the seller is basing the price on that $500,000 profit figure, demand a guarantee. Pay, say, two-thirds of the price and promise the rest if profits in the first year really are as claimed and no unexpected skeletons jump out of the closet.

Before you make the decision to buy, consider one final question: What will you do with this business? If you just plan to go on running it the same way it has always been run, your purchase will probably turn out to be a mistake. You should have a vision for the business. Perhaps it's a mess, and you think you know how to turn it around. Perhaps it's doing okay, but you see how it could be made into something much better. But have a goal for improving the business, and have a plan for accomplishing that goal.

THE FRANCHISE OPTION

When you buy a business you are inevitably somewhat in the position of buying a pig in a poke. If it makes you nervous, you may want to consider buying a franchise. This option is generally intermediate between buying an ongoing business and starting up from scratch. (You can buy out an existing franchise operation, in which case the guidelines for buying a business apply.) Typically when you sign up with a franchise you are buying not a business but (1) a tested business plan; (2) backup and support, ranging from supplies to national advertising; and (3) possibly a location.

Dealing with franchisors is a subject entire unto itself, but there are a few simple rules that can keep you out of some of the more serious pitfalls. (They may be obvious, but there are a lot of franchisees out there with pungi stick wounds.)

1. *Don't think the franchisor will solve your problems.* You have to do the work; the franchisor just gives you the plan. In fact, often the franchisor is part of the problem, not part of the solution.

2. *Check it out in advance very carefully.* Talk to established franchisees—but don't take their word as gospel; often they have motives to paint the operation in colors more glowing than real. Dig up all the dirt on the franchisor, read everything in their fine print carefully, and get a lawyer before you sign the contract or the check. If there is any soiled laundry, such as lawsuits by earlier franchisees, you may be sure that the franchisor will have glib, plausible explanations prepared; don't let them snow you.

3. *Remember that for any retail business the three critical factors are location, location, and location.* Look into the suitability of the location yourself; most franchisors are honest and highly competent, but they may not have the local knowledge of your area that you do. And examine very carefully that part of the fine print that limits how many other, competing outlets the franchisor can place in your area and how close they can be.

BUT WILL IT BE SUCCESSFUL?

Once you have an idea, the next step is to develop it into a *business concept.* To do this you must answer three specific questions:

1. What are the *objectives* of the business?
2. What *kind* of business must you build in order to accomplish these objectives?
3. What will be *distinctive or unique* about your company?

THE TAXONOMY OF BUSINESS

In order to deal with these questions, we must first understand the taxonomy of business. To start with, let's classify businesses by size.

■ *At the low end is what we call the microbusiness.* This is a tiny creature, often run out of the home, a part-time or at most full-time activity for one person, though family members may pitch in. The lemonade stand falls in this category, as do the Amway distributor, the housewife who makes stuffed animals for sale, the carpenter who moonlights doing construction and repair jobs, and the programmer who has a little software business on the side. The microbusiness is seldom incorporated, usually is managed very informally indeed, and has an amazingly low capitalization. Microbusinesses are very inconspicuous and nobody knows how many there are; many are part of the "underground economy."

- *The next step up is the minibusiness.* This is big enough to have more than one person working full time. Usually it has its own premises. A minibusiness may become fairly large, up to perhaps a couple of hundred employees. The defining characteristic is that it is small enough to be managed by one person. The most familiar minibusinesses are small retail outlets—grocery stores, barber shops, restaurants. However, minibusiness-size manufacturers and high-technology companies can be found swarming in industrial neighborhoods.

- *Now we come to the mesobusiness.* This is an organization too large for one person to run, even with the assistance of aides. It requires a real top-management team: a group of people, each of whom has authority to make major decisions in some area of operation. Typically a mesobusiness will have from several hundred to several thousand employees. It may dominate a market in a geographical region, or it may be a minor player in a national market.

- *Finally, there is the megabusiness.* It's possible for a mesobusiness to become so big and so complex that its top-management team can no longer control it effectively. The company cannot just add more people to top management, because the group would become too large to operate as a team. It becomes necessary to split the company into divisions and provide each one with its own top-management team. Most "household-name" companies fall into the megabusiness category.

Taxonomy—the classification of species—may not be the most precise word to describe the classification of businesses. A member of one biological species can never transform itself into a member of a different species. However, business species are not such rigidly closed groups. Small businesses may grow larger. Big businesses may decline and shrink, split up, or spin off smaller entities. And yet there is surprisingly little movement between the four groups we have defined. A typical mesobusiness, for instance, may grow somewhat larger, or smaller, from year to year. But it is very unlikely to make the transition to minibusiness structure, and even more unlikely to grow into a megabusiness.

Of course high-growth ventures cannot reach their goals without crossing these dividing lines. But the transition from one business species to another is not only difficult but dangerous. Many a mini-business has gone bankrupt during the attempted metamorphosis into a mesobusiness.

The Right Size for You.   Before you begin, make a conscious, rational decision about size. In Chapter One we talked about personal aptitudes and goals. Now you must decide what kind of company will satisfy your needs.

If you don't like supervising people, want maximum flexibility, and detest paperwork, stick with a microbusiness. The vast majority of regulatory hassles cut in when a business hires its first employee.

If you believe in keeping a close eye on every detail and feel uncomfortable delegating authority, you can have a prosperous mini-business—but trying to grow beyond that would probably be disastrous. If you decide that your company ought to grow beyond the size that you can run—and enjoy running—plan from the start to step aside at that point and bring in professional big-company managers.

On the other hand, perhaps you enjoy team play and like to work in a structured environment on well-defined problems. You may do very well running a mesobusiness—but if the way there runs through a start-up, watch out. Very few entrepreneurs have the ability, or for that matter the desire, to run a mesobusiness, let alone a megabusiness. If you're one of them, great. But you probably will do better buying a business (as in a leveraged buyout), or doing a major "jump-start" venture (e.g., Genentech) with massive financial backing.

Once you have a clear idea about company size and shape, check it against what the *market* wants.

HOW MARKETS GROW

Your business idea will generally imply, perhaps very specifically, the market area you will be entering. Examine it carefully. Markets have their own growth dynamics.

As shown in Exhibit 1, the growth of a typical market (or industry) may be divided into four phases.

1. *The Primitive Phase.* The Primitive Phase involves a product or service that has not yet really found a market. A few customers are tentatively trying it, unsure whether it's really useful or desirable. Quite likely there is no clear-cut idea of what use it should be applied to. A good example of a market in the Primitive Phase would be microcomputers in the early 1970s. At this point tiny companies like

Exhibit 1. Typical market growth curve.

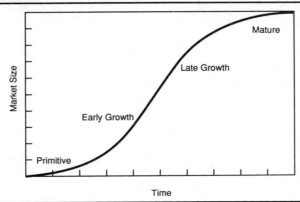

MITS and Imsai were selling a few computers, mostly as kits, to hobbyists and computer professionals. Nobody knew quite what to do with them, but they were fun to play with. Other examples were automobiles around 1900 and air travel in the barnstorming era. Note that customers in this phase are limited to professional experts in the field, or at least enthusiastic amateurs.

An industry in the Primitive Phase is typically populated by microbusinesses and relatively small minibusinesses. Production methods range from handcraft to small-scale systematic assembly. Entry is therefore generally inexpensive; this is the kind of start-up that is financed with personal savings or a second mortgage on the founder's house. That's fortunate, because professional investors seldom consider backing businesses in such a tiny and ill-defined market.

2. *The Early Growth Phase.* An industry enters the Early Growth Phase when its product acquires a clearly defined use and thereby gains access to a significant customer base. By this time one need not be an expert to use it; still, it is not for everyone. The microcomputer might be said to have entered this stage with the introduction of the Apple II. Other examples are automobiles around the Model T's introduction and air travel in the days of the first airlines.

During the Early Growth Phase, the industry is dominated by minibusinesses. Some of these, but not many, are grown-up microbusinesses, survivors from the Primitive Phase. Most are new entries. Entry is still not too expensive, but most start-ups must be financed by professional capital, such as venture capital. At first investors are skeptical, but since the rate of market growth is accelerating they gradually become enthusiastic.

3. *The Late Growth Phase*. The Late Growth Phase of a market is characterized by increasing standardization of the product. There is widespread agreement about how the product should be designed and how it should be used. Paradoxically it is during this same phase that the product splits into specialized versions. Thus the microcomputer market, in the early 1980s, began to standardize on the IBM PC— while splitting into business and home computer segments, not to mention video games, word processors, and portable computers. To take another example, by 1940 the automobile was rapidly standardiz- ing—for instance, the accelerator, brake, and clutch were now in the same configuration in virtually all makes. At the same time, such subspecies as the station wagon, pickup truck, and convertible were becoming clearly defined.

By this time, the industry is consolidating into a relatively small number of mesobusinesses—the notorious "shakeout" is beginning. A few minibusinesses still survive by devoting themselves to specialized niches, and megabusinesses are elbowing their way in, attracted by the now substantial size of the market. Entry, however, has become very expensive. Many millions are required to get a seat at the table. New entries must be financed by a big company, by public offering, or perhaps by the larger venture capital firms. Money is readily available now, though. The industry's growth history has excited investors— but, ironically, it is now too late for them to reap really big returns, since the growth rate is declining.

4. *The Mature Phase*. Finally growth levels off and the industry becomes "mature." At this point, the product is almost fully standard- ized and innovations are rare. Every imaginable customer has been accessed; a company can increase sales only by taking customers from the competition. The highly standardized product offers few opportu- nities for major changes or improvements, so competitive maneuvers consist mostly of marketing ploys and advertising campaigns.

In the mature industry only a few players remain at the table, almost all of them megabusinesses. The product is more or less a commodity, and reducing production costs, commonly by economies of scale, is a crucial concern. Entry is now so expensive that it is for all practical purposes impossible.

This is the normal sequence; however, some industries follow a "pathological" sequence. Consider, for instance, biotechnology. This became an investment fad while still in its Primitive Phase, and vast amounts of money were pumped into it. As a result, it has come to look like a child recklessly injected with growth hormone, a collection of mismatched parts. The industry is dominated by a few large com- panies, uses mostly handcraft production methods, and is considered a hot growth area, but it still has no clearly defined product. There are other pathological patterns.

Before you enter an industry, be sure you understand the dynamics of its market. Is it following the normal growth sequence? If so, what stage is it at? If not, what accounts for the abnormality, and how will it affect the future?

MARKET TIMING

If your start-up is to be successful, you must enter the market with good timing—which means, at a stage appropriate to your company's size and resources. Once you decide what kind of company you want to run, ask yourself: Will this kind of company do well in the market as it is now? As it will be in the future?

An error sometimes made by entrepreneurs, and frequently by investors, is *tardiness*. They wait until success has been clearly demonstrated by the pioneers, then try to imitate them. Apple Computer started in a garage and grew to a $100 million company in a few years. Dozens of would-be imitators followed Apple into the personal computer business and failed. Apple could achieve fantastic growth because—it didn't have to compete with Apple. Sure, successful companies have started in this industry since. But they were innovators, not imitators. Dell Computer, for instance, sold "clones" but created a highly effective new marketing system for selling personal computers.

Starting a new business is risky at best. Starting too late and too small lengthens the odds against you disastrously. Yet this mistake is made amazingly often; apparently, the temptation to imitate someone else's success is hard to resist. One even finds people like Bricklin and DeLorean who try to start new auto manufacturing companies.

Starting too early or too large is another mistake. Entrepreneurs sometimes see a little too far ahead and try to hurry a market that isn't yet ready for their products. Investors may try to obtain greater safety by overfinancing a company. (Yes, this really does happen!) But no amount of capital can make a company grow faster than its market can make room for it. Pouring in excess money is like giving too much water to a plant in a small pot—it merely sloshes over the edge and is wasted. And—sometimes the plant is killed by mildew.

WHERE DO YOU FIT IN?

Some of this may sound a bit alarming. What if it's not your ambition to found the next IBM or Xerox? Is it really necessary to plan for growth to megabusiness size?

The answer, obviously, is no. There are markets that grow very slowly. There are markets that hardly grow at all, that stay in the Primitive Phase indefinitely. Many markets are dwarfs; they level off into maturity at a size too small to attract megabusinesses. And even large markets usually have small but potentially profitable niches where a small company can survive and prosper. You can pick any size and growth strategy you like, as long as you select a market that fits.

TECHNOLOGY-DRIVEN VS. MARKET-DRIVEN

If your product involves technology, you've probably heard that the world beats a path to the door of the inventor of a better mousetrap. Venture capitalists love to refute this famous quotation from Emerson. And they're right; very few products sell themselves, and innovative products least of all. The more radical your improvement, the harder it is to get customers to try it. Dr. Seuss, in *Green Eggs and Ham,* painted a more realistic picture than Emerson.

Unfortunately, many venture capitalists have taken this insight to an unwarranted conclusion. They abhor companies that are "technology-driven." By this they mean a company that is committed to and motivated by its technological innovation and that attempts to persuade customers to adopt its new products. Instead, they prefer the "market-driven" company, in which technology is completely subordinated to accommodating customer preferences.

It's hard to deny the importance of being attentive to the needs of your customers. But in practice, the preference for market-driven companies results in funding a lot of passive, imitative start-ups that wither helplessly when they encounter vigorous competitors. It's true that a technology-driven start-up is attempting a desperate gamble, and most fail. But it's also true that most of the great success stories of American business have been technology-driven companies. Consider Bell Telephone, Ford Motor, and Xerox. These and other big winners did not adapt themselves to customers' traditional habits; they aggressively pushed entirely new types of products in defiance of customer resistance. By their fierce commitment to new technology they *created* new markets. So keep in mind that there is nothing inherently preferable about either the technology-driven or the market-driven approach. They are simply different approaches, each with its own risks and opportunities.

EXERCISE
Classifying Your Business and Market

A. What type of business do you want to run?
- ☐ Microbusiness
- ☐ Minibusiness
- ☐ Mesobusiness
- ☐ Megabusiness

B. How large do you want your business to grow?

Sales:	Employees:
☐ Less than $100,000	☐ Just you
☐ Under $1 million	☐ Five or ten
☐ Under $20 million	☐ A few dozen
☐ $100 million or more	☐ A few hundred
☐ $1 billion or more	☐ Thousands

C. What growth rate do you prefer for your company?
- ☐ High growth
- ☐ Moderate growth
- ☐ Steady state

D. Will you:
- ☐ Stay with the company till you retire?
- ☐ Step aside at some point?

E. Write a brief description of the market you intend to enter.

F. What growth stage is this market currently at?
- ☐ Primitive
- ☐ Early Growth
- ☐ Late Growth
- ☐ Mature

G. Is this a normal market? If not, what unusual features does it seem to present?

H. Do your company's preferred size and character fit the market's growth stage?

WHAT'S *NOT* CRUCIAL

Before we discuss the critical ingredients of your business concept, let's deal with some common misconceptions. Here are some items that are *not* crucial.

- *Money*. Surprised? Entrepreneurs do a lot of moaning about their shortage of capital, and spend a lot of time trying to raise more money. Usually they'd be better off to divert that effort to increasing sales. It's nice to be well financed, but it is rarely the limiting factor. If your business possesses the crucial success qualities, people will come and stuff money in your pocket. If it doesn't, having a Rockefeller for a father-in-law won't help. So don't worry too much about the money. If you do the other parts right, it will be there when you need it. And, as we'll see when we discuss financing methods, you may not need anywhere near as much capital as you initially think.

- *Experience*. Statistically, entrepreneurs tend to be fairly young. Usually they haven't lived long enough to get a lot of experience, but it doesn't seem to hurt them. Being an entrepreneur is a complicated job, and each start-up is different anyway. There's only one way to really get experience in entrepreneuring, and that's to start a company.

- *Prosperity*. It's a common excuse: "The economy is in such bad shape right now; maybe when things start to look better . . ." Fact is, as we'll discuss later in detail, the bottom of a recession is the ideal time to start a company. And a lot of companies do get started in hard times. People who are out of work turn to self-employment in desperation; others moonlight in a microbusiness to make ends meet. Often they are surprised by their success.

TRULY CRUCIAL INGREDIENTS: THE THREE-M THEORY

What *do* you need to succeed in business? There are three factors that are absolutely critical to starting a successful company: market, management, and monopoly.

Market. You might think it obvious that a company can't exist without sales—that there must be a market for what it's selling. Yet many entrepreneurs are so dazzled by the brilliance of their ideas that it doesn't occur to them to ask whether customers will buy. The first step to success is the recognition that just because *you* love your product, it doesn't mean it will sell. No matter how good it is, customers may be unable or unwilling to recognize its superiority. Scientists and engineers are particularly prone to fall in love with their products. This is one reason technology-driven start-ups have such a bad reputation.

If people are buying a product like yours already, at least a market exists. But you must establish this fact and prove it, not merely assume it. If a market does not exist, you may be able to create one. But you must plan how to do so, not just assume that it will happen somehow.

Let's be very clear on what a market is. A market is an ongoing demand for a particular product or service. The critical word is *demand*. Desire is not demand. Customers must not only *want* your product—they must be willing and able to *pay* for it.

> When the People's Republic of China first began to open its markets to U.S. companies, many rushed in to fill the "demand" of a billion new consumers—and got badly burned. Sure, the Chinese *wanted* Western consumer goods; but with a per-capita income of less than $250 per year, they couldn't afford them.

You must be able to look at this question objectively. Don't assume that your customers are just like you. You must find out what their likes and dislikes really are, not just extrapolate from your own. In Chapters Four, Five, and Six we'll discuss market research and marketing in more detail.

Management. Most people think of management as synonymous with supervision. They aren't at all the same thing. Management is organizing work. Whether you organize the work of thousands of employees or only your own, it is management.

You don't have to have experience to be a good manager. There are plenty of experienced "managers" who can't manage at all. You've probably had at least one of them for a boss.

There are three qualifications for management competence:

1. You must know *what* to do; this is effectiveness.
2. You must know *how* to do it; this is efficiency.
3. You must be *willing* to know what needs doing; this is objectivity.

Effectiveness and efficiency are skills; they can be learned. Objectivity, on the other hand, is a character trait; it can be acquired, though not easily. Good managers are rare primarily because objectivity—the willingness to face facts—is rare. Does this seem exaggerated? We can assure you it isn't. You have only to read the business press to confirm what we've seen over and over again in our experience with small companies. You'll find one example after another of businesses—small, medium, and large—that have failed because their managements were guided by emotions rather than reality. An incalculable amount of capital has been destroyed by CEOs who rejected facts because they were unpleasant, uncomfortable, or simply unfamiliar.

When prospective investors consider your start-up, they will look carefully at top management—you. Do you understand business management in general? Do you understand the management needs of your particular industry? Investors may accept either experience or study as qualification. But above all they'll want to know if you are objective, if you can think about your company with a clear head.

Monopoly. No business can be successful unless it has a monopoly. Got your attention, didn't we? Let's hope so, because this is a key point.

Monopoly is not used here in the usual, invidious sense of a coercive control of the market. In fact, having a monopoly in the usual sense is generally counterproductive, because it makes your customers your enemies.

In the late 1980s, American semiconductor manufacturers got together and persuaded the U.S. Government to limit imports of Japanese memory chips. The result, as planned, was a sharp increase in prices. The cartel members, however, reaped no benefit. Expensive memory crippled sales of computers, which reduced demand for microprocessors and other chips that were the most profitable products of the semiconductor houses. And computer manufacturers were not terribly pleased at being gouged by their chip suppliers.

But you should have a monopoly in the sense of *selling a product or service that is distinctive and unique.* You must offer your customers something they want that they cannot get elsewhere, at least not without a great deal of trouble. This is the only way to make money.

Wherever this principle is ignored one finds industrial disaster. The product becomes a pure commodity. Competition becomes price war. Nobody makes a profit. And once everyone is selling at or below cost customers become the ultimate losers, for an unhealthy, malnourished industry cannot properly serve their needs.

Your business must have some unique appeal to the customer. What? There are a number of possible approaches.

- *Product*. Be the only one who sells the product. High-technology companies often seek this position. If you can make a widget that nobody else can make because you have proprietary technology, your position may be very strong—as long as you can protect your know-how by patent or secrecy. On the other hand, in this situation you are alone in the market. The only customers are the ones *you* create. You have no direct competitors to assist you in developing the market. And customers may be especially reluctant to buy an innovative product if they are restricted to a single source.
- *Features*. Equip your product with a unique feature of some sort. This is a less demanding approach. It can be very effective, but the unique feature must be not just an arbitrary add-on but a real benefit to the customer.
- *Price*. Make your price unique. If—*and only if*—you have a superior production process so that your costs are lower than your competition's costs, then you may want to set a distinctively lower price.

Just be damned sure you've prepared for a price war. I don't know how many times I've seen business plans projecting a quick grab of market share by setting a lower-than-market price. Invariably these plans assume that competitors will *not* drop their prices in response. In the real world, they do.

REM

Remember that your price can be unique in another way: It can be *higher* than everyone else's! Naturally there are certain risks involved, but if you can pull it off this strategy will develop an image of unique quality for your product, and produce an exceptionally plump profit margin into the bargain.

- *Location*. Have a unique location. Retail establishments make heavy use of this. Why do you patronize your neighborhood dry cleaner? Probably not because its service is intrinsically better than that of some other dry cleaner but because it's conveniently located. This strategy can also be applied on a larger scale; a good example is the commuter airline that provides service to small airports ignored by its transcontinental competitors.

- *Outlet*. Closely related to the approach of unique location is unique market outlet. You can try to make it more convenient to buy your product by using market channels ignored by your competitors. Sell in retail stores an item previously available only by mail order. Or vice versa. (This is how Sears Roebuck became successful a century ago.) Sell in a different kind of store; L'Eggs pantyhose got a leg up on the competition by pushing its product in supermarkets instead of clothing stores.
- *Service*. Still another strategy is unique service.

> One summer, while in college, I worked in a computer operation of the telephone company on night shift. We had only IBM equipment. I soon learned why. When a machine went down, IBM had someone there within half an hour to fix it—and he did fix it, no excuses or delays. When our billing software failed, we called the IBM programmer who'd written it, long distance. He got out of bed, wrote a patch on the spot, read it to us over the phone, and got us running again. With this kind of service, IBM repeatedly pulverized competitors, some of whom had superior products. Today, with the computer market shifting from main-frames to micros, IBM is finding it hard to offer the same kind of service.
>
> REM

- *One last suggestion*. Consider making your business unique by giving the customer a new way of paying for the product. For instance, there was a time when big-ticket items like cars and houses had to be bought with cash on the barrelhead. The development of installment financing and the standard mortgage revolutionized these markets, and many others. The gasoline credit card had a similar effect.

DON'T REST ON YOUR OARS

Before we leave the subject, we should consider the question: How do you *maintain* superiority? Competitors have a nasty habit of imitating your successes. It's not enough to be unique—you must stay unique.

No matter what your advantage is, there is only one way to maintain it: continuous effort. The only exception is the very tiny market niche—so small it's not worth fighting over. Wherever there's money, there'll be competition. No matter how great your initial success, you can't get away with resting on your oars. You must think ahead, plan for the next step.

If you rely on technology to give you a superior product, you must worship at the shrine of R&D. Sooner or later your patent will expire, your secret process will be sold to a competitor by a crooked employee, or your method will simply become obsolete. *Somebody* will eventually find a way that's even better than yours—it had better be you. Many an engineer has become so proud of his brilliant invention that he . . . never made another. When your Model A has had a tremendous success and is sweeping everything else off the market—that's the time to be hard at work designing Model B.

If your edge is marketing, it's even more precarious. Competitors can easily imitate your advertising, invade your distribution channels, even move next door. You must anticipate their response and have a plan in order to keep one step ahead.

Hardest to get but easiest to defend is the advantage based on service. You can produce a superior widget with little more than a single bright engineer. One hot-shot marketing maven can develop a masterful sales campaign. But to provide truly superior service requires the active participation of virtually everyone in the company. This means building a whole company culture, which is hard work, and maintaining it, which is also hard work. Competitors that try to imitate your service have to follow the same path, and it's slow going. In fact, this is one way in which new companies have the advantage over older competitors. As we'll see in Chapter Three, it's much easier to build a company culture from scratch than to change one already in place.

DEVELOPING THE BUSINESS CONCEPT

Once you've dealt with the issues of market size, growth, timing, and so on, you're in a position to develop your *business concept.*

First, define your company's objectives; begin with your basic idea and take into account your personal goals. Then decide what kind of company meets the objectives. The characteristics of your company—its size, its market, its product, its culture, its organization—must be in harmony with its objectives and with one another. Finally, you must come up with a way to make your company unique. As noted, it could be a new technology, an unusual marketing approach, a perfect location, exceptional service—perhaps some entirely new twist. You needn't limit yourself to being unique in just one way, of course!

EXERCISE
Your Business Concept

A. In twenty-five words or less, describe the product or service you intend to sell.

_____

_____

_____

_____

B. What approach will you take to the market?
   ☐ Market-driven
   ☐ Technology-driven

C. In twenty-five words or less, explain why there is a *need* for your product or service.

_____

_____

_____

_____

D. Who will buy your product? Why? Why are they able and willing to pay for it?

E. What are your management qualifications?
   ☐ Experience—general management
   ☐ Academic training in management
   ☐ Experience—your industry
   ☐ Evidence of objectivity

F. What will make your company unique in the marketplace?
   ☐ Unique (proprietary) product
   ☐ Unique (proprietary) feature
   ☐ Superior technology
   ☐ Location
   ☐ Market outlet
   ☐ Service

☐ Low price
☐ High price
☐ More convenient purchase
☐ Other (specify) _____

G. What approach will you take to maintain your unique advantage in the future when competitors imitate it?

THE ULTIMATE JUDGE

Whatever the source for your business idea, we cannot stress too strongly that you must talk to your market. Perhaps the most insidious disease entrepreneurs have is falling in love with an idea. This can get you broke. Just because you go into a frenzied ecstasy at the very thought of the product doesn't mean customers will do the same. Go talk to them!

Another hazard is dropping an idea that you don't like and then watching some bastard take it up and turn it into the next IBM, while you kick yourself. This can get you a sprained knee. Though an idea doesn't excite you, maybe it will excite customers. Go talk to them!

And we mean, go talk to customers. It's not what you think of your business idea; not what your spouse thinks, or friends think, or even what your banker thinks, that makes the difference. It's what *customers* think of it. Try it out on them. And if it doesn't fly, don't despair. Congratulate yourself on skipping an unpleasant bankruptcy and go back to the drawing board. You thought of one idea. Believe us: There are more where that came from.

CAUTIONARY TALE
Private Profits

Some years ago, I was approached by a salesman who specialized in the sale of private-label products to chains on the East Coast. A private-label product is a copy of a national-brand product that is sold under either the name of the store itself or a house name. It is presented on the shelf right next to the national brand; the packaging is similar in color and shape, and the product is often exactly the same. But there is no advertising cost attached to the private-label product because the manufacturer sells it directly to the store, which puts its name on it. Since advertising and promotion account for a large part of the cost of a national brand, a private-label product can be sold at a substantially lower price. Commonly a successful private-label brand will achieve a 15 or 20 percent market share—partly by eating into the national brand, partly by expanding the market to include some people who can't afford the big-name brand.

In this particular case, the salesman showed me a product called Wet Ones, manufactured and distributed by a company called Lane & Fink (a subsidiary of Sterling Drug). The product is a moist towelette in a cylindrical package. You pull them out one by one, like Kleenex, to clean hands or various other things—largely one end or the other of a baby—when sanitary facilities are not available. He pointed out that this item was extremely successful and that it provided a real opportunity for a private-label imitation. He was sure he could sell millions of them if we could find a way to manufacture them.

The world is full of salespeople who are sure they could sell a million of something or other. With experience, you learn to be skeptical of such claims. But this sounded interesting, so I did a little market research. I went around and talked to representative chain stores and found that, sure enough, this type of product was one of the fastest-growing categories in nonfood items sold by supermarkets and drugstores. So I set forth to run down the cost of manufacturing the product.

There were a number of elements. First there was the plastic container; this consisted of two parts, one of which had to be blow-molded and the other injection-molded. Then there was the fabric for the towelettes, which had to be cut from large rolls and prepared to be placed in the containers. There was a liquid that was used to moisten the towelettes, made up of a number of different chemicals, which had to be formulated in a certain way. There was assembly, of course, and there was packaging.

I traipsed around New York lining up subcontractors, getting costs, and added them up. Lo and behold, they came in—on paper, at least—substantially below what would be required to sell this product at 30 percent off the price of the national brand and still make a very nice profit.

My next step was to make some samples. The salesman went around to his accounts, showed them the samples, and asked if they would buy the product if we could deliver it. The response was immediate and overwhelming. Before we contracted to build the molds for the manufacture of the plastic container—which was the main up-front cost—we already had substantial initial orders from several chains.

I decided it was time to finance and organize this project. Fortunately, at this time I had a partner in another business whose company actually printed labels for private-label manufacturers. So he was a natural to help me in this effort. I put up a couple of thousand bucks and he put in some more to provide initial inventory financing and get the business off the ground. He also agreed to run the business from his existing office. That way, accounting procedures were already in place and the people who would order the materials were already hired. We did hire one young man directly, to worry about the day-to-day running of the business. He was fresh out of business school, but he acted as a foreman, making sure that all the subcontractors performed effectively, with quality products, and in a timely fashion. He spent a great deal of time in the packaging plant checking out the final product. He also kept an eye on inventories, processed orders, answered complaints, and so on.

The overhead of the entire operation was less than $4,000 a month. This approach, moreover, was not only cheap but fast. Within a few months we were in business, we had a product, and we were ready to ship.

It took us only seven months to sign up almost all the major drug chains and food chains around the country. People who had been in the private-label business for years told me they had never seen anything move so fast. There was an extraordinary demand for the product.

In fact, it was a little too much of a good thing. Before very long I could see that this business was getting out of hand. We needed working capital to finance inventory and receivables, and with this spectacular growth the amount was quickly exceeding the means of my partner and myself. The banks were unwilling to finance the business without personal guarantees, because we hadn't been in business that long. Receivables financing wasn't a big problem, because our accounts were with major chains around the country, household-name companies. But the banks had no confidence in our inventory, because we'd turned it over only three or four times since the business had started. So within eight months of start-up, my partner and I had personally endorsed notes to the tune of $3 million for inventory. This was something that made me extremely nervous.

By the fifth quarter of the company's life, we were operating at a level of $8 million a year. This is what you call fast-track growth. We'd obviously found a good thing—so good that it was attracting heavy competition.

Major companies began to sniff around. Weyerhaeuser, St. Regis Paper, and Coca-Cola were clearly intending to come into this market. We had to consider our next step. To stay in the business and be competitive, we would have had to raise a lot of capital. So far we had put next to nothing into plant—just some chicken feed to buy the molds for the plastic parts. But to compete with the big players, we would have to set up our own production line and automate; this would require a big chunk of fixed capital. On top of that we would need massive amounts of additional working capital.

So when the three companies mentioned above put out feelers about acquiring Private Products, Inc., we very intelligently decided to be receptive. We identified Coca-Cola as being the strongest suitor, and toward the end of 1981 we sold the company to them for a very substantial return on the meager equity that we had put into the business.

Some of the tales I tell elsewhere in this book are real bummers, so I'm happy to say that this little project demonstrated my capacity for brilliant timing and implementation.

Private Products was a company with a very clear and distinct business concept. We set out to sell a single, well-defined product to a single, well-defined market. We verified the existence of demand for the product, and our capability to sell it, before putting in a lot of investment. In fact, by contracting out the entire manufacturing operation, we were able to avoid *ever* putting in a lot of investment. We moved promptly to take advantage of a major opportunity, but we didn't skimp on preparation and planning or cut corners. And we kept our overhead low.

But we also recognized the major limitation of the business concept: What did we have that was unique? Just one thing—price. We didn't have a patent, or manufacturing know-how, or a reputation built up over the centuries—we had nothing that could not be imitated by competitors. Our pitch was simple: "Here's a hot-selling item, 30 percent cheaper than the national brand." Anybody could take this approach; we just happened to be shrewd enough to take it first. So the smartest thing I did with this company was to sell it when the selling was good. I had taken my business concept to its logical conclusion.

HDS

Three

BUILDING A TEAM

Two resolute men, acting in concord, may transform an Empire, but an ordinarily resourceful duck can escape from a dissentient rabble.

Ernest Bramah, *Kai Lung Unrolls His Mat*

Only the very tiniest businesses can operate with just one person. If you undertake anything much larger than a microbusiness, you'll find that success requires adding other people to your team. And if you've chosen ambitious objectives, you should consider starting out with a substantial group of cofounders. Experience has shown that start-ups with large founder teams grow better than single-founder companies. In fact, these days it's hard to find professional investors who will finance a one-person show. They strongly prefer to invest in a group of managers who can pool their talents.

As you bring on cofounders, advisers, directors, employees, and all the other people your growing business needs, you are faced with a continuous stream of personnel decisions. It soon becomes necessary to develop *policies* to control these decisions in a systematic way. In the long run, these policies solidify—with or without your intentional guidance—into a complex of goals and attitudes which is sometimes called a "company culture."

Entrepreneurs focus on technology, production, and marketing; the gritty details of personnel manuals, compensation policies, and benefit plans seem boring compared with the excitement of landing that critical sale or getting the first widget off the assembly line. You think: "We can worry about that stuff later, when we're big enough to have a personnel department."

In fact, though, you need to give careful attention to "people

53

matters" right from the start, for two reasons. *First,* the founder or founders can't do it alone. Your company can succeed only if its employees, from top to bottom, are motivated to produce results. Every business success story, from DuPont to IBM to Apple, has involved developing a company esprit. Approaches differ; the methods that work for Toyota may not be suitable for Compaq, and vice versa. But no company succeeds without attention to its people.

Second, decisions in this area are often irreversible. If your product isn't working right, you can redesign it. If your marketing plan fails, you can switch to a new approach. But when you deal with people, decisions once made are harder to change. People resist arbitrary action. They resent sudden changes in policy. They revolt if they perceive you as taking away benefits they've been promised. The day you hire your first employee your organization acquires an inertia in its personnel policies, which makes it increasingly hard to change them. While your company is still on the drawing board, you can establish any policies you choose. Make sure you choose the right ones, because your employees may not allow you to change them later on.

WHAT KIND OF MANAGER ARE YOU?

The first key personnel decision you must make is one about yourself. What kind of manager are you? What kind do you want to be? How can you adapt your company to your personal management style, or vice versa? Much of the management literature speaks of management as if it were a sort of generic skill that comes in a plain white box. The reality is that there are all sorts of ways to manage. Let's begin by surveying six popular organizational setups for small businesses.

Nonteam Management Styles. The majority of entrepreneurs prefer to run their own shows single-handed, because this allows them to maximize their independence. But this does not mean that they are identical in management style. There are at least three styles of running a company without management assistance; we call them the Craftsman, the Coordinator, and the Classic.

The Craftsman. You can absolutely maximize your control over your business if you simply do everything yourself, making your business literally a one-man (or one-woman) show. Obviously this approach limits the size to which your business can grow.

You are most likely to adopt this style if your main concern is the quality of your output over everything else. It's an attitude characteristic of craft types, which is why we call it the Craftsman. However, many entrepreneurs in businesses other than crafts adopt this style.

There are a number of advantages to doing everything yourself. As mentioned, you can be absolutely sure of quality output. Everything is done right, because you do it. Expenses can be minimized. Operating with no employees can *dramatically* simplify your life—no payroll taxes to worry about, no concerns about OSHA, labor unions, workers compensation insurance, and a million other hassles. No hiring or firing, no supervision problems, no need to be concerned about pilferage.

If you adopt this mode it is very desirable to keep your company's administrative structure as simple as possible. You don't need, and certainly don't want, the complications that are associated with most business organizations. Think twice about incorporating; unless you plan to carry a heavy debt load, you probably have no real need for the corporate structure, and a sole proprietorship involves much less paperwork and tax hassles.

The problem with doing everything yourself is that you must do the tasks you don't like as well as the ones you do like. So if Craftsman is your chosen management style, think carefully about simplifying and streamlining those portions of your business that generate work you dislike. You may even go so far as to arrange for someone else to do the things you don't like, which leads to the next type of management style.

The Coordinator. The Coordinator is a style entrepreneurs exploit too seldom. It allows you to run a much larger business than the Craftsman can handle, while retaining complete personal control.

The essence of the Coordinator style is that you job out essentially the entire business. You, the entrepreneur, become simply the coordinator, the person who organizes the enterprise and makes sure that everything gets done.

In principle, you can job out everything. Arrange for someone to manufacture the product for you. Get brokers or reps to sell it. Hire an accounting firm to do your books, and sell your receivables so someone else has to do the work of collecting accounts. You can even retain a contract research lab to do your R&D! You simply sit in your office, coordinate the whole thing, and deposit the checks.

In real life, you generally need to do part of the work yourself, whether it's selling, R&D, or something else. But the Coordinator style allows you to do what you *enjoy* doing, and what you're good at, and get rid of all the other work. Of course you do have to work with other people. All the jobbers who are supplying you must be monitored. However, this is not nearly as much of a hassle as supervising employees. It is a great deal easier to get cooperation and performance when you are a customer rather than an employer. Still, you will have occasional problems. This is particularly true if your business involves tight deadlines; getting suppliers to perform on time is the hardest task.

The Coordinator style allows you to grow your business to a fairly substantial size without hiring a single employee. Eventually, of course, the administrative work becomes too much for one person to handle. It is quite possible to develop into a multimillion-dollar business with this style. If you're willing to hire a few assistants, you can grow even bigger. Some of the Japanese trading companies, which tend to operate in this style, do massive volume with only a few people. Why is the Coordinator style not used more often? We suspect it is due to the notorious cheapness . . . uh, fiscal conservatism, of entrepreneurs. It's a great deal cheaper to do a task in-house than it is to job it out—at least, it usually appears that way. In reality, this is generally false economy. One cardinal error is calculating costs without taking into account the value of your time. It is true that it costs you "nothing" to, say, solder the circuit boards yourself. But is this the best use of your time?

The Classic.   The Classic, the third management style of the entrepreneur, might be described as "watch it all yourself." You hire people as needed to get the job done, but you insist on tight, personal monitoring and supervision. And of course, you personally do all the really critical jobs yourself.

If this is your style, you are probably reluctant to admit it. People criticize entrepreneurs for being unwilling to delegate. Management consultants contemptuously exhort entrepreneurs to reform their evil ways, to cure themselves of the neurotic need to supervise everything personally.

Piffle. This is a perfectly legitimate way to run a company—as long as you recognize and admit that this is your style. Problems so often encountered in businesses of this type do not arise from the management style as such. They arise from the delusion that team management is being used. It's the management "experts" who are at fault. By de-legitimizing the Classic entrepreneurial style they have intimidated entrepreneurs into pretending to delegate. It is okay to delegate, and it is okay not to delegate; it is pretending to delegate that is disastrous.

Because you think you are using team management, you let your business become too big and too complex to run by yourself. So you hire people to join your "team," convinced that you are delegating authority to them. Unfortunately, you don't really trust them. So you keep yanking back the reins. Your subordinates quickly become disillusioned. The best leave, and you lament that "I just can't keep good people, so I have to do it myself." Others turn off, and you lament that "My people just can't be relied on, so I have to do it myself."

The standard prescription is psychotherapy. You must, you are told, cure yourself of your aversion to delegation, your neurotic phobia of losing control. We have a different viewpoint: Whose business is it anyway? (In both senses of the phrase!) Where do they get off telling you to revise your psyche? Just exactly why do you have to delegate?

Our advice is simply this: Decide whether or not you are going to delegate. Then make sure your company plans are compatible with that decision. If you are not going to delegate authority, you must limit the complexity of your business. There is simply a limit to the number of different tasks you can cover personally. There is thus a trade-off involved in adopting the Classic style. If your chosen business is very complex, it will have to be kept small. If it is simple, you can grow fairly large.

※　※　※　※

All of the single-manager styles involve limitations on your business. You cannot grow indefinitely unless you are willing to take on other people and give them authority.

However, most entrepreneurs don't want to build or run Fortune 500 businesses. If you choose to adopt single-person management, make a conscious decision: How big do you want to be when you grow up? Then evaluate whether your management style will be able to handle that size.

A tip: Most who write about entrepreneurs warn that when you take on too much you tend to make bad decisions. But our experience indicates a different symptom: If you take on too much you *tend not to make decisions.* If you find that you're having trouble making up your mind—on business, personal, or even trivial issues—chances are you're suffering from decision overload. Delegate some authority, or simplify your operation.

Team Management Styles. Businesses over a certain size cannot be run by a single person; a management team is required. What is the size limit? That depends on the complexity of the business, which is primarily a function of the industry involved. Manufacturing, particularly if it involves high technology, can be very complicated even on a small scale. But mass-assembly operations can be far simpler. The same applies to service companies; running even a one-plane commuter airline is a very intricate operation. But, at the other end, brokerage organizations can be very simple, and one person with a couple of assistants can manage an operation that generates many millions in revenues. This may not apply, however, to import-export brokers, where the business is much more complicated.

For a complex business, you must build a top-management team, with several people, each of whom has decision-making authority in a particular sphere. This means real delegation, which might be described as, "You make the decisions in this area. I will never overrule you; if I find one of your decisions truly unacceptable, I will fire you."

Team styles of management can be divided, somewhat arbitrarily, into three types: employee teams, small partnerships, and big-team ventures.

The Entrepreneur Plus Employee Team.   This style gives you, the entrepreneur, more control than other team styles. In this method, you delegate authority to key employees. But you retain final control because you have the option of firing them (or, less intelligently, retracting authority) if you are dissatisfied with their decisions.

You can't very well start a company with this management style, since you probably won't have many employees at first. High-level people hired at the start are generally partners, for the simple reason that high-quality managers won't hire on at a start-up unless they get equity. So if you are adopting the entrepreneur plus employee team style, you probably are switching the organization from another style, most likely the Classic, due to company growth.

This sort of transition is not as easy as you may think. As we've said, you have to delegate sincerely and knowingly. You may find it hard to convince your employees of your sincerity. And your employees have a tendency to feel there is an implicit contract that things will stay the same. So when you introduce delegation, they think you're "changing the rules"—which of course you are. The foremen who are used to dealing with you directly may feel that having to go through your new production manager amounts to a demotion.

It is best to make the transition as sharp as possible. Don't set up delegation gradually. Do it all at once. Be firm and explicit. Announce to one and all that you are changing the way you do business. Tell them the company has grown, and is successful, so much so that the old ways of doing things won't work any more. Point out the opportunities for promotion for those who qualify—and make an effort to promote from within.

The Small Partnership. The two- or three-person partnership, once a common mode of management organization, is now a rarity. However, it may be making a comeback.

You have considerably less control over the management of the business if you adopt this style. You now must share not only tactical but strategic decisions with your partners (who may be partners in the legal sense, or more likely cofounders who share equity in a corporation).

In compensation for this loss of control, you receive a substantial advantage: the assistance of managers who, like you, have a real stake in the company and are motivated to make it succeed in a way that no employee ever can be. Like you, they are hungry, and that can make a real difference for the growth of the company.

One of the most effective ways to organize a small company is the "inside-outside partnership." One sees this setup over and over again. One partner takes on the "inside" tasks—operations and administration. The other is the "outside" partner, handling marketing and sales. This divides responsibility along a natural fault line and commonly results in highly effective two-person teams.

Another lesson from experience with many entrepreneurial companies: If your founding team consists of just two people, try to avoid a fifty-fifty split of the equity. It will work out only as long as things are going swimmingly. When companies get into trouble, or disagreements arise, the even division of power is a prescription for civil war. In the traditional partnership, there was always a senior partner, and there are good reasons for it. If your partner's ego is too touchy to let her be Number Two, it's too touchy for her to handle the day-to-day give-and-take needed for a co-equal partnership. Let her be Number One, or find another partner.

The Big Team. In the viciously competitive economy of the 1990s, you can't keep a good thing to yourself for long. If there's money to be made, competitors will be nipping at your heels within months, perhaps days. What this means is that if you find a market with real growth possibilities, you must exploit it rapidly. You cannot grow slowly, or the competition will take the market away from you. You must have a growth company set up right from the start.

This means you will need access to a lot of capital. So forget about control; the venture capitalists will insist on taking the lion's share of the equity (though a public offering may give you a better deal if the stock market is ripe). But more to the point, you are going to need a growth company management team.

This is the big-team venture. You're going to ride the tiger, which means you have to be prepared before you saddle up. Once you're in motion, it's too late to make changes or additions. You won't have time. Sign on a complete management team right at the start and make sure they're good people. You can't afford to skimp. Time is not on your side. If you try to hoard your equity, you're going to read in *Forbes* about the brilliant entrepreneur who built an empire in a brand-new industry—and it won't be you.

You Takes Your Pick . . .   You now have six options for your management style. You need to pick one that is compatible with your way of operating. Look to the past for guidance. When you were a kid, did you play (and enjoy) team sports, or individual sports? Are you a perfectionist? Do you have a history of trusting other people with important tasks, or did you stay up all night to decorate the auditorium for the Senior Prom yourself, to make sure it got done right? Be honest with yourself; there are no right or wrong answers and there's nothing to be ashamed of either way.

And don't tell yourself that you've decided to change your ways and be a perfect delegator from now on. Stick with the style that is comfortable for you.

But as you develop the plan for your business, keep in mind how you plan to manage it. Ask yourself whether your management style is really effective for a business of this particular size, shape, and complexity. If the answer is no, modify your plan.

What if you encounter irreconcilable differences? Perhaps you have an idea for a major growth company, but looking over your past you see that you have always been a lone-wolf type. What then? Shouldn't you change your style?

Well, if you really think you'd miss your big chance, okay, give it a whirl. But don't think it will be easy. You'll have to keep a very tight rein on yourself. Like a dieter who finds himself in the kitchen at two a.m. with an empty plate in front of him and no memory of the previous fifteen minutes, you will suddenly realize in the middle of the night as you complete some crucial project with your own hands that you've backslid again. Try to avoid reforming yourself during a start-up. You're going to have enough worries. Accept what you are and make the best of it.

Delegation Redux.   We have a few more remarks to make on the subject of delegation. It used to be said, "If you want something done right, do it yourself." This is an old-fashioned attitude. It may have applied to the workers of fifty years ago, but these days a more appropriate saying would be, "If you want it done at all, do it yourself." People who can be relied on to do the work, and do it properly, even when the boss is not watching, are increasingly rare— indeed, almost an endangered species. If you hire very carefully, and have some good luck, you may have a few of these exceptional people on your staff. But if your business is to grow, sooner or later you must rely on more or less "ordinary" people.

Since you cannot do everything yourself, and you cannot rely on your employees to do properly the things that you do not do yourself, you must be certain that the tasks you perform personally are the critical ones. If you head a growing company, you *will* delegate—the only question is, *what* will you delegate? If you're smart, you will arrange things so that you are doing only the critical jobs and nothing else.

I must confess that my thinking on the issue of delegation has regressed over the years. In my younger days, I was very impressed by the arguments of the management literature on the importance of delegation. Let your subordinates do it; sure, they'll make mistakes, but the company will survive, and they'll learn while you save time.

Experience has taught me that this advice should be heeded by middle managers in big corporations. But a small company often will *not* survive a mistake. If you let George do it and he fumbles, it's not ten cents a share off earnings; it's the sheriff putting a padlock on your door. The conventional wisdom on delegation amounts to advising you to cut off your arm so you won't have to waste so much time washing your hands.

REM

WHEN IT COMES TIME TO HIRE

In the early days of your company be very conservative about hiring. Think twice, think three times, before you establish a new position. Then be sure to insist on quality. When you're working a ninety-hour week, it's tempting to compromise, to take on somebody who really isn't up to your standards. You're desperate for help, and you don't want to take time to search for the best. Resist the temptation to settle for second best; you'll soon regret it if you give in.

Later, when the company is successful and expanding, you'll need to set up controls to keep from loosening up. When managers feel flush, they are apt to hire carelessly. By this time you probably won't be able to personally vet each candidate. You'll have to establish—correction: You'll *have to have established*—a set of rules.

The economy of the 1990s, tumultuous and heavily regulated, puts an enormous premium on low head count. You should add to staff only when there is a compelling reason to do so. Before you create a new full-time position, consider the alternatives. Could you job out the task? Bring on a temp for a while? Get someone part time? (Sometimes a CFO or other expensive executive can be "shared" among several small companies.) Get someone to do it on an independent contractor basis? (But be very careful to meet IRS guidelines!) Make maximum use of "flexible staffing."

The Present vs. the Future.

A major problem for any growing enterprise is dealing with people who may not be able to grow as fast as their jobs. Suppose you hire a production manager to supervise the ten assembly workers you have now. In a couple of years you expect to have 500 workers. If this woman doesn't have the ability to handle 500, you'll have the embarrassing and unpleasant task of replacing her. If she does, she may go crazy with boredom working with only ten people—and you may go broke paying her the market price for her credentials.

There is no good answer to this dilemma. No matter how you handle it, sooner or later you'll face some distasteful options. If you're doing a team start-up, you should select cofounders who are qualified at the very highest levels. However, if the management slot in question is to be filled by an employee, we'd suggest the opposite approach. Bring in fresh talent who can handle your present needs and who are ambitious. Make it very clear right from the start that they must grow with the job or see newcomers brought in over their heads. Monitor them carefully, do your best to train them, and if they start to fall below your expectations let them know at once. Those who can't measure up may be unhappy, but you'll find that many are relieved to be eased into a subordinate position, provided they aren't publicly humiliated.

Nepotism.

If you're running a family business, nepotism is unavoidable by definition. But nepotism, broadly defined, occurs almost everywhere in the business world; big business or small, people get hired because of their family, friends, race, religion, or old school ties. It's been said that since nepotism is unavoidable, it's better to be the nepoter than the nepotee. And as a practical matter, many entrepreneurs choose their cofounders and early employees from their families or friends.

But there are real dangers in nepotism:

1. There is the obvious objection that your son or sister-in-law may not be competent to do the job.

2. Nepotism is violently resented, especially by your best workers (who have the most to lose if considerations other than merit control promotion).

3. Nepotism results in new conflicts in your personal life, because business disagreements now mingle with family matters.

4. Professional investors, particularly venture capitalists, regard the presence of family members on the management team as a serious red flag.

So what do we advise? It's best to avoid nepotism if you can. Sometimes you really can't. In that case, put specific limits on it.

> Mitsui, the great Japanese trading company, has for centuries had a rule that members of the owning family may sit on the board but may not take an active role in management.

Many family businesses make it a rule that scions of the founder must start at the bottom and work their way up. Others require family members to work for another company for a few years before coming into the family business. Some reserve certain management slots for family members and others for outsiders. The key point is to have firm, explicit, public rules, established in advance, that delimit the employment of family members in some way. Other workers will best tolerate nepotism if they know just where they stand and have some protection from arbitrary treatment.

Husband-wife partnerships present special problems. They're beautiful when they work, but when they don't the fireworks are spectacular. As with other partnerships, the odds of success are best when the spouses' duties within the company overlap as little as possible, and one spouse has a clear leadership role.

THE HIRING PROCESS

Once you decide that you really do need to hire somebody, how do you go about selecting the right person? Most managers think they know how—until a candidate comes in for an interview. Then they find themselves wondering what to say, what to ask, how to fill up the scheduled time. Successful hiring, like so many other aspects of business, is a matter of preparation. If you do your homework at the start you'll have less trouble when it's time to interview candidates.

Here is a simple five-step procedure for personnel selection. We've put it in terms of hiring an employee, but the same method, with slight modifications, works for selecting a cofounder, a director, a lawyer, or anyone else who has to work with you on a regular basis.

Step 1. Write a Job Description. It's hard to believe, but an amazing number of managers hire without having a clear idea of the nature of the job they are filling. Frequently they just have a vague feeling that they're understaffed and that having more hands would be helpful. Get down on paper a complete job description. Exactly what will be this person's responsibilities? To whom will he report? Who will report to him? Make it very explicit. Be sure to avoid evasion words like "assist," "supervise," "handle." Not "will assist me with the bookkeeping" but "will make all journal and ledger entries and do the trial balance every month." Not "supervise Station Two" but "monitor output quality at Station Two, make sure preventive maintenance is done, and keep operators supplied with parts." Not "handle routine correspondence" but "compose and type letters in response to credit inquiries and accounts-payable disputes."

The more detailed you make the job description, the better. If you have trouble coming up with this kind of specification, recognize that you have a problem. Maybe you don't need anybody after all. Maybe you do, but you're reluctant to delegate the tasks involved. Maybe you've failed to organize the work properly and don't have a good idea what needs to be done. Back up and rethink your needs.

When you're looking for a cofounder rather than an employee, it's even more important to define the job strictly. Decide what *specific* tasks you will expect this person to accomplish.

Step 2. Define Job Qualifications. Now that you know precisely what job needs to be done, you can decide what qualifications are needed. What does the candidate need in order to be able to do the job? Again, be very specific. Most qualification factors fall into one of the following six categories.

1. *Credentials.* These include college degrees, licenses, certifications, and so on. Though often a legitimate requirement, credentials

are frequently overemphasized. Where they are required by law, by contract, or perhaps by custom, they may be necessary. Otherwise, why pay for them?

2. *Experience.* If you are currently doing the task yourself and you plan to show the new chap exactly how you want it done, why pay a premium for experience? On the other hand, if you need somebody to do gene splicing and you don't know diddly about it yourself, better be sure you hire somebody experienced. Again, the key is to be explicit. Not "five years' experience in polymer coatings" but "has personally developed new coatings for high-performance electronic components." The idea of an experience qualification is to get somebody who *has already done* what you are hiring her to do. How long she's done it, or when or where, is not nearly as important as that she's done exactly the thing you're looking for.

3. *Knowledge.* This is often confused with credentials and sometimes confused with experience. If it is knowledge as such that you need, buy that and not something else. Knowledge might be a significant qualification for, say, a librarian or researcher: "Must know where the locate information on health effects of any chemical pollutant."

4. *Skills.* This is very frequently confused with experience or credentials or both. The mistake can be expensive. If you want somebody who can write accounting programs in COBOL, specify that skill. Don't pay a big premium for an M.S. in computer science, or for three years' experience with one of the Big Six accounting firms. It's useful to distinguish "talent" skills, such as computer programming or playing the violin, from "craft" skills such as cabinet making. The former don't require much experience (though it's certainly helpful), but only certain people can do them well. The latter can be done by almost anyone, but almost everyone needs a long apprenticeship to do them well.

5. *Intelligence.* Most jobs require a certain amount; too little and she can't perform, too much and she's bored.

6. *Creativity.* This is needed by artists, scientists, engineers, writers, and so on. The hiring manager is often reduced to quivering helplessness by a creativity requirement. You needn't be if you remember two things. First, define just what you want created. You don't want a "creative electrical engineer," you want somebody who can design a microcomputer-controlled television aerial rotator.

Second, look at past performance. Note that this is not necessarily the same as experience. Often the most creative people are young, fresh out of school. But they can still show you tangible evidence of creativity. An artist who's never had a job may come in with a portfolio of strikingly effective drawings. A freshly graduated scientist may show you an ingenious undergraduate research project. Never hire "creative potential"; always look for evidence of accomplishment.

Step 3. Get Applicants.

With qualifications specified, you're ready to *generate applicants*. There are various routes you can pursue to bring in qualified people.

- *Advertisement.* First select the right medium. It has to be seen by the people you want. If you need a chemist, you wouldn't advertise in *Science,* which is read mainly by biologists. If you want only local candidates, use a local newspaper. Timing is part of the medium. For instance, in *The Wall Street Journal,* Tuesday is job ad day; if your ad runs on Friday, it will get much less response.

Second, write an ad that specifies the essential qualifications. A vague ad may bring in a lot of resumés, but that just adds to the burden of answering (and yes, courtesy does require that you answer every one). Don't worry about excluding good candidates; if you developed honest qualifications and didn't overspecify, an explicit ad won't turn away anyone you want to talk to.

- *Blind ads.* You may want to run an ad under a box number for one reason or another—for instance, to conceal a new project from the competition. But blind ads don't draw the best applicants. Usually people use one because they fear a flood of applicants writing, phoning, dropping in. If this is your problem, perhaps your ads are underspecified; consider tightening up on requirements.

- *Headhunters and agencies.* The former can be useful in special cases. When you want to hunt out top talent, you may need to call in these professionals to handle the tricky task—especially if you're trying to pirate someone from the competition. Employment agencies, on the other hand, are seldom cost effective. It's tempting to turn recruitment hassles over to the pros, but few of the best job applicants use agencies. Because their inventory—job hunters—has a short shelf life, agencies seldom have in stock a person with specified qualifications and may end up sending you a lot of round pegs to fit in your square hole. And finally, agencies, though not as pricey as headhunters, are still a very expensive way to hire.

Government employment agencies, where people register when they collect unemployment benefits, are a special case. It costs you nothing or next to it to use one. The applicants they send you are a mixed bag; many are hopeless losers, but sometimes you get a real gem and at a bargain price.

■ *The Old Boy Network.* Using personal contacts to locate candidates is a good method, but you have to work at it, not just make a few phone calls. Contact everyone you can think of, and ask each one to suggest additional names. Follow up every possibility your contacts give you, and don't forget to thank them. Be wary of careless vetting of candidates from this source. Too often a friend's recommendation is taken totally on faith. Try to interview and judge candidates from this source just as you do the others. One final point: Keep in mind that the Old Boy Network seldom sends you many girls—or boys who aren't white.

■ *Current employees.* These days many companies rely heavily on referrals from employees. This has several advantages. The new people are likely to get a good feel for your company from their friends, and so are better prepared to work there. The employee who recruits a candidate will feel some responsibility for her recommendation and will make an effort to help the new person work out. This practice enhances morale and group spirit. Beware, however, of becoming too inbred.

■ *Temporary agencies.* Consider one more option: Can you get someone for the job from a temporary employment service? Hiring a temp can let you cover a gap without making a permanent commitment. You get a chance to evaluate the person they send on the actual job and can easily ask them to send you someone else if you're not getting the performance you want. And if the temp turns out to be top-drawer, you can make him an offer for a permanent position.

Step 4. Choose Applicants to Interview. Once you have that pile of resumés on your desk, you need to select candidates for interviews. You may find there is a shortage of good applicants. Try to resist lowering your standards. Consider rewriting your ad, pursuing other media, or sweetening the compensation (or just giving it more prominence in the ad). However, keep in mind that many otherwise good people lack job-hunting skills. Try to look past an unattractive resumé to see if there might be a strong candidate behind it.

Step 5. Interview Candidates. The purpose of the interview is to give you a chance to evaluate the candidate on three factors:

1. Qualifications—is the candidate *able* to do the job?
2. Motivation—does the candidate *want* to do the job?

3. Character—is the candidate the *kind of person* you want in
your company and in this job?

Qualifications. Judging the candidate's *qualifications* is
the easiest part. You have her resumé. Now, with the job description
in front of you, dig in and get the details. Go down your list of
specifications one by one and satisfy yourself that she's got what you
want. Some items cannot be evaluated from the resumé, or even from
probing questions. You can check credentials and experience by calling
her college and her former employers. *Always* do so—you may be
surprised how many liars there are in the world. A plant tour is another
good way to check on experience if you use it shrewdly. Does she
obviously know her way around and understand what's going on? Does
she ask intelligent questions?

If knowledge is a criterion, a few well-prepared questions can
quickly settle any uncertainty. Judging skills is much harder. Lead the
candidate to talk at length about her past work; have her describe *how*
she did it. Listen carefully; with a little practice, you'll be able to hear
the difference between the confidence of talent and the hesitation and
evasion of bluff. Another good technique is the "what if" question:
"How would you handle such-and-such?"

Of course, simple skills such as typing can be subjected to direct
test. Intelligence you can generally judge pretty well from conversation, but always try to back up your evaluation with some sort of check
against real performance; some people are lousy at talking but very
good at doing—or the opposite. Creativity, as already mentioned,
should always be evaluated on past performance. Somebody who
comes up with bright ideas during the interview should not be overestimated; look for proof that she can carry through her ideas to a
finished product.

> Before using any sort of test as part of the hiring process,
> get legal advice. Federal and state antidiscrimination laws
> often tightly restrict what is permissible. General-ability
> tests such as IQ tests are generally *not* permissible. Even
> a customized test which specifically examines the actual
> skills and abilities needed to do the job may put you on
> the receiving end of a lawsuit.

Interviews also provide you with an opportunity to evaluate some
less obvious or less tangible qualifications. If social skills are part of
the job—and they frequently are for management jobs—take her out
to lunch. See if she has basic table manners, if she can carry on a

social conversation effectively. You may discover in this process that she can't resist a second martini—or a third. Watch how she speaks to a waiter; if she's curt or rude to this "menial," that may be a hint about how she'll treat her subordinates. Be sure to introduce her to all the people she'll be working with if hired (and later ask their opinions).

Motivation. *Motivation* can never be taken for granted. Of course, a candidate who seems unenthusiastic at the interview can be discarded as a poor risk. But a gung-ho attitude is hardly a guarantee of real motivation—it's too easy to fake. To judge motivation effectively, remember what it is: First and foremost, motivation is *enjoying the job.* In the long run, even the most conscientious worker will slack off if he's not enjoying his work. So ask questions about what he likes. "Do you enjoy your current job? *What* do you like about it? What do you dislike? What part of your work do you enjoy the most?" John Molloy suggests an excellent question: "Describe the last time you got real personal joy from your work."* Note that these questions focus on past or present. Questions about the future ("How would you like . . . ?" or "Where do you want to be in five years?") are unproductive. People don't really know their future feelings, so you'll get either a vague generality or a snappy trick answer from some "how-to-get-a-job" book.

Character. Evaluating the *character* of a candidate has an old-fashioned ring to it, so these days people usually refer to "psychological factors." Call it what you will, but recognize the importance of this criterion.

First you need to know: Is this person a winner or a loser? Sometimes you can spot a loser, almost at a glance. She trudges into your office apathetic, sad, obviously defeated by life. Usually it's not so easy, but there are ways.

- *Winners feel responsible for themselves.* They believe that their own actions determine what happens to them. Losers believe they are controlled by forces outside themselves. In conversation, probe for these attitudes. Bring up the subject of luck. A loser blames bad luck for his failures. The winner, if hit by a meteorite, would say, "I shouldn't have been standing there." Influence is another telltale subject. As Molloy points out, a favorite saying of losers is, "It's not what you know, it's who you know." The winner says, "It's who you know—so it's up to me to know the right people."

Molloy's Live for Success (New York: William Morrow, 1981), p. 18.

- *Winners are energetic.* Look into the candidate's hobbies and sports activities. It doesn't matter much what they are, so long as he's clearly active. Oddly enough, the chap with no outside interests probably won't be a tiger on the job. The loser can just barely struggle through a thirty-five-hour workweek; the rest of the time he naps or watches TV. The real winner may play tennis and chess, be a miniature railroad buff, and write haiku in his spare time—in addition to a heavy work load.

- *Winners have self-esteem.* They never plead or grovel, even when desperate. They project a calm conviction of their own value. Losers, on the other hand, typically slide into the extremes: either self-criticism and supplication or bluster and bragging.

Never hire a loser—never. Beware of pity. The guy who had "bad luck" in his previous job will have "bad luck" in your company. If his last boss was "prejudiced," he's going to sue you for discrimination. Harden your heart and send him away.

Check for another quality: integrity. A resort to polygraph examinations or handwriting analyses is not recommended. All you need is one simple psychological principle: People almost invariably assume that other people are just like themselves. In this specific application, it means that a dishonest person, given the opportunity, will assume you are a crook also and will speak and act accordingly.

A new employee suggested to me a way to, in effect, cheat the employment agency through which I hired him of part of its fee, to our mutual advantage. It wasn't quite blatant enough to justify firing him, but as I declined I made a mental note to keep an eye on him. Still, when he left the company, he took some of my money with him.

REM

As you converse with the candidate, probe her attitudes with remarks about unpopular organizations. If she expresses the feeling that it's all right to cheat an insurance company, or a bank, or the phone company—watch out. She may just as easily convince herself that she's justified in cheating *you.*

A lot of the traditional rules of interviewing may seem like nitpicking, but they do have some validity. They are based on the fact that at the interview you are seeing the candidate at his best. A minor deficiency that shows up at the interview may presage a major deficiency after hiring.

I didn't want to be old-fashioned and arbitrary. He showed up for the interview without a tie, but I hired him anyway. He showed up for work without a shave.
REM

When time comes to make your choice, you may find you're not happy with any of the alternatives. After all this work you are reluctant to give up and start over—but maybe you'd better. It's easy to hire someone. But if you have to fire her, it's not very pleasant. After you've done a couple of firings, you'll realize that you'd rather go three rounds with a sumo wrestler. Hire carefully—very carefully.

CHECKLIST
Before You Hire

☐ Have you evaluated the candidate on every qualification in the job description?
☐ Have you checked with the candidate's job references?
☐ Have you checked with references *not* provided by the candidate?
☐ Is there evidence that the candidate has enjoyed in the past doing the kind of work you're offering?
☐ Does the candidate have adequate social skills for the position?
☐ Has the candidate been introduced to potential coworkers?
☐ Is the candidate a "winner"?
☐ Is the candidate honest even when being honest exposes him or her to ridicule?
☐ Did the candidate show up for the interview clean, groomed, and properly dressed?
☐ Do you feel really comfortable with hiring this candidate?

MAKING THINGS CLEAR

Make your choice, make your offer, and when it's accepted, make damn sure the new employee knows the score. Give her a job description in writing; you may want to rephrase the one you wrote at the start of the hiring process, but keep it just as specific. State in writing what is expected of her, and also what she can expect in terms of compensation, vacation, benefits, salary or promotion reviews, and so on.

There's always a temptation to gloss over any uncomfortable questions; and too often the new worker, eager for the job, will refrain from rocking the boat. But any hand waving or "we'll worry about that later" may plant the seeds of future trouble. Keep in mind that the embarrassing question unasked now may mean a lawsuit or a union organizing drive later on.

These days, hiring is also subject to a thicket of antidiscrimination laws. Unfortunately, it's impossible for us to guide you through this jungle because the rules change constantly, and often retroactively. You need professional advice and a constant effort to keep current with the latest regulations. *Do not* assume that being honestly unbiased is enough—it isn't.

COMPENSATION AND MOTIVATION

When you hire someone, the question of compensation comes up. Nobody has yet devised the perfect compensation system, and you'll have to develop something suitable for the specific situation in your business. However, certain principles may prove helpful.

■ *Compensation should support.* Compensation must include an irreducible minimum that will provide basic financial security for the employee. This also applies to cofounders, and to *you*. You may take a substantial cut or even skip a paycheck or two when cash flow is in a fade, but don't try to show off by starving yourself and your family. It can lead to some very bad decisions.

■ *Compensation should motivate.* This can be tricky. For instance, profit sharing is overrated. It has two faults. First, it's too dilute—employees know that individual efforts have only a small effect on profits, so why bother? Good motivational systems reward employees for *their* results, not the company's.

Second, no employee—except for the CEO—really has control of, or responsibility for, profits as such. A good system ties employees' rewards to factors under their control. However, be careful: Don't set up a conflict among the workers. A little competitiveness is fine, but not a system where one worker gets rewarded at the expense of another. Try adding a component based on team performance.

■ *Compensation should be immediate.* A critically important principle: *Reward in real time.* A year-end bonus waits much too long to tell people what they're doing right or wrong. Any monetary reward should appear in the paycheck immediately following the performance to be rewarded.

—But not too immediate. Stock-purchase plans or stock options present problems of their own. What if somebody doesn't work out? You may not want a disgruntled ex-employee as a stockholder. If he's a cofounder, he may own an annoyingly large hunk of your company, and use it to make a lot of trouble as you essay your next financing. You can limit this difficulty by using buyback provisions, but keep in mind that the cash necessary for a buyback may not be readily available when you need it. Also, various legal restrictions may hamper your ability to buy back stock. Try to avoid awarding stock up front; instead, feed it out as it's earned by performance. Consider provisions that transform common stock to nonvoting preferred if the owner leaves the company.

▪ *Compensation should be fair.* Make a real effort to tie rewards to objective, tangible, indisputable criteria. A bonus based on "attitude" or other subjective, vague standards may encourage favoritism and other abuses. Also, anticipate the need to extend rewards to those who will come aboard later. Don't be so generous with the early participants that you run out of goodies to distribute.

Before you start hiring—before you talk to the first prospective cofounder, if possible—think out the principles of your compensation system very carefully. And before you finalize the details, talk it over with your lawyer and accountant.

THE SUPPORTING TEAM

You will need professional *counselors*. They are part of your team too. Many entrepreneurs choose a lawyer or accountant very casually on the recommendation of an acquaintance. If you're inexperienced, you may never realize that the person you've retained is a total dud. If you already have a lawyer or accountant handling your personal affairs, the instinctive course of action is to retain him for your company's needs too. This may not be a good idea.

You want to have a good business lawyer, someone familiar with corporate and business law, from an early stage. You are usually better off selecting a lawyer on the basis of a personal recommendation than out of the Yellow Pages, but even if she gets rave reviews from a friend, check her out. Does she have other clients like you? Is she experienced in this type of work? We laypeople tend to think of lawyers as generalists, but modern legal practice is extremely specialized.

As you investigate, remember that a lawyer, like a stockbroker, should give good execution. When you need something done, will she get right on it—or dawdle? When Anthony Trollope created his famous fictional law firm, he named it Slow & Bideawhile. Be sure you don't retain them; things move faster now than they did a century ago. You want someone who is efficient and gives good service even to a small client.

You probably can't afford, and don't want, the services of a top partner in a major law firm. This leaves you with two choices: a small firm, or a junior person in a large firm. There's much debate over the relative merits of these two options. It seems likely, however, that the former is the best choice for a small, stable niche company, and that the latter is better for a growth company.

A tip: Legal services can be quite expensive. When you need a legal document, such as a contract or a patent application—avoid asking your attorney to write it. Look around for a similar kind of document, and draft what you need yourself by copying shamelessly. Then submit it to your attorney and ask her to suggest revisions. This saves a lot of time and reduces the amount you spend on fees. Also, it helps to ensure that your lawyer understands clearly what you want the document to accomplish.

You also need an *accountant*—again, from an early stage. It is possible for a layperson to set up and operate the accounting system of a small business, but only a masochist would want to. Bookkeeping and accounting are easy; it's dealing with taxes that no civilized person should have to endure.

Your accountant, like your lawyer, should be carefully vetted before you retain him. Remember that this fellow will be handling all your taxes; you will have to rely on him, and if he makes a mistake, the IRS could wipe you out. Again, good execution is critical. Talk to some of his clients. Does he get out financial statements and tax returns *on time?*

Also be sure he is familiar with small-business accounting and with your industry. Accounting has become just as specialized as law.

Accountants, like lawyers, prefer to use "canned" systems, because they're easier and cheaper. If your company has special needs or unique practices, being shoehorned into a generic white-box accounting system may cause serious problems. We therefore advise you to learn elementary accounting and bookkeeping yourself, so that you can discuss your needs with your accountant in an intelligent manner. Insist on statements that provide you with the information you need; many accountants prefer a format that simply rephrases the contents of your tax return and is incomprehensible to nonspecialists. Go into all this *at the start;* if your accountant is unwilling to cooperate, try someone else.

THE BOARD OF DIRECTORS

If you use the corporate form, you'll be legally required to have a board of directors. In legal theory, the directors run a corporation. They are supposed to perform four functions:

1. They select, and if necessary fire, the CEO and other members of top management. Also, the directors should be involved in the development of new members of management.

2. They represent and protect the interests of the stockholders. Specifically, they are responsible for watching over the corporation's financial affairs to make sure no hanky-panky is occurring. They also must make certain decisions where management could have a conflict of interest—setting management compensation is an obvious example.

3. They formally decide major questions. There's no consistent rule as to what is a "major" decision. Usually it's a decision where the stakes are high enough that the CEO is afraid to face the music alone if something goes wrong.

4. They pitch in as general high-level handymen whenever their specific talents are needed, giving advice, providing contacts, helping with negotiations.

In practice, the board is usually a rubber stamp for management. Entrepreneurs, like other captains of industry, almost always seek the weakest board they can get away with. But a strong board of directors can be a tremendous asset, especially for a growing company.

We recommend that you choose strong people for your board. They will fall into three categories: members of management (you and your cofounders); major stockholders or their representatives; and outside directors. One good policy is to have roughly equal numbers of these three types. You, as CEO, will have a strong voice in the selection of directors, but as the company grows you will come under increasing pressure, especially from investors, to put other selections on the board. One way to maintain effective control is to take the initiative in bringing in outside directors. Don't wait until the venture capitalists force their candidates on you. Find people you have confidence in, preferably other entrepreneurs with strong credentials.

Never take the board of directors for granted. Select directors with care, keep them informed, stay close to them. Big investors will expect to name their own people to the board. That's fine, but insist that their candidates meet your standards. Put up a fight, if necessary, but don't let Mr. Moneybag's incompetent brother-in-law sit on your board. All directors must bring with them useful talents, knowledge, and if possible prestige. Every director must have integrity. Every director must be compatible with the rest of the team—don't ever allow your board to split into factions. And above all, every director must be *willing to work*. Expect each member of the board to take an active interest in the company; to visit, investigate, question, advise; to be continually on the lookout for ways to help.

Okay, we admit it. All this splendid advice falls into the "nice-work-if-you-can-get-it" category. Recruiting competent outside board members is hell these days. As soon as you make the approach, you'll be asked about your directors' and officers' insurance: Are you providing coverage against getting sued? Since D&O insurance premiums are crushingly high, you probably are not. Still, try to get good people. Remember, a board member doesn't have to be rich and famous (though it helps). A bright rising star may be willing to join your board as a career move, figuring there's more to gain than lose.

Many entrepreneurs, especially in technology businesses, recruit a board of advisers—prominent scientists or other experts. This is great if you really use them for advice (and of course prestige). But it is not a substitute for having a real board of directors.

THE COFOUNDERS

Your earliest and most crucial personnel decisions involve cofounders.

If you did the self-analysis recommended in Chapter One you should have a list of tasks that you don't want to do, either because you're not good at them or because you don't enjoy them, or both. Many of these tasks may be of the sort that relatively low-level employees can handle. Others may demand top-management attention. Look for cofounders to take on these important functions that you don't want to deal with. Don't accept cofounders at random, people who are friends or relatives or who are just looking for a good thing. Write job descriptions and go through the five-step hiring process described in Chapter Three. Never forget that the *only* valid reasons to take on a cofounder are to relieve you of work that you don't want and to provide essential talents you don't have.

It's not uncommon for a new entrepreneur to take on partners she doesn't actually need simply because she's unsure of herself and feels insecure. Watch out for this tendency.

You may feel guilty about taking the good stuff yourself and making someone else do the unpleasant parts. Don't worry about it. If you've got the right cofounder, she'll *like* doing what you consider the unpleasant parts. This principle is the key to forming a compatible top-management team. Good people seldom fight over money or recognition, but they'll fight like minks over responsibility. The only way to keep the peace is to minimize overlap between cofounders' interests. Clearly define each one's domain; good fences make good neighbors.

You'll probably find that a person who likes doing things you hate has a personality different from yours. Welcome this. Too many start-up teams are overly homogeneous. A bunch of engineers can definitely use a marketing type to remind them that their better mousetrap won't sell itself. A group of high-flying salespeople will do much better if augmented with a controller who can bring them back to earth on occasion. If you're an optimist, be sure there's a pessimist on your team. If you're a pessimist, be sure there's an optimist.

Another area of concern is commitment. There are a lot of people out there who *think* they are eager to get in on the ground floor of a new business. Your selection process should aim to weed them out. Test the commitment of each cofounder in three stages.

1. *Will he work?* As you develop your business plan, be sure each cofounder is given tough assignments as his contribution. Slackers should be politely excused and replaced.

2. *Will he invest?* Pay all expenses yourself during the planning phase, but make it clear that all cofounders are expected to chip in at incorporation. (Each should contribute roughly the same amount, by the way. Money talks, and a VP who puts in ten times the amount the others do may start talking too loudly.) Those who don't write a check at incorporation should be dropped courteously but mercilessly. It makes no difference whether they are unable or unwilling to invest.

3. *Will he come on board?* When you actually start operations, it is time for your people to cut the umbilical with their employers and work full time for the new company. Make no exceptions. The chap who wants to play it safe will leave you in the lurch just when you need him most.

Finally, compensation is especially tricky when dealing with co-founders. In addition to the principle we developed earlier, keep in mind the importance of *clarity*. There is a deadly temptation to come to a rough agreement on touchy questions like stock apportionment and leave the tedious details to be settled later. When "later" comes—especially if a cofounder is being dropped—you may be in for a fight. Right at the start, define what each cofounder's responsibilities are and precisely how he is to be paid. Leave no detail unspecified, and *put it in writing*. When verbal agreements are made, people hear what they want to hear.

Cofounders usually get their major compensation in stock. We pointed out earlier that stock should seldom be awarded up front. Let's reiterate that here, for the stakes are much higher. Each cofounder should purchase some stock at incorporation. The rest should be awarded, by the board of directors, based on the performance of explicitly defined, previously specified tasks. This probably has to go for you too.

BUILDING A COMPANY CULTURE

There is nothing mystical about a "company culture." A company culture is simply the sum of attitudes, motives, and policies of your individual employees. Every company that survives develops some sort of culture. If you do not actively define a culture by intention, your employees will randomly define one by default.

The kind of culture depends on the kind of company you have—or want to have. Consider, for instance, the typical telemarketing company. Such a company is likely to develop a company culture that emphasizes aggressive selling—get your foot in the door (or rather phone), blast down the customer's sales resistance with a petard of high-pressure sales techniques, and leave him dazed with a purchase he had no intention of making. The best-rewarded and most admired people in the boiler room are those salespeople who can move the largest amount of product each month. The danger in carrying this culture to its limits is that, having been encouraged to abuse their customers, employees are not likely to show great respect for the company or for each other. The company culture will thus include a great deal of disloyalty and infighting.

To understand a company's culture, first ask: What are its employees most proud of? At Toyota, it might be turning out a high-quality product. At Genentech, it might be technological leadership. At Saatchi & Saatchi, it might be creativity. What do you want *your* employees to be proud of?

Company Culture and Motivation.

Company culture is the best way to motivate employees. Experience has shown again and again—in big companies, in government bureaucracies, in socialist economies—that you cannot get real effort out of people over the long term solely with carrot-and-stick tactics. Rules, quotas, bonuses, merits and demerits, even the whip will not make them put out 100 percent. To get their best effort you must engage their loyalty and enthusiasm.

How do you do it? There are four things you must do.

1. *Set an example.* Employees are never better motivated than top management. If you want them to work hard—*you* must work harder. If you want them to drop everything and rally round when a customer has a problem—*you* must take the lead. If you want them to keep costs down—*you* had better be conspicuously frugal.

2. *Make sure your management control systems harmonize with your company's goals.* Everything you use to make sure things are done properly is part of your management control systems. Vacation policy, accounting procedures, work rules, quality standards—any rule, procedure, or policy constitutes an official statement of what you want your company culture to be. Thus every item should be carefully examined to determine how it fits in with your objectives.

Suppose you want your employees to take the initiative in spotting and correcting quality problems—but your assembly-line work rules require the worker to get permission before going to the bathroom. Suppose you want new inventions from your R&D group—but every new idea must pass a strict evaluation process before getting approval. Suppose you want every employee to be oriented toward solving customer problems—but promotions go to those who are prompt and accurate with their sales reports. If this sort of contradiction is common in your controls, your employees will be frustrated and turn off. Most will serve their time and try to get by with minimum effort. The best will leave.

3. *Go and find out.* Don't settle for an "open-door policy"—go out the door and actively seek out grievances to resolve. Don't just put up a suggestion box—ask people for suggestions in person. There's only one way to find out how your control systems are working, and that is to examine them in action. Set aside a certain number of hours each month for "inspection"—informal and unscheduled, not the white-glove type. Drop in on the production area, talk to the janitor, ride along with a salesperson for a day.

On these occasions, you must have an open, noncritical attitude.

Don't lay down the law, ask questions. Avoid, however, vague queries. "How are you doing?" "How do you like it here?" "Do you have any problems?" Instead, get down to specifics. "What do you think about this design—could it be made easier to assemble?" "Would you say we're throwing away scrap that could be salvaged?" "When you need a firm shipping date to close a sale, would it help to have a hot line to Production that you could call?"

4. *Motivate attitude with the intangibles.* You'll recall that basing tangible rewards such as salary, bonus, or promotion on attitude is a poor idea. Tangible rewards (and punishments) should always be based on objective criteria of performance. The complement to this principle is that attitude, effort, and enthusiasm should be rewarded with the intangibles: praise in front of coworkers, or better yet in front of family; a letter of commendation in the personnel file (with a copy on the bulletin board); an award ceremony; a plaque or trophy. These are the appropriate ways to applaud those who put out for the company. (Often, of course, they will go to the same people who are getting bonuses for specific accomplishments.)

There are, however, two traps to watch out for. First, never use intangible rewards as a consolation prize. If someone deserves a raise, give her a raise—not a medal.

Second, beware the "employee-of-the-month" program. Sooner or later—usually sooner—a month comes in which nobody has done anything outstanding. If you give it to a second-rate worker just once, you make all the previous winners feel defrauded and, by cheapening your reward, destroy its future value. Never make a commendation a routine event; it is esteemed because it is exceptional.

If you follow these rules, your company will have a culture that complements your goals and makes them effective. You'll never have trouble hiring or keeping good people. Union organizers will hit your company and bounce. And your company will be a happy and pleasant place to work for your employees—and for you.

CAUTIONARY TALE
Insecurity in Security

Some time ago I was invited to serve on the board of directors of a company I'll call Digitensor. Pat Chroman, the founder, chairman, and president, was an engineer who had developed some technology that could be extremely valuable to the security industry. There is a persistent, ongoing need for methods to check people out before allowing them access to business premises or military facilities or computers and so on. Chroman's gadgetry used electronic means to determine, very reliably, whether an applicant for admission was authorized or not. Don't ask me how it worked. He often tried to explain it to me, but I'm not a technology type, and all I can remember is that it had something to do with determining whether a person was contravariant or covariant.

With all the concern these days about computer crime, terrorism, and security in general, you can see what a tremendous market opportunity was available, if the device could be developed and marketed properly. That was where I came in. Digitensor had made a public offering, but was trying to raise even more money to finish development and start marketing.

Chroman's background was essentially pure engineering. He had founded a previous company, which had failed. I didn't hold that against him; on the contrary, I prefer to work with entrepreneurs who have had some acquaintance with adversity. Those who have never experienced anything but success may crumple up when things get tough. Digitensor had a really exciting product and presented an interesting challenge. Chroman had attracted a fine group of engineers, but at this point it was time to build a complete team; supposedly the product was about ready to come out of the lab and get into the market-place. Digitensor needed a skilled chief financial officer to handle the considerable amount of money already involved and to assist in raising more. It also needed to add a sales manager with some extensive marketing experience, and a production manager competent to develop a reliable manufacturing process for a new and very complex device.

Unfortunately, almost as soon as I took my seat on the board, there began to be friction between the CEO and me. Chroman was an engineer's engineer, and for him it all began and ended in engineering. He paid lip service to the need for strong people in marketing and sales and finance and production, but in his heart of hearts he was loyal only to his own god. As an engineer, he felt that if you perfected a fine product, everything else would take care of itself. The market would knock down your door. Money would pour in, and any kind of financial controls or accounting would be unnecessary. Production would be trivial, because the item was so well designed and easy to manufacture.

In short, product design was to him the creative and important part of a business venture; the other activities were merely incidental. This sort of attitude makes it difficult to build an effective management team. In fairness to Chroman, I have to say that this "my-specialty-is-the-only-thing-that-counts" attitude is not confined to engineers. I've encountered it among sales, marketing, financial, and production people also.

Chroman and I quickly tangled over the selection of a sales manager. I had managed to identify a number of candidates who in my judgment had the background and temperament that would be necessary to fill the job. Chroman refused even to interview any of them. He had been "fortunate" enough to encounter someone who had expressed an interest in the product. This individual worked for a major computer manufacturer as a divisional sales manager. He was extremely enthusiastic about the Digitensor security device—so Chroman hired him as sales manager.

Our new sales manager, though well-meaning, simply did not have what it took to promote a new product in a skeptical marketplace. He was used to working with the resources and support of a large organization, selling established products. His task was somewhat complicated, to say the least, because the product was always under redesign. Chroman had great difficulty letting go and pushing the product out into the marketplace. He always wanted to make it more and more perfect.

As chief financial officer he hired an accountant who had worked in his father's accounting firm. This fellow was a perfectly competent CPA, but he simply was unable to cope with the start-up nature of the business. He didn't have any idea of how to manage the finances of a growing enterprise. Eventually this poor chap was replaced, but unfortunately his successor was no better.

Then there was the production manager. Chroman hired a man who had worked for him in his previous, unsuccessful venture. He had pretty much a job-shop background and lacked the experience needed to set up from scratch a full-scale production facility.

What these people and indeed the entire management team had in common was weakness—not just weakness in qualifications for their particular jobs but personal weakness. Chroman kept them all under his thumb and ran the company as a dictatorship. He could not brook any opposition. As a result he was surrounded by yes-men, and that is the last thing you want in a growth business. Independent viewpoints from all the various disciplines are necessary. One man can never have all the answers, particularly if he has an extremely narrow background and experience.

I began to realize that Chroman, in spite of real talent as an engineer, was extremely uncertain about himself. He felt fundamentally inadequate because he didn't understand marketing, didn't understand finance—didn't understand business, in short. He was superb in technology, but management issues made him feel insecure, threatened by anyone who really knew these areas.

This insecurity was also the source of the company's persistent inability to get its product design finalized and start selling. In my frustration I sometimes felt that all Chroman really wanted to do was sit at the bench and make that machine do more wonderful things than it had done the day before, irrespective of whether it ever got onto the market. In fact, that turned out to be pretty much the case. If he got out and actually did business, then he would no longer be relying on his strength as a creative technology person. He would have to deal with all sorts of nontechnology issues that made him uncomfortable.

The result of all this was that Digitensor went nowhere. Nobody really knew what to do. The product just sat in the lab, being "improved" and adapted, under various contracts, for specialized applications. Digitensor didn't have a single commercial site. Naturally, this couldn't be Chroman's fault, could it? So he began firing his yes-men and replacing them with other yes-men. Pretty soon the company had a revolving door of key personnel, and it hurt the company badly. The customers lost faith because every time they called there was a different sales manager in place. The financial community lost faith because chief financial officers kept coming in and going out.

After about eighteen months, I was fed up and left the board of directors. Digitensor still exists, the last I heard, but has gone pretty much nowhere.

I want to emphasize that this is not a case of an incompetent or neurotic entrepreneur. As head of a contract engineering company, Chroman would have been perfect. With just himself and a few assistants, working on the leading edge of technology and not needing to worry about manufacturing, marketing, or financial issues, his talents would have been put to ideal use.

I think Chroman instinctively knew this, because what he did, in effect, was to run Digitensor as if it were a contract engineering company. But Digitensor was based on a very bright idea for filling a very important need in the market. The market demanded a solution to its problem; it needed a real product, and to supply that product Chroman *had* to build a growth company. As is often the case, the decision to tackle a certain market problem virtually compelled certain decisions about the company.

Given that, what should have been done? First, of course, Pat Chroman should have confronted his own problems with delegation, and accepted that he could not run a public, high-growth company out of his hip pocket. Next, he should have built a strong board of directors. I probably was a poor choice as a director; somebody with more knowledge of technology might have communicated with him more effectively. And to have a dissident like myself on the board was in itself a problem that should have been resolved earlier, one way or another. Above all, there was a need to have a system—some sort of rules or principles—for hiring top management. It's easy to criticize Pat Chroman for letting his personal insecurity result in poor hiring decisions, but all of us are subject to similar tendencies. That's why you need a *policy* to guide you in hiring.

HDS

Four

MARKET RESEARCH

It is a capital offense to theorize in advance of the facts.

Sir Arthur Conan Doyle, "The Adventure of the Second Stain"

Most new companies fail. And the most common cause of failure is simple starvation—inadequate sales.

A new venture is particularly vulnerable because, unlike an established company, it does not have ongoing sales. You must build sales from scratch. So the first question you should ask is: Do you have a *market* for your product or service? Are there customers out there—people who *need* and *want* what you plan to sell?

Your estimate of future sales provides the foundation of your business plan. As we'll see when we discuss financial projections in Chapter Ten, everything is based on your sales projections. Your estimates of costs, profits, cash flow—all depend on sales, and all are pie-in-the-sky unless your sales projections are reliable. This is the first (but not the only) reason you need market research. Before you jump off the diving board, it's wise to make sure there's water in the pool.

"TOP-DOWN" MARKET RESEARCH

Investors look for *evidence* that your venture's sales will be high enough to make the company profitable. When they pick up your business plan, the first thing they do is flip through it to find the key paragraph that addresses this question. Suppose you do your market research the way it's usually done. Then they'll read something like this:

> According to an authoritative study done by *Mushroom Age* in 1990, there are 10,000 mushroom farms in the United States alone, and each spends an average of $20,000 per year on mushroom-cutting machinery. Thus the total market is $200 million per year. On even a pessimistic estimate we can take 2 percent of this market the first year, and so we project sales of $4 million . . .

At this point the investor closes your business plan, tosses it into the "reject with regrets" basket, and picks up the next plan. You just blew it.

But, you protest, you're estimating only a 2 percent market share. Surely it's perfectly reasonable to expect that you can attain it—such a tiny percentage!

Is it? Try the following experiment. Go to one of the established companies in the industry, Monolithic Mushroom Machinery. Talk to the CEO. Tell him: "Our new company, Incandescent Fungoid Cutters, Inc., is going to compete with your business. We want to take away some of your market share—just a *little*—you'll never miss it!" See if he thinks that's "reasonable."

This is why "top-down" market research, performed in the library, is of limited value. It doesn't matter whether it's 1 percent of a $1 billion market or 100 percent of a $10 million market. Either way, you're going to be taking those sales away from someone else who has them now (or would like to have them), and he's not going to give them up without a fight. In fact, he's going to fight like a Tasmanian devil.

The top-down method of market research merely establishes that there *is* a market—people are buying this kind of product, and plenty of it. There are a number of sources you can use. Market research firms produce studies of markets they consider interesting. If a recent study exists for your market, you can buy a copy—for several thousand dollars, typically. Fortunately, major conclusions are commonly published in trade magazines, so you can read at least that much for free. A publication called *Predicasts* provides a summary of these studies every year, indexed by industry (SIC code, to be exact). You can usually find a copy in the nearest B school library. If you are planning to sell a consumer product or service, census statistics available—again at a hefty price—from the federal government can be invaluable in defining the demographic and economic characteristics of a given geographical area. You certainly should familiarize yourself with as much of this kind of information as you can manage to acquire—but *don't stop there.*

For some years I worked with a company that built retirement centers and observed a number that had failed. These projects are not inexpensive to construct, and the housing and facilities are designed specifically for the needs of the elderly and can't be easily modified, so if you don't attract your intended market you're stuck with a lot of empty units and a real financial disaster.

Each of these failures resulted from reliance on census information without actual research on the ground. The developers went to major accounting firms and paid them to do so-called "feasibility studies." These involved getting the census data for the appropriate tracts and determining how many elderly there were in the local population, their incomes, competitive housing available, and so on. After careful analysis, the accountants came out with wonderful studies that confirmed that indeed there was a market and that demand for their units would be strong.

In each case the project, once constructed, went into bankruptcy because the promoters had not bothered to talk to anybody in the community. There was never a face-to-face conversation with people who would actually be buying into these apartments. It was all done by statistics—and goods and services are not bought by statistics but by people.

In one case the promoters arranged for a local Jewish temple to sponsor the project. Naturally they assumed that every Jewish person over sixty-five in the area—of whom there were many, according to the census data—would move in. So they didn't bother with little details like asking their prospective customers what size and shape and design of apartments they would like, or how much they would be willing to pay.

In another case the promoters chose to locate the project in a town that had an Italian-dominated city government. Unfortunately the prospective customers, who were almost exclusively WASPs, refused to live under this jurisdiction. Because of this prejudice the project could not be filled. Again, this problem could have been avoided if the promoters had gone out and actually talked to the customers.

HDS

In short, statistical studies of your market and its growth are very useful, but you still need to produce tangible evidence that *you* are going to be able to make significant sales.

MARKET RESEARCH FROM THE GROUND UP

The only way to get reliable sales projections is to do "ground-up" market research. Suppose the investor looks for that key paragraph and finds this:

We interviewed 100 randomly chosen mushroom farmers (see Appendix C for details) and showed them our prototype hot-wire mushroom cutter. Three of them gave us written purchase commitments on the spot, and five more stated that they would almost certainly buy one of our cutters as soon as we are in production. We expect that we will make 2,000 sales calls in our first year, and if we can maintain a 3% close ratio we will sell 60 machines. At $20,000 per unit, that projects first-year sales of $1,200,000 . . .

This is the kind of market research that makes an investor's checkbook itch. She is going to read on with real interest, because your plan stands out very favorably from most of the others in the stack. Every day she reads and rejects a dozen business plans with good products but no real market research. You, on the other hand, have demonstrated that there is a real need and desire for your product. And your actual contact with customers improves your credibility as someone who can not only investigate the market but sell to it.

Generating Sales Projections. Of course, the "bottom-up" market-research approach has a serious drawback—it involves an awful lot of work. The intimate details of preparing sales projections are beyond the scope of this book, but here is a simplified outline of what you will need to do.

1. *Select a random sample of your market.* And try to make it really random. If your research sample consists of your best prospects, you're in for a nasty surprise when you try to sell to the other guys. If you talk only to prospects in New York, you may later find out the hard way that Californians are different. Getting a truly random sample is not easy, but do your best. By the way, note that selecting those prospects who are easiest to locate does *not* give you a random sample.

2. *Interview your prospects.* You'll get the best results if you can do it in person. Telephone interviews are adequate. Surveys by mail are not so good but a lot better than nothing. If someone does not respond, do *not* drop her from the sample; count her as someone who will not buy. Use a written list of questions and be sure every prospect is asked *all* the questions and the *same* questions.

3. *Analyze the results.* Make a *conservative* estimate of the sales you can achieve. Keep in mind that just because you could "sell" 10 percent of the people you interviewed, you are *not* entitled to assume that you can sell 10 percent of the total market. Will you have enough salespeople even to call on everyone in the market? Will your salespeople be as convincing as you are? Will your sales arguments remain

convincing after your competitors have had a chance to counter them? And above all, how many of those "sure sales" will still be sold when it comes time actually to sign a check?

A market test needn't take long, especially if there isn't any market! While I was running Sedgwick Printout Systems, I was approached by a man who wanted to start a company in a related area. At about that time, technology had become available that made it possible to print text onto microfilm at high speed directly from computer tapes. He was sure there would be a huge demand for this service, which would put large amounts of information into a small space very quickly.

I looked at his business plan and did some very simple market research. I called up various computer operations in the New York area to see how much information they or their customers needed to store as a permanent record. It turned out that most of the data spewed out by their computers using line printers was of strictly temporary value—used for a short time and then thrown away. There just was not, at that time and place, a significant need for a magnetic-tape-to-microfilm service.

So I declined to participate in this venture. This chap went ahead, got funding, and opened up seven or eight microfilm service centers, and went bust after eighteen months. He really should have listened to his market.

    •   **HDS**

The need for realistic sales projections is the first reason you must do market research, but it's not the only reason, or even the most important. Even if you do a good job, your sales projections may not be very accurate. In fact, they could be way off. First-rate market-research professionals—top experts—told Ford that the Edsel was just what the American car-buying public wanted. A very good study done for Xerox (then called Haloid) predicted that its first copier would be a flop. Customers don't always do what they say they'll do! You must generate those sales projections, but go on to examine something even more important.

Understanding Your Market.   Here is the second reason you need market research: You need to *understand* your market. Getting valid sales projections is difficult because customers are not good at predicting what they will do in the future. What's more important, it doesn't tell you *how* to make the sale.

So the most important function of your market survey is to answer questions like the following:

▪ *Who is your customer?* Who actually makes the purchase decision? Be sure you don't end up aiming your sales presentation at someone who is unable to buy. If you're selling a retail item, it's not enough to say, "We're aiming at families in the $20,000 to $35,000 bracket." Define who buys it—Dad, Mom, Junior, Sis, or the whole family in conclave? Suppose you're selling to industry. What companies buy your type of product? Who within those companies sets the budgets, writes the specs, signs the purchase order? It may well be three different people, and you may have to sell all three of them— each in a different way and with different sales arguments.

▪ *What does the customer want?* The key to getting good results with this question is to focus on the past and present, not on the future. The usual practice is to say, "We're planning on having this feature in our product—would you like it?" This produces fuzzy and unreliable responses. Instead, ask what the customer has bought in the past, and why. What did he like about the unit he purchased last time? What did he dislike? What are his key concerns—price, quality, reliability, service, style?

▪ *How does the customer buy?* Again, focus on the past and present. How often does she buy? When was the last time? How much does she buy at once? Are there other items that she usually buys at the same time? Did she shop around last time? Whose products did she look at? How did she decide? Did she consult anybody for advice? If it's a retail item, how did she pay—cash, check, credit card?

▪ *How does the customer like to be sold?* What ads did she find memorable or enticing? Did she encounter sales tactics that turned her off? Was some sales argument particularly persuasive?

When I was sixteen, I took $40 that I'd saved up from my job in the Chemistry Stockroom and went to buy a slide rule. I wanted one rugged enough to use in the lab without concern. The salesman selected a K&E Deci-Lon—and threw it across the room. Then he went over, picked it up, and hammered it against the counter. It wasn't even scratched. I was sold on the spot. You probably remember from your own experience a similar case. As you talk to customers, be alert for these highly effective arguments or demonstrations; when you find one, use it!

REM

▪ *What does the customer think of your competitors?* Which ones is he familiar with? What is his image of each? What—in *his* opinion— are their strong and weak points? From whom does he buy now? Why? Does he switch brands readily or is he loyal to one supplier? When did he last switch? Why?

HPLC is an important technique for chemical analysis, and many companies have tried to enter the lucrative market for HPLC "columns." Newcomers, however, have encountered difficulty due to seemingly irrational customer brand loyalty. Customers often refuse to switch to a new brand, even though it's cheaper and performance is better. It turns out they won't switch *because* performance is better.

The reason: Developing a new analytical method using HPLC is a tedious process—even though, once the method is developed, it is fast and simple to do repetitive runs. Thus a new column's superiority works against it; the better performance means that the procedures worked out with the old column are no longer applicable and the method development work must be done over again. That can take thousands of dollars worth of an expensive chemist's time—dwarfing the $300 cost of a column.

A good market survey may tell you such interesting facts as that you are planning to sell the wrong product—or perhaps the right product for the wrong use.

You know Velcro—the sort of fuzzy tapelike fastener material. The company was founded originally by a wealthy Canadian friend of mine named Ben Webster. He didn't invent it, but bought the rights to the patent.

I became involved with him in a very minor way, but I remember a conversation we had about the business. He contended that Velcro fastenings would make the zipper obsolete. I suggested to him that he should first talk to people in the garment industry who bought zippers and determine what they required. For instance, would they reject Velcro because it was bulkier and less durable than a zipper? I also suggested that he look at the market in more general terms—not just zippers but buttons and snaps and buckles and so on.

Webster persisted in going after the zipper market. After some early hardships Velcro became a big success, and as we all know it is now being used to replace every kind of closure imaginable. Yet somehow zippers are still with us!

The point of this story is not that I was smarter than Ben Webster, but that nobody, no matter how smart, can safely enter a new market without a real knowledge of customers and their needs and wants. It's all very well to linger in the dining room with a decanter of claret and a fine cigar and speculate about the market, but that's no substitute for getting out there and talking to your customers.

HDS

In addition to familiarizing yourself with your customers and their characteristics, you must also understand the dynamics and standard operating procedures of the sales process in your industry. Particularly if you are selling to an industrial market, you must take into account the sales cycle and the purchasing process.

The Sales Cycle. Individuals who purchase retail goods or services are (usually) spending their own money. This is a natural source of sales resistance. Industrial purchases, whether of paper clips or jet aircraft, are made by people who are *not* spending their own money. So companies develop institutional procedures to create an artificial sales resistance. The standard method of controlling spending involves separation of the buying decision into three steps, with (in all but small companies) three different people involved:

1. Someone (generally a department manager) must *budget* the purchase, that is, authorize the expenditure and set an upper limit on the amount.
2. Someone else (often a specialist or technical person) must *specify* the purchase, that is, decide exactly what is needed.
3. Someone (usually the purchasing agent) will *select a vendor* and carry through the purchase.

So, if you are selling to an industrial market, you must know who these three people are in your customer company and how to sell to each of the three.

That's not all. This process takes time. Many promising start-ups have foundered because they failed to determine the length of the *sales cycle* for their product. This is the period from the first approach to the customer to the receipt of the money. (''The sale isn't made, until you get paid.'') It can vary from a few seconds to over a decade. If it's very long, you may starve to death while you are waiting. So you must find out in advance: How long will it take a customer to buy this product?

The sales cycle is critical for your start-up because there are substantial costs associated with waiting until the sale is made. You must pay to advertise, pay salespeople to sell, pay to manufacture the product, and pay to keep it in inventory. The longer it takes to make a sale—the longer the sales cycle—the longer you must carry all these costs before you get paid. A long sales cycle can have an absolutely devastating effect on your cash flow. The more expensive the product (and, the bigger the customer) the longer the sales cycle, because it

takes customers longer to make up their minds when a lot of money is
at stake.

Sales Size. So one of the most critical questions for any
start-up, and one of the most seldom asked, is: How big will a typical
sale be? The answer to this question determines how many sales you
must close to meet your total revenue objectives. Why is this important? Because it costs money to complete a sale. You must pay for
advertising to attract a customer; you must pay salary or commission
or bonus, commonly, to have a salesperson make the pitch and close
the sale; you must pay, often, a clerk to do paperwork; and you may
need to pay people to provide training or handholding or service to the
new customer.

A number of software firms have encountered serious
problems with service costs (or "support," as it's referred
to in the industry). Coming from a mainframe or minicomputer software background, where a program license
would cost thousands of dollars, they took it for granted
that customers would get hundreds of dollars worth of
advice and assistance in getting the program running for
their needs. But a microcomputer program that sells for
a few hundred dollars cannot justify this kind of support.

So if the typical sale is too small, it may cost you too much to
make it. On the other hand, if the typical sale is too big, it may take
you too long to make it. You need to check out this factor in advance
and be prepared.

The smaller the typical sale, the greater the proportion of your
costs that will be due to selling rather than production or other factors.
If you expect your typical sale to be very small, you must have an
eagle eye on your sales costs; you cannot afford to spend much sales
time on any one sale. Look at a newsstand: A fifty-cent transaction is
involved, which takes only seconds. If it took hours, or even minutes,
to sell a newspaper, it would be impossible to make a profit at that
price. Even supermarkets, with a much larger typical sale, suffer heavy
selling costs at the checkout counter. Hence the investment in scanners
and automatic changemakers so their sales clerks can spend less time
on each customer. As a bonus, they please their customers, who also
prefer to minimize the transaction time. So, for the small sale, keep
things moving—and the less paperwork the better.

There is of course one crucial exception to the "don't-waste-time-making-a-small-sale'' rule and that is the first sale. In some businesses you have many small sales but a few big customers—people who buy not much at a time, but buy often and regularly. It can be worthwhile—indeed essential—to spend time on the first sale or the first few sales to establish a regular customer. In this case you must regard the cost as a capital expenditure; though you take a loss on the early sales, it is made up over the years.

> The newsletter business is a good example. Commonly, the cost of the direct-mail advertising needed to get a new subscriber is so high that the subscription results in a loss for two or three years. But if renewal rates are high, the subscriber will eventually become profitable.

Large sales have their own advantages and perils. If your company can make very large sales—over $100,000, say—it can achieve growth in very large spurts. Furthermore, very large sales give your start-up credibility. A really large sale is not just a transaction, it is a news item. You can put out a press release and get some nice exposure. In doing so, you give your company the image of a solid organization.

On the other hand, the large sale has serious disadvantages. Your customer is likely to be a large company, since a small customer couldn't afford to spring for such a big invoice. They may have too much power over you. As noted above, the sales cycle on a large sale tends to be long—years, sometimes. Finally, don't forget that the large sale can take you up like a rocket—and down like the stick. When you are making small sales, losing any single sale is a small hit. When a typical sale is a third of a year's revenue for your company, losing one sale can wipe you out.

The Market-Research Process. There's no end of questions you can ask your customers. Carefully consider the structure of your questionnaire, to gather the maximum amount of important information without making the subject impatient. This is why face-to-face interviews work better than phone interviews, which in turn get a better response than mail surveys. People will take more time for a direct interview. You may want to split your questions among two or more groups. Ideally, you would want to do two or even three independent surveys so that results can be cross-checked for bias. You may want to improve response by thanking your subjects with a small gift; this practice is common, particularly when mail surveys are used.

There are a couple of other pitfalls we should mention. Be sure you do not neglect *geographical differences*. If you plan to sell your product nationwide, be aware that consumers may have very different tastes and attitudes in various parts of the country. This is true of industrial as well as retail customers. Of course if you plan to sell overseas, this becomes even more critical. But geography can be significant even on a block-by-block scale for a neighborhood retail store.

You should also consider the *timing* of your survey. Some markets—such as the semiconductor industry—are extremely subject to the business cycle. During the boom, they frantically race to expand capacity as backlogs build to months or even years. Then it all turns to bust. They lay off workers by the thousands and dispose of warehouses full of inventory at fire-sale prices. If these are your customers, conducting your market survey during the expansion phase may lead to overoptimistic estimates of the market, resulting in an extremely unpleasant shock when the crash comes. Once again we must emphasize that it is insufficient to ask customers what they are doing or plan to do in the future. You must probe their behavior in the past, and if they are part of a cyclical industry be sure you examine their behavior in all phases of past business cycles.

The *size* of your survey will depend, of course, on the size of the market you are investigating. The number you must sample to achieve a specified confidence level for the results can be calculated mathematically. It turns out that a surprisingly small survey will give good results if the sample is carefully chosen to be random. The national polls taken by the Harris and Gallup organizations can predict election results to within 3 percent, yet only about 4,000 people are interviewed.

Of course, the size and sophistication of your survey will also depend on your resources, and must be intelligently adapted to the size and complexity of your proposed business. If you're going to start a hot dog stand, simply standing at the proposed location, counting the lunch-hour crowd, and talking to passers-by may give you as much information as you need. On the other hand, if you propose to raise $50 million in venture capital to launch your new chocolate-coated mainframe computer worldwide, you'd better budget for a really substantial market-research program.

CALLING IN THE PROFESSIONALS

You may want to consider having your market research done by a professional company. This has certain advantages. Potential investors may be impressed by a prestigious consultant. Very large surveys can be done without drowning in paperwork. It's much easier to maintain anonymity, if you wish. Professionals can help you use techniques such as focus groups that can be a bit difficult for the inexperienced to handle properly.

On the other hand, it's expensive. Even a lousy survey costs thousands of dollars, and a good one will set you back even more. If you are planning to sell a consumer item nationwide, it may well be justified. But if you go this route, be sure you remain intimately involved with the whole process. Don't just toss it in their laps and wait until they give you their nice pretty book with the results in it. Insist on looking over their shoulders. Examine the design of their survey and ask them to explain what they're doing and why.

One advantage a professional market-research firm *may* provide is objectivity about the market. Unfortunately, you can't count on it. Consultants are in business too, and being marketing experts, they have a very strong predisposition to tell the client what he wants to hear.

ACHIEVING THE IDEAL

As we've mentioned before, what people *say* about what they plan to buy does not necessarily predict accurately what they actually *do* buy. That's why the very best way to do market research is to actually peddle the product.

Now, admittedly, many start-ups simply cannot do this. In many businesses you will need to raise money—perhaps millions of dollars—and spend it—before you even have Serial Number 0000001 in hand. Even so, with a little thought, effort, and determination, the vast majority of start-ups can do some sort of test marketing for new products.

If you are doing high-tech stuff, ask your engineers: "What's the least amount of money we would have to spend to get a prototype that we could take to customers?" Whatever they respond, cut the amount by a factor of ten and insist that they produce *something*—perhaps a simplified model with fewer features (which, incidentally, may sell much better than their more elaborate visions)—within that budget. If you and your team make a whole-hearted effort, surprisingly often you can produce a primitive, stripped-down version on a shoestring, which can then be taken out to beta sites and get you real-life feedback from the market.

If you can possibly build sample quantities of product, do so and take them out and sell them. If you can't, try to sell from a model or mock-up or an artist's drawing. If you can't do that, consider getting a temporary sales job with a competitor, just to get a feel for what the industry's customers are really like.

We cannot emphasize too strongly *early presence in the market.* The deeper that presence, the better. If you speculate about your market, you'll probably fail. If you talk to your market, your odds are better. If you physically get out there and sell to your market in the very earliest stages of your planning, your chances improve dramatically.

CHECKLIST
Market Research

A. Choosing a sample:
- [ ] Sample includes entire geographic area being addressed.
- [ ] Sample contains members of all market segments being addressed.
- [ ] Sample is chosen randomly.
- [ ] All members of sample are questioned consistently.

B. Data for sales projections:
- [ ] Each prospect gets standard presentation of product.
- [ ] Purchase commitment is requested.
- [ ] Commitments are classified and tabulated.
- [ ] Prospect is asked *when* he or she will buy.

C. Identifying the customer:
- [ ] Retail or [ ] industrial product.
- [ ] Individual, [ ] family, or [ ] group purchase (retail).
- [ ] Customer specifies, [ ] budgets, or [ ] purchases (industrial).

D. Retail sales—most likely customer:

Sex_____

Age group_____

Marital status_____

Income level_____

Ethnic group_____

Occupation———————————————————

Geographical location———————————————

Educational level———————————————————

E. Industrial sales—most likely customer:

Company business———————————————

Company size———————————————————

Geographical location———————————————

Other factors———————————————————

F. Customer needs and desires:

Past purchases, likes and dislikes———————

Benefits desired———————————————————

Features specifically mentioned by customer as
desirable———————————————————————

Ranking of concerns:
☐ price
☐ quality
☐ reliability
☐ durability
☐ service
☐ style
☐ other———————————————————————

G. Customer buying habits:

Frequency of purchase———————————————

Date of last purchase———————————————

Size of typical (or last) purchase———————

Seasonal item?———————————————————

Business-cycle effects?———————————————

Concurrent purchase of related items?—————

Extent of shopping around before purchase————

Criteria for decision———————————————————

Information or advice relied on_____

Payment: cash, credit card, check (retail)_____

Payment terms (industrial)_____

H. Selling media and arguments:

Media where customer expects ads_____

Ads customer found memorable or motivating_____

Sales tactics that offended customer_____

Sales tactics that impressed customer_____

I. Sales cycle:

Stages in customer's purchase decision_____

Time involved in previous purchase_____

J. Competition:

Competitors of which customer is aware_____

Customer's evaluation of competitors_____

Customer's current supplier(s)_____

Brand loyalty_____

Most recent switch: When and why?_____

COVERING YOUR TRACKS

In some cases, before doing your market research, you may want to
consider setting up a dummy organization and a cover story to conceal
your true identity and intentions. Word of your survey may get back
to your competitors, and if they're on the ball they'll respond. A
description of your prototype may be very useful to them. If they can
find out who you are, how you're financed, what your plans are, they
are in a position to launch a preemptive strike against you at a time
when you are most vulnerable. They can use all sorts of tactics,
ranging from predatory price cuts to lawsuits to vicious rumors.

That said, we must point out that most start-up entrepreneurs err
on the side of excessive paranoia. Established companies commonly
are contemptuous of start-ups. Often they don't even bother to search

out or track new entrants to their industries. Be cautious, but don't let secrecy considerations interfere with your relationships with prospective investors, suppliers, or, worst of all, customers.

There are other reasons for anonymity. Established companies frequently do anonymous surveys, not just to avoid tipping the competition, but to get an unbiased judgment of themselves and their competitors. Customers may tell quite different stories, depending on whom they think they are talking to. Consider using this ploy yourself; let your customers think you are one of the old-line companies in the industry.

GAUGING THE COMPETITION

Of course, you yourself must make every effort to thoroughly know and understand your competitors. Market surveys provide crucial information about customer perceptions of competing companies, but this is only the beginning. Fill out the picture with information from the trade press, industry gossip, any other method you can think of short of industrial espionage. Public companies publish annual reports and must submit financial data which you can access. Private companies are usually more secretive, but there are ways.

One valuable technique is to obtain Dun and Bradstreet reports on competitive companies. Your banker or a friend in a large company may be able to get them for you. They provide information not only on credit history but on ownership, employees, quality of their plant or office, officers' names and biographies, and sometimes even a financial statement. Unfortunately, D&B reports are notoriously inaccurate, so try to verify the information independently. Incidentally, this should also be considered from a defensive point of view. You won't be in business long before D&B sends an agent around. Decide in advance how much to tell them—enough to reassure your suppliers, but not so much that you lay yourself naked to the competition. Decline to give a financial statement.

We were close to starting when we got word that another company was showing signs of interest in the same area we planned to enter. We knew this company could be a formidable competitor if it made a strong move into this technology. We got a D&B on it and discovered that the management had recently bought out the previous majority owners. A look at the company's financials—which they had generously and incautiously provided to D&B—indicated that the resulting debt burden would preclude any major R&D effort for some time. We concluded—correctly, as it turned out—that we could safely go ahead.

REM

New entrepreneurs commonly make the mistake of regarding competitors as stationary targets. They proudly proclaim that they have thoroughly investigated the competition and found it wanting. Like a white belt in karate, they attack as if their opponents were a target bag waiting to be kicked. In real life competitors move, change, respond—and fight back.

The Marketing VP's presentation was smooth and professional. He conceded that the start-up's product—a word-processing widget—would face strong competitors like IBM, Wang, and Lanier. However, he pointed out that the company's own product would be technologically far ahead of the others and loaded with new features that prospective customers raved about.

After the presentation I asked one of the venture capitalists who attended what he thought. "These guys are comparing their prototype to IBM's current model," he replied. "By the time they get it on the market, IBM will have a new model out, and it will be at least as good as theirs."

I've forgotten the name of this start-up. So, I'm afraid, has everyone else.

REM

Our discussion so far has dealt with competitors who are (1) direct competition and (2) current competition. That, however, is not all you have to worry about. You will always have *indirect* competitors, because customers always have other possible uses for their money. Some of these alternative uses may provide the same satisfactions as your product. Your market research should therefore look into why customers buy your type of product rather than other items, and you should keep an eye on trends in the broad marketplace.

If you sell, say, fax machines, you are competing with other makers of fax machines. But you are also competing with the post office, Federal Express, electronic mail networks, and the plain old telephone.

Even when we consider only direct competitors, the market is seldom static. Companies are always moving in and out of markets. Your competitors tomorrow may be a completely different set from the ones you have today. New players may enter your market without warning, posing a serious danger. Old players may suddenly leave, presenting a major opportunity—if you are alert. You must always keep your market research and market planning up-to-date, and have an eye on future possibilities.

EXERCISE
Assessing the Competition

A. Identify and list *every* competitor, no matter how big or small, that sells into your market.

B. Obtain the basic statistical information on each competitor—size, profitability, whatever details are available.

C. Examine and evaluate your competitors' products. Assess their strengths and weaknesses, and compare your evaluation with that of your customers, as shown by your market research.

D. If your industry is innovative, also attempt to predict the most likely improvements competitors might make in their next models.

E. Research the history of the industry. In particular, see how major competitors have reacted in the past to major events. How have they responded to a technological breakthrough? A new entry into the industry? A competitive price cut? Piracy of personnel? What does this imply for how they might respond to your start-up?

F. Look into likely new entrants to the industry among large firms. What are their habits? Do they tend to start new divisions or buy into the industry by acquiring an existing company? Do they push price, technology, or service?

G. Check into the weaklings of the industry. Who are their customers? How can you eat up their market base and push them out?

H. Develop a written security plan. Decide what information about your start-up would hurt if it got to the competition, and make sure you have policies in place to protect it—but not at the cost of inhibiting your customer contacts.

I. Assign one of your team to monitor the competition. This person should be required to give you a written report updating your information on competitors at least every six months, and in a fast-moving industry every month.

FINAL WARNING
Our experience indicates that lack of good market re-
search is the most common single factor that causes start-
ups to fail.

CAUTIONARY TALE
A Landslide Defeat

Simulmatics was started by a group of social scientists, political scientists, and computer scientists. In 1960, this company developed a computer model of the American electorate that could be used to test various political strategies and simulate the response of the voters. The company sold this scheme to the presidential campaign of John F. Kennedy. I came in at an early stage because the head of the company, Edward Greenfield, was an old friend. I had known Bobby Kennedy at Harvard, so I made an introduction and sat in on the meetings where the deal was worked out. Simulmatics did a good job for the campaign, particularly in advising them on the issue of Kennedy's Catholicism and how it should be handled. I had played my part by bringing the parties together and had nothing more to do with the company for a couple of years.

With the election over, Simulmatics needed something else to do with its computer model. Management decided to use it to simulate Americans in a consumer, rather than voter, mode, and sell the results to advertising agencies. The idea was that Simulmatics could predict how many people a given ad campaign would reach, what media would give the best coverage, how the product should be promoted, and so on. Clearly this sort of information would be extremely valuable to advertising agencies.

In the early 1960s, there was a nice new-issues market for a while; it was a good period for going public, so Simulmatics did so. It raised $1.5 million (that was real money in those days) and set out to conquer Madison Avenue. It never occurred to management to do any market research because of course the value of the service to the customer was so obvious that any fool could see it.

Somehow, though, the company didn't do so well, and this is where I came in again, in 1962. I was asked to join the board of directors, since I was the only person affiliated with the company who had any prior business experience. I went on a few sales calls to the advertising agencies with salespeople, attended some meetings, and soon realized that the agencies simply were not going to buy.

First of all, the advertising community, in spite of all the up-to-the-minute hype, is very conservative. Ad agencies used computers for accounting and payroll, but they had never heard of mathematical models or simulation.

Second, they already had a method of evaluating their results—the Nielsen ratings and other measurement services. These old-fashioned methods weren't very good, but the agencies saw no reason to change. As a matter of fact, they were afraid that newer, more accurate measurement techniques might inform clients that their ads weren't effective. And Simulmatics had to charge an up-front fee of $15,000 to $20,000 to reprogram for a particular agency's application.

This brings us to the third point, which is that advertising agencies never spend their own money. They only spend the client's money and they add on 15 percent before billing. No way were they going to pay out of their own pockets to try out a new system and see if it made sense for them.

I went back to the board, reported my findings, and recommended that the company drop the whole approach and fold up the operation as it then existed. Its $1.5 million had already dwindled to a couple of hundred thousand and it was essential to stop the bleeding quickly. Then we sat down and brainstormed.

There was really only one chance for the company at this point, and that was to sell simulation services to the government. Our personnel included a lot of visible and successful political scientists and social scientists with solid achievements and credentials—they were at Yale, Harvard, Johns Hopkins, names that impress bureaucrats. It was a Democratic administration, and we of course had some very good, high-level contacts because of our work for the Kennedy campaign. So we went down to Washington and made some sales calls, and we got some very significant contracts.

For the Department of Health, Education, and Welfare we did a simulation of a water fluoridation referendum. At that time, districts all over the country were considering fluoridation to reduce dental problems. A lot of them were deciding against fluoridation, and HEW was very upset. We did a simulation and played out various strategies so the department could see what ways of pushing fluoridation were most persuasive with the voters.

We got another contract with the Defense Department. We sent a dozen or so people to Vietnam to try to figure out why we were losing the war. We simulated a Vietnamese village so the military could experiment with counter-insurgency tactics without taking real-life casualties.

For a couple of years we did very well on government contracts; we met the overhead and made some money. We got a lot of attention in academic circles and learned journals published great articles about us. There was even a novel written about the company. But all these contracts were relatively short-term projects. We had to go out and land another big one every few months in order to feed the programmers and the computer. The federal government is very large indeed, but even a market of that size can be saturated. There were a limited number of senior people scattered among the agencies who were intrigued by simulation and wanted to play with it. When they'd had their fun, they went on to other ways of spending the people's money. There was no ongoing, routine demand for our services, and eventually it just got too hard to make more sales. That was the end of Simulmatics.

This case illustrates what happens when you go into business without doing market research. Our brilliant academic experts assumed that the value of their work would be as obvious to others as it was to them. In reality, there was no market at all on Madison Avenue—and there was a much more limited market

than we thought even in the government. Had we done a real market survey—
and done it early enough—we probably could have found a viable market for
our services. (Perhaps the marketing departments of the big consumer-goods
companies would have been interested.) It's really rather ironic. Simulmatics
made a business of asking members of the general public their opinions on any
subject under the sun, but never thought to ask its own customers what they
wanted and what they'd be willing to pay for it.

HDS

Five

FINDING YOUR NICHE

Do one thing at a time, and do that one thing superbly.

Astronaut training rule

Your market strategy implements your business concept by providing specifics. You must answer two questions: (1) To whom do you sell? This defines your market. (2) What do you sell? This defines your product. Your market research should provide you with the information you need to formulate your strategy and find your niche in the market.

Most entrepreneurs seem to feel that a formal market analysis and market strategy are unnecessary. The standard prescriptions for big-business marketing strike them as unrealistic. And in fact small-business marketing is quite different.

MARKETING FOR BIG BUSINESS

Classic big-business marketing emphasizes the following principles.

- *Selling the same or similar products in diverse markets.* Maximizing unit volume is critical to the large company, for economy of scale is the primary justification for its existence. Thus each product must be sold in as many markets as possible. Quaker State, for instance, sells motor oil by the quart to consumers through hardware stores and auto shops; by the case to service stations; and by the tank truck to commercial fleet operators.

■ *Exploitation of each market with peripheral products*. Once a foothold has been gained in a particular market, it should be followed up by the addition of peripheral or even unrelated products for sale to the same customer. Thus Sears, which sells household goods to middle-class consumers, successfully added a completely unrelated product—auto insurance—for the same market.

■ *Careful attention to regional differences*. Advertising, packaging, and even the product itself may have to be modified specifically for each geographical market. For mass-market consumer goods, this segmentation may be taken almost to the city-block level. In New York City, for instance, Coca-Cola billboards are an excellent indicator of neighborhood ethnicity: In Puerto Rican neighborhoods the text is in Spanish, in Harlem the models are black, and so on. In Brooklyn supermarkets, each Coke bottle cap is marked to indicate that the contents are kosher.

■ *Emphasis on image-oriented advertising and brand consciousness*. Large companies, operating in mature markets, can seldom gain by product innovation. Gaining market share by price cutting is scarcely attractive. The best solution is to develop loyal customers by stressing a favorable *image* for the company and its brands, using slogans ("You can be sure if it's Westinghouse"), fantasy characters ("Mr. Goodwrench"), appeals to self-image ("the Pepsi generation"), and various other ploys.

MARKETING FOR SMALL BUSINESS

For a small business, marketing strategy is dominated by a different set of considerations. This is not to say that we have nothing to learn from the way big companies go about it. But there is great danger in the unexamined importation of standard methods. Effective small-business marketing generally requires a rather different approach.

■ *Strict concentration on a single market segment*. Economy of scale is of little importance to a small business. Far more critical is the effective deployment of desperately inadequate marketing resources. To sell into two discrete market segments will nearly double marketing expenses, because it is essential to custom-tailor the approach for each segment. You will have to pay for two market-research surveys, artwork for two sets of advertisements, two sales training programs, and so on. General Motors can afford this sort of thing; you can't. Even more important, your top management will be stretched very thin just selling to a single market segment; if you try to approach several segments at once, none of them will get enough attention.

- *Concentration on a single product or a limited line of related products.* The only exception is the retailer or distributor in a business where "one-stop shopping" is a customer demand. Even in this case you frequently find it's an advantage to be more specialized than your larger competitors. For the small manufacturer, a diversified product line is generally disastrous, because it dilutes not only marketing but production resources.

- *Reliance on close customer contact and intuitive knowledge of the market.* Large companies rely heavily on detailed statistical studies, not because they enjoy doing them but because it's impossible for their marketing executives to stay in personal contact with the market. Their markets are simply too vast and too complex to be comprehended without statistical analysis. The small business, by contrast, usually sells to a small and relatively simple market. It's possible for one or two marketing people in the company to be thoroughly familiar with the entire market—and to talk daily with a broad cross-section of customers. A certain amount of quantitative analysis is still essential to provide objective data, but the small company can and should rely on intuitive understanding of the market to a degree that would be quite unsafe for a mass marketer.

- *Restriction to a single geographic region, or to a national market with few or no regional peculiarities.* Again, the small company simply does not have the resources to handle regional or ethnic diversification.

- *Emphasis on substantive superiority of the product or service as the source of competitive advantage.* This is not to say that image is unimportant to a small business, but usually it should not be the primary marketing focus. A new company, in a growth market, should concentrate on providing superior value to the customer—and its marketing should concentrate on letting the customer know it. Image-creation advertising, conspicuous charitable deeds, and similar techniques are usually a waste of resources.

With these distinctions in mind, let's consider the development of market strategy for a start-up. How should you answer the two interlocking questions: (1) Who is our market? (2) What are we selling? Neither question can be properly answered without reference to the other.

MARKET TYPES

In Chapter Two we discussed market growth cycles and classified markets according to their growth stages. Now let's reexamine market classification from a practical perspective: What market strategy is appropriate for each type of market?

The Radical Product.   The most primitive type of market is the market that does not exist at all: The customer does not have a need for your product. In order to succeed, you will have to begin by creating a need in the customers—make them want something they never wanted before. This is extremely difficult but not quite impossible. Consider the personal computer. As late as 1970 the idea of a powerful, individually owned computer was such an offbeat concept that it did not show up even in science fiction. Who needed his own computer? What on earth would he use it for?

If you wish to tackle this type of marketing problem, the best approach is to experiment; try out the product with the most adventurous and innovative people you can find. Better yet, see if someone else has already done such a test wittingly or unwittingly.

> During the 1960s, MIT had a PDP-1 computer, which had been donated by Digital Equipment Corporation for student use. The PDP-1 was the first minicomputer; it filled a room, but only a small room. The most frequently used programs written by MIT students for this computer included "Expensive Typewriter," a very primitive word-processing program; "Space War," a simple video game that threatened to monopolize the machine until it was outlawed; and a music program that played the Minute Waltz in 57.5 seconds, as well as a variety of Bach fugues. Today, word processing, video games, and "synthesized" music are major uses of microcomputers.

Bringing out a product that is so radical is comparable to a Marine landing: You face a desperate fight just to get a beachhead. The odds are you'll be pushed right back into the sea; even if you manage to maintain a toehold, further progress will be slow. And, to continue the metaphor, it's very likely that you'll suffer such heavy casualties that the follow-up troops (that is, me-too competitors) will make the big gains and reap the big rewards. This is exactly what happened in the personal computer industry. Who remembers the Altair 8800 now?

The way to get that first market beachhead is to piggyback in on an existing market. For the early personal computer makers, this was the electronics hobbyist. There was an existing market for do-it-yourself electronics kits: Hobbyists built their own hi-fi components, television sets—why not a computer? This is exactly how you do it: Present your product not as a blue-sky innovation but as a variation in an existing market. More examples? The airplane was originally sold to the military market as an improvement of the reconnaissance balloon—and to the civilian market as a new type of carnival ride.

Once you secure the initial market you can try to expand your customer base by exploring new needs your product can satisfy. If you're lucky and the market takes off, you must nimbly jump from the initial market into the emerging market. And your timing must be perfect—too soon and you'll starve, too late and the competition will have all the best claims staked out. The latter case is the common one. In personal computers, for instance, IBM and Apple, though relative latecomers, took over from the early, hobbyist-oriented companies like MITS and Altair.

The New Product. Less ambitious and less difficult is the marketing of a product that is new but not radical. An example of this type is the pocket calculator. It's interesting to note that this product was marketed initially not as a portable version of the familiar desk calculator—the most obvious approach—but as a replacement for the slide rule. This illustrates an important principle: When introducing a novel item, address a small but adventurous market segment first; then expand into larger but more conservative markets. Hewlett-Packard made a tidy piece of change selling its early calculators to scientists and engineers; had it started with office managers it probably would have failed. Of course once the ice was broken and the product was familiar it easily invaded the much larger office-calculator market.

The new product, as we use the term here, satisfies an existing customer need in a different way. What does this imply for market strategy? One consequence is rather obvious: If there's a recognized market need, most likely there is an existing market with existing products filling that need. Thus the initial question is whether to annex part of the existing market or to expand it. Consider again the pocket calculator. It actually annihilated the slide rule, and it ate up much of the desk calculator market. But it also expanded the market; today many people use it for simple arithmetic that would once have been performed with paper and pencil. In fact, it has made it possible for mathphobes to do arithmetic which, without a calculator, they would not have attempted at all.

If you propose to introduce a new product of this sort, you have to choose between annexing a share of the existing market and developing a new market segment. *Don't* try to do both at the same time; focus your marketing effort.

The Direct Approach. To access existing customers you must take sales directly from competitive, established products. These competitors will not willingly relinquish market share. Under what circumstances should you adopt this direct approach?

One important criterion is, of course, weak competition. If you're going to slug it out, it's well to challenge inadequate opponents. Perhaps the existing products are grossly obsolete, so that your innovation has a decisive advantage. Competing companies may be old-fashioned, stodgy, out of touch with their customers—just going through the motions. Or competing firms may be concentrating their efforts elsewhere, regarding the market you've chosen as a sideline. Naturally it's also helpful if your competitors are small, weak, and in financial trouble.

A second—and strong—indicator for direct attack is frustration among existing customers. If the people who are buying the existing product don't like it, but can't find anything better; if they're dissatisfied, irritated, or just plain bored—there's your cue.

The Indirect Approach. Your alternative is to choose an indirect approach to the market. Surrounding many an existing market is a halo of "almost-customers." These are people who have a need or desire for the product but don't buy it. Perhaps the existing product doesn't quite fit what they want. Perhaps they "can't afford" the product—that is, it doesn't have enough value. Perhaps they aren't aware that the product even exists, or that it can solve their problem. Perhaps there are cultural, religious, or political obstacles to buying the existing product. This marginal or potential market is hard to identify and characterize. But often it does exist, and under certain circumstances it may offer the best entry for a new product.

This indirect approach is clearly indicated if the existing market is dominated by strong competitors. Rather than immediately climb into the ring and take on several strong, fast, and ferocious opponents, it's advisable to say, "Let's you and him fight," while you pick up the goodies they've neglected. After you've developed and served your new market segment, you'll be stronger—and the competition may have been weakened.

The Improved Product. The introduction of a product that is an improved version of an existing product presents a somewhat different problem. If you take this approach, chances are you'll be entering a market in the Late Growth Phase. Recall that during this phase a market is characterized by increasing product standardization, combined with the emergence of a clearly defined product subspecies. Also, during this period large companies are likely to be forcing their way into the market, while a shakeout of the weaker players may be occurring or imminent. In short, you'll be entering a very treacherous environment that will call for some careful footwork—one false step and you're sunk.

One approach to this situation is to attempt to standardize the product by yourself. "Our new improved widget has ten ventricles, and the frammistan is on the left. This is clearly the optimum design, and from now on it will be the widget industry standard." Obviously, it won't be a trivial task to carry off this bold proclamation over the protests of your outraged competitors. As a newcomer, your credibility is unlikely to be sufficient; normally, this approach should be left to megabusinesses that possess the prestige—and muscle—to get away with it. (IBM did this with microcomputers.) Still, it may be just possible to self-standardize the product in a dwarf market; if the market is very small, the competition very weak, and your improved product very superior, you may want to consider this strategy. But it remains high-risk; have a contingency plan for wiping the egg off your face if it fails. A far more viable approach to this type of market is to define and stake out a new product subspecies.

Sony, in the 1950s a relatively small company, used a new technology—the transistor—to improve an existing product, the radio. Instead of trying to standardize the console radio on transistors rather than vacuum tubes, it carved out a new product subspecies: the portable radio.

Osborne Computer, in the 1980s, tried to do much the same thing in the personal computer market. It succeeded in defining a product subspecies—the portable computer—but after an initial period of spectacular growth, it suddenly slid into bankruptcy. What went wrong? Business school students will be analyzing this case for decades, but two problems stand out. First, Osborne had no technological edge. Its product was shrewdly designed to meet an unfilled need in the market, but there was nothing to prevent competitors from following quickly with imitations. If Osborne had not been under such heavy competitive pressure, it might have been able to weather its second major error: under-estimating the urgency of the market push to standardization. When Osborne prematurely announced a forthcoming model with IBM compatibility, sales of its current model dried up.

Before trying to enter a late growth market, make sure your market strategy has the following components:

- *Start with a clear description.* Describe the product subspecies that you will try to establish. There are a number of approaches you might take. Make the product more personalized (for example, the executive or corporate jet). Make it more portable (the folding baby stroller). Make it more convenient to use (the auto-dialing phone). Make it more rugged, for heavy-duty use (the Jeep). Make it more fun to use (the sports car). Your concept should of course be tested carefully by market research.
- *Provide for a high barrier to entry.* Commonly this consists of superior technology, but there are other alternatives. Just be sure you have *something* to keep the competition at bay.
- *Do a detailed study of competitors.* Potential megabusiness competitors may be interested in your industry. Do not kid yourself or indulge in wishful thinking; the giants *will* come in, and they *will* take big chunks of market share. Accept this and plan for it. Develop a scenario for the next few years. Who are the most likely new entrants? How will they behave? What will be the effect? How will you deal with it?
- *Study the weaklings of the industry.* When will they be shaken out? How will they behave when they're thrashing around in their death throes? There will certainly be an orgy of price cutting—how will it affect you, and how will you respond?
- *Plan for industry standardization.* It will happen, and you must go along, like it or not. It may be frustrating if you know a better way, but you just can't afford to fight the market.

The Me-Too Product. The most "conservative" strategy is the most risky one for a small business: entering a mature market with a noninnovative product. To introduce a new brand of soap is a major campaign, with a significant risk of failure, even for Procter & Gamble.

For a small business, and most particularly for a start-up, to go head-to-head with the giants is generally asinine. There is really only one viable approach to this problem, and that is the loyalty niche. Not just a niche; "niche marketing" is not a panacea. The megabusiness players in a mature market are so competitive that they will shed blood for peanuts. There is no niche so small that they don't want it. Your only chance is to find a niche that they *can't* get into because they're too big.

> Here's an example of a niche that looked good but wasn't. When Detroit stopped making convertibles, several small businesses sprang up to exploit the opportunity. They bought sedans and made them into convertibles, or modified customers' cars for a fee. But in the viciously competitive auto business, even this tiny niche did not last long. Soon the behemoths started limited production of convertibles again.

What is a loyalty niche? It's a market segment that is loyal to your company for reasons a big company finds hard to duplicate. This may involve providing a level of service so high it is impossible for a large, bureaucratic organization to achieve. Or, you can appeal to ethnic, political, or religious solidarity with your customers. You can appeal to snobbery; smallness can provide a guarantee of exclusivity, so that you make an asset of your inability to produce large quantities. Another approach is to ask for preference over big companies on the basis of your smallness itself, either appealing to "fair play" or a "David and Goliath" image, or claiming that your business, being small, is morally superior to a big company.

> Many small dry-goods retailers sell high-quality but otherwise rather ordinary items, which customers buy even though they could get them cheaper at a department store. Image is the key. A piece of clothing with an L. L. Bean or Land's End label can be a trademark for your lifestyle.

> Goya, a canned food company, holds a lucrative niche in the Hispanic market. Bigger companies can make the same foods and label the cans in Spanish, but they have difficulty presenting themselves as members of the Hispanic community. Similarly, on a much smaller scale, ethnic grocery stores—Jewish, Italian, Japanese, Korean,

Filipino, and so on—continue to thrive at a time when the traditional mom-and-pop groceries have been nearly exterminated by the supermarket chains. The chains can easily stock ethnic foods, but they can't provide clerks who can gossip with the customers in their native language.

A small company, Ben & Jerry's Ice Cream, became a large company by emphasizing its devotion to politically correct values. By contrast, John DeLorean's attempt to market an image of moral superiority to Detroit suffered a fatal blow when he was indicted for trafficking in drugs—even though he was later acquitted.

If you choose the loyalty-niche approach, you must recognize that it will probably put a limit on your growth. By expanding too much, you risk losing the qualities that make customers loyal.

EXERCISE
Market Strategy—Industry

What kind of market do you plan to enter, and what approach do you plan to use?

☐ Primitive market
   ☐ Piggyback on existing market—specifically:

_____

☐ Early growth market
   ☐ Access existing market.
   ☐ Develop new market segment—specifically:

_____

☐ Late growth market
   ☐ Set industry standard.
   ☐ Define new product subspecies—specifically:

_____

☐ Mature market
   ☐ Develop loyalty niche, based on:

_____

JUST WHAT ARE YOU SELLING?

Let's turn to another viewpoint on market strategy. What is your product? This is a treacherous question. The classic example, which has become a cliché among market strategists, is the small drill press. The company that makes this item thinks it's selling drill presses. But, the marketing expert portentously tells us, the man who buys it sees it only as a means to an end—namely, making holes. Thus the company isn't really selling drill presses, it's selling holes.

Or is it? Suppose the company believes this analysis, and decides to satisfy the customer's needs directly instead of indirectly. It approaches him in his basement workshop and offers, for a fee, to drill the holes for his bird-feeder project. What kind of response should the company expect? It seems this chap is not buying holes, he's buying the pleasure of making holes himself. The logical response to this conclusion might be to rent rather than sell the drill press. Yet this approach, too, mysteriously fails. Let's observe the customer more closely. Watch him showing off his workshop to the fellow next door, gloatingly fondling the gleaming machines. Our hypothetical company now has the key to this market: To hell with what kind of holes it makes, design a drill press that *looks* impressive! It is not selling tools; it is not selling holes; it is not selling entertainment; it's selling a status symbol. The company that realizes this can clean up, while its mystified competitors wonder why an "inferior" product sells so well.

The lesson is this: What you think you're selling may not be what the customer is buying. If the customers' behavior seems "irrational," chances are it's because you don't understand their needs. Please note that this applies in industrial as well as consumer markets.

Let's consider what kinds of product might exist. There are as many different products as there are human needs and ways to satisfy them. It's a bit dangerous to limit this array for classification—feel free to go beyond our analysis—but most products can be fitted into one of seven categories:

1. Consumption goods
2. Durable goods
3. Services
4. Entertainment
5. Information
6. Status items
7. Social satisfactions

In using this or any other classification scheme, keep in mind that different customers may use the same product to fill different needs.

(Sometimes the same customers use the same product to fill different needs!)

The way customers classify your product has profound implications for your market strategy. Let's consider the possibilities.

Consumption Goods.

A *consumption good* is a physical, tangible item that is intended to be "used up" over a fairly short period of time. Many successful businesses have been based on the decades-old trend by consumers to reclassify durable goods as consumption goods. Disposable napkins, disposable diapers, disposable kitchenware are now old hat. Has the trend run out of steam yet? It's clearly slowing and in some areas reversing, especially due to environmental concerns.

Consumption goods are usually best marketed by stressing *intensity* of satisfaction. Focus your effort on providing the customers—and letting them know you provide—a strong benefit, even though it may be short-lived. As a corollary, it's well to stress a single benefit rather than promote a variety of benefits.

Durable Goods.

Durable good has a specialized technical definition in statistical economics; we just use it to refer to a physical good that lasts for a relatively long period of use. Recently there has been a tendency for consumers to return to long-lived products, to an emphasis on quality, durability, and tradition. People have become increasingly inclined to buy "classic" rather than "fashion" goods—in clothes, furniture, automobiles, and other goods.

Generally, durable goods should be marketed with an emphasis on long-lasting satisfaction. It's less effective to stress intensity of satisfaction; ecstasy is a one-shot experience, not an everyday sensation. For a durable good, long product life is a major value by definition. Note that this means not only physical durability but also protection from obsolescence. You may also want to stress a variety of benefits from the product, because a product that will be used over a long period of time raises the specter of boredom.

The distinction between the consumption good and the durable good corresponds roughly to the accounting distinction between the expense item and the capital expenditure. This is true in both industrial and consumer markets. Customers not only regard the *products* differently, they regard the *expenditures* differently. Often there are special procedures or restrictions for capital expenditures. A hospital administrator, for instance, may be required to get a formal vote of approval from the Treasury Committee to buy a $10,000 lab instrument—but she spends $250,000 a year on laundry with essentially no oversight. Similar paradoxes abound among retail consumers. A family may agonize for weeks over the purchase of a $300 TV set, yet expend $2,000 per year on beer and cigarettes without a second thought.

Ironically, this distinction sometimes provides a reversed incentive. The thinking seems to be that money spent on a consumption good is gone, but when a durable item is purchased one has "something to show for it." Many businesses, for instance, prefer to buy a piece of production or office equipment even when accounting analysis shows it would be more economical to lease, or contract out the work. There is something comforting to management (and their bankers) in seeing that they have something "permanent" and "valuable" for their money. Consumers often show the same phenomenon. A shrewd marketer can turn this attitude into a useful selling tool.

Services. You're selling a *service* when you perform work for the customer—whether changing the oil in her car or flying her across the continent.

The key factor in marketing a service is dealing with customer nervousness. A service, even more than a consumption good, leaves the customer with the prospect of "nothing to show for his money." Like a consumption good, once it's "used up," it's gone; unlike a consumption good, it's not visible or tangible even before it's used up. Thus, selling a service, especially an expensive service, requires special attention to reassuring the customer. Your market strategy should take this into account. Here are some approaches you might use.

• *Credentials are important in a service business.* If you're selling a tangible good you can point to its appearance and performance; as long as it works well the customer needn't know, and doesn't care, whether the engineer who designed it graduated from MIT or Podunk Junior College. It's hard to point to a service, so the credentials of the people who provide it matter. This is why doctors, lawyers, dentists, and beauticians prominently display their framed diplomas.

• *Appearance counts.* A service business can afford less than any other to look tacky, dirty, or cheap. Everything that the customer sees—your premises, your literature, your advertising, and your people—should convey the image of class, quality, and permanence.

• *Add something tangible to the service.* Service businesses often "give away" some item—the house magazines of the airlines are a good example. As typically used, this is merely an advertising technique—a calendar, mug, or desk blotter keeps your name in front of the customer. But it's also an opportunity to reassure the customer, if used properly. Consider bundling into your service a related physical good—and make that good very obviously a premium product.

> Organizations that put on expensive "seminars" or "workshops" generally learn to hand out textbooks, course outlines, portfolios, and similar tangible items that the participant can take home. Purchased in bulk, even high-quality products can be surprisingly inexpensive, and a $10 portfolio can add $100 to the customer's perception of value.

Entertainment.   Isn't entertainment a service? Not quite. Service is doing work for the customer; *entertainment* is helping her have fun. Even more important, what you think of as entertainment—say, a vacation at a posh resort—may actually represent status or social satisfaction to the customer. Such a misconception can result in a badly targeted marketing campaign.

If the customer is coming to you just to have fun, not to impress people or to meet a prospective spouse, then you're selling entertainment. How do you sell it?

By word of mouth, mainly. Movies, music, novels—all entertainment vehicles succeed or fail primarily on word of mouth. So your primary advertising medium is your customers. Don't worry too much about print ads or television spots. Think about how you can send out your customers in the mood to tell their friends about you.

If you want repeat business, you must take into account another principle: When it comes to fun, people want novelty. The customer comes the first time because her friends told her it was fun. She comes the second time because it was fun the first time. She doesn't come a third time because the second time wasn't as much fun as the first time. This is why amusement parks constantly add new attractions.

Information.   Selling *information,* again, is not quite the same thing as a service business. The economy is relentlessly moving towards products with higher information content. A hundred years ago, sand was a significant industry; today, computer chips are. They're both silicon dioxide, but the chips have a lot more information in them.

One key to selling information is appreciating the role of the *medium.*

> A mail-order company sold a self-improvement course on cassette tape. It tried using various mailing lists, including lists of people who had attended self-improvement seminars. Results were very poor. The company finally achieved an excellent response simply by mailing to a list of people who owned cassette tape recorders.

Examine your market carefully. What media do your customers prefer to use? This variable includes not only the physical medium but also the style of communication. Some people like detailed explanations; others prefer a simplified exposition with many illustrations. Some customers accept a chatty, informal style; with others, you will lose credibility if you fail to take a portentous, authoritative style.

The choice of medium also depends on the durability of the information being sold. News, for instance, is similar to a consumption good, and a very perishable one at that. News media appear frequently and are quite ephemeral. On the other hand, information of longer-lasting value, such as reference data, is more likely to appear in a book with quality binding. For information that (supposedly) lasts a lifetime, still other media, such as a college education, may be appropriate.

> Inappropriate medium choice is a frequent killer of magazine start-ups. Undercapitalized magazines commonly lower their expenses by publishing on a reduced schedule; for example, quarterly instead of monthly. If customers need the information more frequently, such ventures will probably fail. The magazines would have been better off cutting expenses some other way.

Finally, choose a medium that enhances the apparent value of the content. Information, again, is an intangible; the customer should be reassured that she is "getting something for her money." She often does judge a book by the quality of its cover, or the credentials of the author.

Status Items. The status item is a product that frequently appears in disguise. Of course, it would be quite correct and reasonable to consider a Mercedes a durable good, a vacation in Biarritz entertainment, or a Harvard education an information product. But each of these is also, and in most cases primarily, regarded by the customer as a status item.

Products that are purchased for the sake of the status they confer on the owner are worth considering separately because of the major part the struggle for status plays in human behavior. It's extremely important to realize that this struggle is not confined to the upper crust; rich and poor, men and women, old people and young children, individuals and corporations—all strive for status.

I drive to work through a semi-slum neighborhood. The billboards are dominated overwhelmingly by ads for cognacs, liqueurs, and premium whiskeys—usually featuring a couple in expensive evening clothes. Apparently a bottle of costly liquor is one of the few status symbols the inhabitants can afford.

REM

With the possible exception of some very primitive tribal cultures, every human society provides a variety of possible routes to status. Most of them, however, can be boiled down to one of four categories.

1. *Power*—the oldest and most fundamental source of status. Products that are seen as enhancing power (for example, the notorious dark business suit) sell best to people in structured, authoritarian environments: politicians, bureaucrats, managers in big companies.

2. *Birth*—a surprisingly important factor even in the United States. Although constitutionally we have no aristocracy in this country, many middle-class people are willing to pay a handsome price for clothing or other appurtenances that give them the appearance of belonging to "the best families" or the "old rich."

3. *Wealth*—the currency of status as well as of exchange. Money confers status in this as in most other cultures, but it's of no value for this purpose unless it is displayed. Such displays have sometimes been as blatant as a potlatch, but these days more subtle methods are in style. There is a substantial market indeed for products that discreetly flaunt the owner's wealth—or, better yet, allow him to appear even wealthier than he is.

4. *Talent*—superiority in sports, the performing arts, or intellectual pursuits—the route chosen when all else fails. Products that help customers excel and excite the envy of their peers can find a market of this type.

One of the classic advertisements of all time was based on the appeal to status enhancement by way of talent. It was headlined, "They laughed when I sat down at the piano . . ."

Be aware that status products may be negative as well as positive. The obvious status item appeals by its exclusivity: "Buy this; nobody else has it (well, hardly anybody) and therefore it will increase your status." But there are also status items that appeal to the fear of exclusion: "Buy this; everybody else has one, and if you don't your status will be lowered." The latter argument is an even better motivator than the former, and you can sell a lot more units. The really smart marketers start with the appeal to exclusivity, and then, when that market segment is saturated, switch to the "don't-be-left-out" approach!

Social Satisfactions. Our final product category consists of items people buy for social satisfactions. Consider, for instance, membership in a hobby club. This product is intangible; yet the customer may get little or no service, information, or status for her dues. She is buying primarily a social benefit—the opportunity to socialize with other people who share her interests. A singles bar, a health spa, a computer dating service—many businesses that seem to be selling services are really selling the ability to better fit into society.

Success in such a business depends on seeing past the obvious product to the true product. The customer's objective is to enhance her social interactions. Some products that contribute to this are (1) introduction to, or better, insertion into a desirable group; (2) acquisition by the customer of characteristics, appearance, or possessions that will help her join a desirable group; and (3) removal of handicaps that prevent the customer from acquiring the friends or lovers she wants.

If you enter a social-satisfactions business, you should be aware that the interactions among your customers may be more important than the relationship between you and your customers. If you own a cocktail lounge, for instance, customers will probably care much more about who the other patrons are than how friendly the bartender is.

This, incidentally, brings back the point we made earlier about the importance of marketing to a homogeneous group of customers. The more alike your customers are, the easier and cheaper it is to focus your marketing efforts. But also customers frequently prefer to rub elbows with other customers who are like them. In a social-satisfactions business this factor is crucial, but it applies also to other types. For instance, airlines know that their business-class customers intensely dislike having vacationers with kids or infants sitting in adjacent seats.

EXERCISE
Market Strategy—Product

A. Select one or more of the following categories to characterize your product.
- ☐ Consumption goods
- ☐ Durable goods
- ☐ Services
- ☐ Entertainment
- ☐ Information
- ☐ Status items
- ☐ Social satisfactions

B. Cite evidence from your research to show that your *customers* view your product in this way.

C. If you have checked off more than one product classification, examine your market research again. Do all or most of your prospective customers see your product as filling more than one need? Or are there several market segments, each of which views the product differently?

CAUTIONARY TALE
The World's Smallest Conglomerate

After I failed to get tenure and was cast out of the ivory tower into the cruel world of profit and loss, I became the first employee of a little start-up called Lifesystems Company. One might say I got in on the ground floor—literally—since, before this, Lifesystems had been operating in the basement of one of the founders. The company started in 1977, in an old mill on Boston's famous entrepreneurial corridor, Route 128.

The founders were Paul, a brilliant young biochemist, and Oliver, who had a background in engineering and project management. Briefly, the concept was as follows.

Every living organism—every living cell—is a complex chemical factory. Thousands of chemical reactions go on constantly and simultaneously, controlled by molecular processors called enzymes. Among other functions, enzymes make sure that there is not too much or too little of any particular chemical in the cell. Normally, when one wishes to alter the chemical balance in the cell—say, to cure an illness—one puts in certain chemicals: drugs. Annoyingly, the enzymes immediately try to get things back to "normal," destroying the compounds they consider in excess.

Paul was aware of recent advances that made it possible to intervene in living systems much more selectively and much more efficiently. This involved designing certain molecules that would destroy specific enzymes. By using these, one could alter chemical balances within the cell much more efficiently, preventing the enzymes from interfering with one's work. Lifesystems Company was set up to exploit this technology by making new pharmaceuticals.

Paul and Oliver were not so naive as to think that with a capitalization of under $100,000 they could saunter into the pharmaceutical industry, with its massive R&D requirements and years of testing for each new drug. So they did little practical work on their drug ideas. Instead, they looked for a product that they could handle more quickly and use to grow big enough to become a viable drug company. As it happened, the big drug companies were way ahead of them anyway; when I went to the library to check on patents, I discovered that Merck and Richardson-Merrell had Paul's drug designs pretty well locked up. But Paul's really brilliant idea was that this same concept could be applied to agricultural products.

When I came on board, they had developed a compound that could alter the nicotine levels in tobacco plants. Currently, low-nicotine cigarettes are made by chemical treatment of the tobacco leaves after harvest—a process that is relatively costly and causes certain pollution and safety problems. Lifesystems' approach was a chemical that could be sprayed on the plants shortly before harvest. By properly timing the spraying, one could harvest plants that contained as little as one-third, or as much as three times, the normal amount of nicotine. They demonstrated this in greenhouse experiments. (Incidentally, though you might think that tripling nicotine levels would be useless, in Turkey and several other countries very high-nicotine cigarettes are popular.) My job was to synthesize new compounds to test.

Though fairly frugal, the two partners were spending money, and nothing was coming in. They had no clear plan for tackling the tobacco companies and made no particular progress in getting their innovation to market. They responded to the developing cash crunch with a two-pronged strategy: raising more capital, and turning some cash by opening another line of business.

Both approaches were moderately successful. They brought in some more money from small private investors. Meanwhile, the company got into the research chemicals business, making a line of reagents useful in certain aspects of cancer research. They chose these particular items because Paul was familiar with them from his Ph.D. thesis work. It became my job to make them in the lab.

Unfortunately, sales were not very high; the market was small and easily saturated, and they sold through a distributor who took the lion's share of the markup. Lifesystems continued to bleed cash. I suggested expanding our line of research chemicals—and selling them direct, since the distributor was raking off most of the profit margin. However, Paul and Oliver decided to diversify into still another line of business: analytical services. We bought (and leased) some instruments and began doing various sorts of analyses—mostly polymer studies—for local companies. This involved hiring some technicians, as well as an expert in analytical chemistry.

Soon the company was bustling. Lifesystems expanded from its original three rooms to take over the whole floor, then part of another floor. Our instruments hummed continuously; we added more to handle new kinds of analyses; and there was a rapidly growing flow of customer samples, reports, invoices, and even checks.

Trouble was, the analytical services business was (and is) quite competitive. A lot of people in it were operating out of their garages, with very low overhead. We were under constant pressure to quote low prices to get contracts. By this time I was spending all day standing at a chromatograph running analyses—not the kind of work I was trained for—and I exercised my mind by analyzing our costs. It turned out we were selling analyses at a negative gross margin.

I communicated this result to Paul and Oliver. They thought it over for a while, then responded very logically by letting me go. I had to admit that it was not particularly economical to use an expensive Ph.D. synthetic chemist to do work that could be performed quite adequately by a low-paid technician.

The company lasted for another year and a half. The two partners were co-equal in their holdings—generally a poor arrangement—and as the company's problems worsened, personal friction developed. Eventually there was a rather unpleasant bankruptcy and the company was liquidated.

The story of Lifesystems Company is depressing because the opportunities lost were so vast. The founders were good people—very intelligent and very competent, and initially they got along beautifully. The business concept was absolutely brilliant; if they had followed through on the agricultural chemicals opportunity, Lifesystems might well have been in the Fortune 500 by now. The potential applications were not limited to tobacco; perfume oils, rubber, turpentine, more nutritious grains—the possibilities were staggering.

Why did Lifesystems fail? Quite simply, this tiny company acted like a conglomerate. It was involved in four entirely separate and unrelated lines of business. It ended up successful in none of them. Had they stuck to one product and studied their prospective market carefully, these highly talented entrepreneurs would almost surely have succeeded.

REM

Six

THE MARKETING FUNCTION

All progress is based upon a universal innate desire on the part of every organism to live beyond its income.

Samuel Butler, *Notebooks*

The marketing function within the company has five major tasks: (1) market research; (2) market strategy; (3) sales organization; (4) pricing and positioning; and (5) advertising and promotion. We discussed market research in Chapter Four and market strategy in Chapter Five. Now let's cover the other functions.

THE PROBLEM OF DISTRIBUTION

Between thee and thy customers is a great gulf fixed. It's called "distribution." Your product cannot achieve its mission of satisfying customers unless you can get it into their hands. You must attract their attention and their interest, present your product to them, and make the sale. To do so you must deal with our country's distribution system, and there is no greater obstacle for the small or young company in today's viciously competitive economy.

To put it bluntly, the pipeline is full. You may think your biggest problem is competition for the customer's money. Wrong. In most industries today, you must chop through a phalanx of competitors and wade through gore just to get a shot at competing for the customer's *attention*.

THE SALES ORGANIZATION

How do you access customers? You need a sales organization, a channel of distribution. There are four basic distribution approaches:

1. *Direct marketing.* In its purest form, this method involves no salespeople, only order clerks. The sale is made by the advertisement, which may appear in various media—"junk mail" (direct marketers *hate* that term!), catalogs, magazines, television, and so on. Customers then place their order by phone or mail, or, increasingly, fax.

2. *In-house sales force.* In this case, you use salespeople who are employees of your company.

3. *Sales reps.* In this case, the salespeople are not your employees; they are, or work for, independent brokers or agencies.

4. *Systematic distribution.* This involves working through companies that not only act as sales intermediaries but also carry an inventory of products.

No law requires you to confine yourself to one marketing avenue. You may, however, be restricted by custom; in some industries (and consumer markets), customers have a definite prejudice as to whom they will deal with and how they will be sold. Another consideration is competition between sales channels. If you use both reps and in-house salespeople, for instance, there may well be considerable friction between the two groups.

Direct Marketing. Direct marketing (which used to be known as "mail order") is an extremely powerful selling technique. Widely used, it offers several important advantages:

1. *The sales process is under the direct and immediate control of your marketing management.* The whole problem of motivating, supervising, and monitoring field salespeople is bypassed.

2. *Direct marketing is fast and flexible.* To hire and train a sales force takes months; a direct-marketing campaign can begin as quickly as you can do the artwork and get it through the printers. What's more, if you decide to change your sales pitch, you can turn on a dime—you have no sales force to reeducate.

3. *It is easy to test your sales approach and improve it.* By measuring the response to different ads, you can find which is most effective. (Of course, in principle, you could do this with a field sales

force. However, in practice, variation in the personal selling effectiveness of the individual salespeople makes it almost impossible to get valid quantitative data.)

The big disadvantage of direct marketing arises from the lack of close customer contact. It's not possible to tailor the initial sales pitch to the individual customer. If customers telephone their orders, you get some feedback and can adapt the sales close as needed. Even so, in the absence of face-to-face contact, it's very difficult to keep in touch with your market. You really have to work at it.

There is a persistent canard that direct marketing is unsuitable for expensive products, though Sears Roebuck disproved this decades ago (and Hammacher Schlemmer has carried the practice to the point of absurdity). Some product categories, however, are obviously inappropriate. A service, or a product with a strong service component, is likely to present problems. A very complex product may need a salesperson to explain it. A product that requires careful customization to the specific customer can be difficult to handle by direct marketing.

Direct marketing has evolved into a specialized science. A detailed treatment of the sophisticated methods used in modern direct marketing would require more space than we have; see the Reading List for further information. However, let's cover some of the essential principles.

Direct marketing is unique in that the advertisment must more or less make the sale. You must therefore give the closest attention to your ad and to the media in which it appears. And since you'll have little if any opportunity to meet and talk with customers, you have only one good way to gauge the effectiveness of your approach: testing. Test different offers; test different prices; test different media; test different advertising themes. If you're using mailing lists, test different lists. It's been known for a tiny change, such as using a different-colored envelope, to substantially improve response. (However, your priority should be to test the major factors before you descend to trivia.)

Understand the volumes involved. If, for instance, you send out a mailing and get a 5 percent response rate, you'll have achieved a phenomenal success. One percent is good; a fraction of a percent is typical.

Remember that customers are buying sight unseen. They don't get to examine the product in advance and they don't get to meet you either. Naturally this results in a certain amount of nervousness, especially if you're selling an expensive item. For this reason the "money-back guarantee" is practically mandatory in direct marketing. It's also been shown that quality, "classy" advertising pieces have a positive effect on customer confidence. But above all you must *perform*. You must absolutely keep your promises on product quality and shipping date—to the letter—or you'll be in big trouble with your customers, and possibly with Uncle Sam.

In-House Sales Force. The in-house sales force has only one significant advantage over other marketing channels, but it is a very valuable advantage indeed: You can easily maintain intimate contact with your customers. Your own people are out there talking to customers every day. Properly monitored, these contacts can provide you with a continuous flow of timely information about the market.

The big disadvantage to the in-house sales force is its cost. Every salesperson you hire represents a substantial fixed expense: salary (straight commission is rare these days), training, travel, expense accounts—it's appalling how quickly all this mounts up.

Hiring your own sales force works best for a retail store. Your salespeople are right there on the premises, so you get the greatest advantage at lowest cost. If you must go visit customers, especially over a large geographic area, the cost of maintaining a sales force explodes. Not only do you pay for travel, meals, and lodging, but your salespeople are selling only a small fraction of the time. Mostly you are paying them to ride airplanes, drive cars, and sit in some purchasing agent's waiting room. Furthermore, though your salespeople are in close touch with the market, you may have trouble staying in contact with them if you have a far-flung sales operation.

With an in-house sales force, the twin keys to success are training and follow-up. Consider this: How many kids do you know who want to grow up to be salespeople? Most people in sales have drifted into it from other jobs, and have little or no formal education in sales. To be effective, they must get proper training. Be sure they are thoroughly familiar not only with general sales techniques but with the specific methods that work best in selling your product. In addition, they should know your product inside out. Last but not least, they should be trained in the importance of gathering market intelligence.

But it's not enough to run them through a course—even a very good course—and send them out to sell. You must follow up; keep an eye on their problems, their needs, and their performance. Every member of top management should regularly schedule time to work with the sales force.

Sales Reps. Sales reps, or brokers, or agents, are essentially freelance salespeople. They sell your products, for a commission, but are not on your payroll and do not carry any inventory. There is one very solid advantage to using reps: The up-front and fixed costs are low. If you need to build a large sales network quickly on a small budget, this is the way to go.

Private Products, the company I started to market private-label towelettes, was a classic case of the ideal situation for using sales reps. We were not relying on high technology or management genius. The whole idea was to get this simple product out and exploit a substantial market quickly, before the big boys realized what a gold mine they were missing.

Speed was everything, and there was only one way to expand sales rapidly enough: sales reps—or, as they're known in the grocery industry, food brokers. We hooked up with a master broker in New York who had been in the private-label business for years, and who had relationships with his opposite numbers in other major cities all over the country. In short order he developed for us an entire national sales force.

Through this loosely affiliated network of sales reps we were able to start supplying forty-four of the major food and drug chains within a twelve-month period. It was this national coverage that a few months later attracted Coca-Cola and persuaded it to acquire the company.

HDS

There are, however, some serious disadvantages to using sales reps. The rep is your "representative" to the customer, and thus he has a major influence on how your company is perceived by the customer. Yet he has no inherent loyalty to you, and you have very little control over his behavior. He is representing not only your company but several others, some of which may be direct or indirect competitors. But worst of all, the rep *insulates you from the market.*

You must realize that brokers tend to be paranoid. The rep lives with the constant fear—sometimes rational, sometimes not—that buyer and seller will get together and "cut out the middleman": *him.* He therefore may see it as in his interest to minimize your contact with the customer. He may even try to keep both of you in the dark, by "buying" your product himself and "selling" it to the customer. This prevents "conspiracy" between you and the buyer, and it gives the rep the opportunity to cut himself an extra large slice. But such an "order" puts you at substantial risk; if the rep doesn't come through, you have no recourse. He's just pretending to be a distributor; he is nothing but a desk and a telephone, and has no resources to back up his commitment.

If you don't have any sales talent on your founding team, your start-up may become dangerously dependent on sales reps. The rep seems like the answer to your prayers. He, the expert, offers to take all those unpleasant sales problems off your shoulders. It's tempting, especially when you're working eighteen-hour days trying to debug your production process and you "have no time for sales calls." But this is misuse of a potentially valuable marketing channel. There is no substitute—ever—for controlling your own sales effort.

Sales reps are useful by virtue of their flexibility. It's unlikely that you'll want to use reps as your major marketing channel on a long-term basis. Instead, use them when you want to build a sales network fast; follow with a gradual shift to your own sales force or to distributors. Use reps for other temporary tasks: selling products with a short market life, such as fad items; test-marketing a new product; investigating a new group of customers; or penetrating a new geographic area.

Distributors.   Most complex of all marketing channels is the use of distributors. For this discussion, we define a "distributor" as a middleman who *carries an inventory of your product*. It may be a retail outlet or a warehousing operation; in some industries there may be several levels involved. The distributor may actually buy your product for resale (as do grocery stores) or take your product on consignment (as do bookstores). Also included is the value-added reseller (VAR), who enhances your product or combines it with other products or services before selling it to the ultimate customer.

The distributor, like the sales rep, gives you the opportunity to develop a large sales network rapidly and with minimal up-front expenditure. Unlike the rep, the distributor offers a relatively permanent sales channel. Another advantage is that a top-rank distributor can provide your product with instant credibility. Products selected by J. C. Penney or Neiman-Marcus benefit from the presitge of the outlet that has thus endorsed them.

On the other hand, the distributor's cut is usually very hefty; markups between 50 and 200 percent are common. Distributors, like sales reps, insulate you from your market. Selling becomes complicated; you now have two customers, the ultimate buyer and the distributor, both of whom you must satisfy—and sometimes what pleases one displeases the other. And a large distributor, like any big customer, may develop too much power over your business.

When should you use distributors? Normally you should do so only if carrying a substantial inventory at the point of purchase is needed to sell the product effectively. In selecting and negotiating with distributors, never forget that you are paying them to carry an inventory of your product. That, and only that, is what entitles them to mark up your product 100 percent or more and resell it.

Exclusivity. An important issue that often comes up in dealing with distributors (and sometimes with reps) is *exclusivity.* You may be offered a temptingly large order—on condition that you sell your product solely through one outlet. This is a tough decision. Often that one big order is the break you've been waiting for. However, the exclusivity deal can enslave you to your distributor.

It's best to resist the exclusive distributor arrangement if you possibly can. But if you feel you must go this route—and sometimes it's the right thing to do—make two nonnegotiable demands. *First,* don't get locked into option agreements on future products; negotiate exclusivity on one product at a time.

Second, don't settle for a single big purchase order; insist on guaranteed, regular future purchases. The customer must agree to buy a certain amount every year, or better, every month. These demands are quid pro quo for exclusivity, but don't tie them together in the contract. Don't accept an agreement that says, "We agree to buy 100 units per month until we decide to let the exclusive lapse." If you do, you give up the option of developing other customers and make yourself totally dependent on a single one who can unilaterally terminate his purchases at any time. He's quite likely to bug out just when you need him most.

KEY FACTOR: SELLING EXPENSES

A crucial factor in your decision about sales organization is the cost of making a sale. How much will it cost to push the product through the distribution channel—and is there room in your profit margin to pay for it?

We don't have any ironclad rules for deciding on cost—only some general guidelines: Distributors are usually best for relatively low-priced items that must be sold in volume. Use your own sales force only if a typical single sale is large; you can easily average several thousand dollars in selling costs per sale. In direct marketing, selling costs can be very low, or quite high, depending primarily on response rate. When using reps, keep in mind that in the long run you'll probably switch to another channel, so project your ultimate costs carefully.

Circumstances alter cases, however, so you need to check out the specifics involved in your case.

To begin with, for your type of product, what marketing method (direct, in-house sales force, reps, distributors) is currently being used by the competition? If more than one, which has proved most successful?

Your customers may have something to tell you about preferred distribution channels. Some years ago I was involved with Esteem, a start-up that aimed to sell special cosmetics to women recovering from plastic surgery. It was a newsworthy venture and our initial publicity campaign resulted in considerable media attention. We got a lot of calls from women who had seen an article and wanted to buy some, so we did a little mail-order business—not much, since we couldn't color-match through the mail.

However, our marketing concept was to distribute the product through the plastic surgeons' offices. That would put the doctor's authority behind the product and access the customer with precise targeting and perfect timing. As it turned out, neither the doctors nor the nurses had any great inclination to spend time peddling cosmetics. Even making up special kits with the doctor's name on the package didn't work.

Then we tried to set up a system of independent distributors on the Mary Kay model. That didn't work either; we had a huge turnover of these amateur salespeople and the process was too inefficient.

Finally we used up our initial start-up capital, about a million dollars, and had to shut down. All this time, mail-order sales had continued to trickle in despite our doing nothing much to promote them. Perhaps if we'd gone with direct marketing from the start . . .

HDS

Develop a sales-expense projection. Begin by defining a "sales presentation": This is a sales pitch and close attempt to a customer. In pure-form direct marketing, this is the advertisement; otherwise it is a salesperson's pitch. For your product, and for the marketing channel you propose to use, estimate the effort and expense required to carry through a sale. *Don't guess.* Base your estimate on actual experience or observation (testing, in the case of direct marketing). Example: You plan to sell cellular phones at retail. If you haven't sold this sort of item yourself, go into the stores that do and discreetly watch. You might find that the salesperson has to work with the customer for, say, about twenty minutes on average before closing the sale. Filling out the paperwork and completing the transaction takes another fifteen minutes. You can use these numbers to estimate sales costs for your planning.

Once you have a number for the cost of making a sales presentation, you must estimate the fraction of presentations that will result in a sale. Again, avoid guesswork. Find a competitor or someone in a very closely comparable business and observe its results. Then assume that you'll do half as well.

Now it's a matter of simple arithmetic to calculate projected direct-sales expense: To make X sales, you have to make Y presentations, which takes Z salesperson-hours. You'll have a certain amount of sales overhead, of course, and don't forget that each successful sale will tie up the salesperson a while doing the paperwork and completing the transaction.

If you are going to use direct marketing or an in-house sales force, you can plug the figures you have just generated directly into the financial projections for your business plan. However, if you are going to use reps or distributors, you must also estimate what proportion of their selling effort will go into your product in comparison to other products in their line. In this way you will have an idea of their costs, which you can use when you negotiate with them.

CHECKLIST
Direct Expense of Sales

A. Direct marketing:
- ☐ Cost to buy or rent mailing lists
- ☐ Cost per name to develop your own list
- ☐ Cost to clean your list
- ☐ Cost of ad composition
- ☐ Cost to run ad (magazine, TV, and so on)
- ☐ Cost to print ad (direct mail)
- ☐ Postage costs (direct mail)
- ☐ Reception medium (post office box, 800-number phone line)
- ☐ Reception personnel (order clerks)

B. In-house sales:
- ☐ Salespeople's salaries
- ☐ Salespeople's commissions, bonuses, and so on
- ☐ Sales training (not just the cost of the trainer; don't forget you're paying the salespeople to sit there and get trained!)
- ☐ Point-of-sale advertising and literature
- ☐ Demonstrator models

    ☐ Travel, meals, lodging
    ☐ Telephone expenses
    ☐ Management time and travel to close major sales

  C. Sales reps:
    ☐ Rep commissions, bonuses, and so on
    ☐ Product literature and training aids
    ☐ Point-of-sale advertising and literature
    ☐ Management trips to assist and monitor reps

  D. Distributors:
    ☐ Costs of acquiring and negotiating with distributors
    ☐ Distributor markup
    ☐ Point-of-sale advertising and literature
    ☐ Management time and travel to monitor distributors

PRICING AND POSITIONING

Deciding how much to charge is a perilous process, especially when you bring a new product to market. Here's a simple rule of thumb: If a proposed price seems reasonable to you, it's way too low. Consider doubling it.

Anybody who works much with new companies quickly discovers that there's one mistake they make more often than any other, and that is underpricing the product. The founders, for all their brave talk, are very nervous about sales and seem to view a low price as a sort of insurance policy. There's also a common tendency—particularly among engineers—to adopt a "cost-plus" pricing policy: Figure the costs and add a "reasonable" profit.

The reality is that *your costs are utterly irrelevant to your price*. The customer will pay whatever your product is worth to her. She will not pay more than it is worth to her just because your costs are high. Why should you let her pay less than it's worth to her if your costs are low? This point is so important that we'll repeat it: *Your product's value is what it is worth to the customer; your cost and your profit margin have nothing to do with it.*

I made the mistake of setting a price that was too low when I set up Private Products. You'll recall that we jobbed out all the production and packaging. I went around and got the costs, added them up, added a factor for profit, crossed my fingers, and set a price.

What happened of course was that I underestimated our costs. In spite of my care I didn't account for mistakes in production, loss of product, certain overhead costs—it turned out to be just about enough to wipe out most of our projected profit.

The guy who put together our sales force, the food broker, told me that we had to come in at 35 percent under the name brand. Looking back on it, we could have come in at 20 percent or even 15 percent under and done very well. But the salespeople wanted low prices to make their job easier. Letting Sales set prices equals trouble; it's a formula you can usually rely on.

As it happened, in this case we lucked out. The low price helped us to expand distribution rapidly, and Coca-Cola came along and bought the company before we had to face the problem of increasing prices in order to keep the company going. Incidentally, *they* promptly began to raise the price, and within eight months they had it up to just 10 percent under the name brand.

HDS

You should set your price high. First, to correct for the natural tendency to set it too low. Second, because if your pricing decision is wrong, it will be easier to lower your price than to raise it. Third, because a high price enhances your product's reputation for quality and value.

How do you know if your price is too low? One indication is persistent inability to meet demand. This doesn't necessarily apply if you run into an unusual production snag. But if you're running into not one but a series of production or quality problems; if you just can't seem to expand production fast enough; try a price increase. Chances are you've been selling too cheap, and that's a mistake. Frustrated customers, who can't get shipment, provide a royal road to entry by competitors. Meanwhile, your company develops a reputation as a Mickey Mouse outfit that can't serve its market properly. By underpricing you are leaving money on the table—money that will be desperately needed to expand production and meet competition. As you run flat out at capacity, you raise your costs and risk a major quality fiasco. Finally, this situation tempts you to expand too rapidly—leaving you, when the fever cools, with too much capacity, high fixed costs, and a crushing debt load.

Underpricing can badly distort your perception of the market and make you think you are much more successful than you really are. You may be saying to yourself, "We've got this terrific business selling $10 bills for $9 *and we can't keep up with demand!* We've got unlimited sales potential and the only thing that's holding us back is the need for more working capital. If we can just get another infusion from the

venture capitalists. . . ." But it's easy to make sales when you're selling at a loss! The challenge is to make sales at a profit.

Some marketing theorists advocate a preemptive strategy for new product introductions. The idea is that a high introductory price attracts competitors and creates an umbrella for them. Instead, one should start with a low price, thus expanding sales and production quickly. This builds a dominant market position and cuts costs, because the high unit volume will push the company rapidly down the learning curve. It should be clear that we don't agree with this analysis. The theory is beautiful, but in practice it has shown an ironic flaw: Although the idea is to accept a short-term restriction in order to gain a long-term advantage, the actual result is usually the opposite—short-term success followed by long-term disaster. The preemptive strategy works only if it succeeds in deterring the competition. But what if the competition adopts the same strategy and attempts to deter *you?*

The preemptive pricing strategy is simply a modern, stylish revival of what used to be known as "predatory pricing" back in the days of the robber barons. Unlike Standard Oil, your little start-up probably doesn't have to worry about being broken up under the Sherman Act. But you may find, as Standard Oil did, that this method simply doesn't work. One oil man likened it to "trying to sweep back the ocean with a broom so you can have a dry place to sit."

A strategy with a better track record is "creaming" the early market. Start with a high price and don't drop it until you need to in order to meet the competition. The key to making this work is twofold. *First,* concentrate on raising sales by understanding and satisfying your customers' needs rather than by cutting prices. *Second,* work continually at improving your production methods and cutting costs. In reality you travel down the learning curve by *learning,* not by just mechanically pumping out product. Lower costs result not from volume as such but from the effort to manage production more effectively.

Similar principles apply to products that are not new. Perhaps you're trying, not to protect your market, but to take market share from established competitors. In such a fight there are many weapons you can use. Price cutting can be a devastatingly effective weapon in the market; indeed, one might call it the atomic bomb of marketing. Like the atomic bomb, it is a weapon one should try never to use. In a price war, like a nuclear war, there are no winners. Instead, concentrate on becoming the low-cost producer and letting your competitors know it. Deter them from lowering prices by making it clear that you will respond in kind, and that you can take it better than they can. The threat is stronger than the execution.

EXERCISE
Price Changes and Profit Margins

Before you commit yourself to a price change you need to calculate the effects. Use the following formula.* The question is this: If you lower prices, how much will unit sales have to rise to give you the same dollar amount of gross profit? Or, if you raise prices, how much can unit volume fall without loss of gross profit? Here's the formula:

$$\text{New unit volume} = \frac{\text{Gross Profit Margin (\%)}}{\text{Gross Profit Margin (\%)} + \text{Price Change (\%)}}$$

For instance, if your current gross profit margin is 40 percent and you contemplate a price decrease of 12 percent, the formula gives $40/(40-12) = 1.43$. In other words, unless it increases unit volume by at least 43 percent, the price change will cost you profits.

Positioning. Price positioning is another factor to consider. In most markets there is a range of products, with "premium," mid-range, and "economy" models. A large company often tries to cover all or most of the market by selling several models; General Motors, for instance, consciously positioned its five divisions to cover the entire auto market. Your small company cannot afford this approach. Instead, pick one position; then make sure your total marketing approach is compatible with it. If you've decided to be the Cadillac in your market, don't use a Chevrolet marketing approach—and vice versa.

CHECKLIST
Pricing Your Product

Place a checkmark beside each statement that is true for your company.

☐ Customers complain sometimes that our price is too high.

*Presented by Charles W. Kyd in *Inc.* magazine, April 1987.

☐ Our salespeople frequently suggest that we should cut prices.

☐ We have developed sales arguments to justify why our product is worth more than our competitors'.

☐ Our capacity utilization is not higher than 90 percent.

☐ We are able to ship on time without exception.

☐ Our prices are not lower than those of our competitors in our market segment.

Are there any statements *without* checkmarks? If so, your price may be too low.

ADVERTISING AND PROMOTION

Whether you develop your own advertising or hire an agency there's only one simple principle you need in order to produce good advertisements: *The purpose of advertising is to gain access to potential customers.* There are exceptional cases, such as direct marketing, but in general you should focus on this objective to create effective advertising.

What do we mean by gaining access to potential customers? Quite simply, getting people who may buy into contact with your sales channels. Let's break it down into four steps:

1. *Target your best prospects.* On the basis of your market research, develop a profile of the person most likely to buy your product.

2. *Locate the targeted prospects.* Choose an advertising medium that will give your ad exposure to large numbers of this selected group—and not to a lot of poor prospects. Whether you're buying magazine space, a slot of television time, or a mailing list, minimize paying for people who aren't prospects—you can't afford it.

3. *Communicate with the targeted prospects.* The objective is to let them know that you have a product or service that will satisfy their needs. Don't try to write an ad that will appeal to everyone. Don't try to write an ad that will appeal to the target prospect and also to marginal possibilities. Visualize the person who wants what you have and talk to him or her.

4. *Motivate the targeted prospects.* This step is where most ads fail. The prospective customer should do one of two things as a result of seeing your ad. Either he should come to you and offer you a chance to sell him, or he should identify himself and invite you to come to him. The corollaries are obvious. Let him know how to do

it—should he come to your store; circle a number on the "bingo card"; phone you? Make it easy for him—if your shop is hard to find, draw him a map. Give him a reason to respond, and to respond immediately before he forgets—whether it's an offer of free literature or an entry in a million-dollar lottery.

Effective advertising focuses on the prospective customers and their needs and desires. The ad therefore should emphasize benefits rather than features of your product. The customers probably don't care that your widget has ten ventricles; they want to know why a ten-ventricle widget will give them better satisfaction than an eight-ventricle widget.

Beware of certain pitfalls in advertising. Don't offend or patronize your customers. Don't imply that they're stupid, ignorant, or irrational. They probably aren't; if you sincerely believe that they are, you're in the wrong business. Don't irritate the customers with ads that are too repetitive, too aggressive, or too shrill. In some markets it's become necessary to reassure the wary prospects that they won't be pestered: "No salesman will call." Don't omit important information. Modern consumers are pretty sophisticated; if you leave out a key item (such as the price), they may assume it's because you don't dare mention it.

Should you hire an agency or produce your own advertising? If you lack the specialized skills required, you'll have no choice but to get professional help. Even large companies, for instance, don't try to produce their own TV ads. On the other hand, if you're short of funds you'll have to limit yourself to advertising you can design yourself. For very innovative products selling into specialized niche markets, lean toward the do-it-yourself approach. For products intended to appeal to large, established markets, turn it over to the pros if you can afford it. Keep in mind that you have the option of maintaining control but hiring professionals for specific tasks. The world is full of starving artists who will do your artwork for peanuts.

Of course, advertising costs money. What about publicity, which is free—and often more credible? It can be very effective, providing you ensure that, like your advertising, your publicity is *targeted*. Don't get caught up in attention-getting gimmicks that expose your company to the general public. Instead, focus your effort on becoming known to prospective customers. Whatever approach you use—press releases, magazine articles, demonstrations, stunts—ask yourself: *Who* will see this?

Many entrepreneurs believe that if they get that story in a major business magazine or place a full-page ad the orders will flood in. Wrong. You've got to keep at it continually.

This I learned in politics. When I was running for office on the Upper East Side of Manhattan, I at first had the idea that the announcement of my candidacy would cause the whole world to stop and listen to me. In fact, nobody even noticed my existence until a constant stream of mailing pieces, radio spots, television appearances, public meetings, and sound-truck tours slowly began to take effect.

I applied this lesson at Sedgwick Printout. As one of my competitors said to me, "Damn it, Sedgwick, every time I turn around, there's your name." It was true. Every time he opened up a trade magazine, there was an article. Every time he opened his mail, there was another mailing piece. Every time he attended a meeting, there I was, giving a talk. We were ubiquitous, and it worked.

HDS

YOUR COMPANY NAME

One of the greatest pleasures in starting your own company is selecting the name and logo. All of us feel highly competent to do this and are disinclined to listen to advice. However, there are a few points that should be covered.

In my Enterprise Forum experience I've several times encountered entrepreneurs who stubbornly refused to change company names that clearly hurt them in the market. The best meeting transcription service in New York, for example, is called "Rainbow Enterprises," with a very frivolous-looking logo. The founder fiercely defended her choice against the panel's unanimous criticism of its negative impact on her potential customers—mostly Fortune 500 corporation managers who probably felt a bit uncomfortable with handing an invoice from "Rainbow" to their companies' humorless and steely-eyed controllers. A similar criticism of "UFO Software" (it stands for "user friendly oriented") met with the same defensive response.

REM

The name of your company is its most ubiquitous advertisement. It really helps for it to say something about what your company does for a living. This is one good argument against using your own name for the company.

The Julius E. Holland-Moritz Company makes specialized pliers for orthodontists. Would you know it from the name? Does this name help the company get new customers? Incidentally, this company is no longer owned by the founder, so the name doesn't even identify the proprietor.

There are several other good reasons for not using your own name. What if your company goes under? What if it is highly successful, you sell it, and *then* it goes under? It can be rather embarrassing to have people asking, "Are you connected with the Joe Blurpsky Company that was indicted for polluting Lake Michigan?" You can of course explain that yes you were but not anymore and it wasn't your fault. . . . But why get into this situation? Why put your name in the control of other people?

Of course, it's traditional for law firms and other professional businesses to use founder names. And if your name is very well known (to your *customers!*) it may have marketing value. But in most cases a name such as "Smith Enterprises" doesn't do much for your credibility. Its cautious generality suggests that you are trying out several lines of business and lack a clear definition. This may indeed be the case, but if so you should try to conceal it from your customers. Also to be avoided in most cases is "Smith & Associates." A lot of people who get fired or laid off set up as consultants under a moniker of this type. Few clients will be naive enough to believe in the "associates"—even when they actually exist!

Names consisting of initials tell the prospective customer *nothing* about your company or its products. They don't work well for start-ups; such names must be earned over decades. Once everybody knows who you are and what you do, you may be called by your initials, as IBM is.

Also to be avoided is the pretentious name.

A Route 128 company with a dozen or so employees made a very ingenious little computerized gadget that kept track of vending-machine sales. It provided a good method of keeping the maintenance people who go around to collect the money from the coin boxes honest, and it created valuable data for market analysis. Its name—International Totalizing Systems—was probably more a hindrance than an advantage to this excellent little company; whom was it fooling?

Another pitfall is the cutesy-pie name. Basing your company name on a pun—even a very ingenious pun—is likely to have you and your employees cringing eventually. Even the funniest joke gets stale after a few years. (One possible exception: if the product you're selling is humorous.)

Finally, be very careful not to arouse the prejudices of your customers—or your neighbors. People in this Politically Correct era have become very touchy, and a word or phrase that seems totally innocent to you may outrage women, blacks, gays, or other groups. It's not always obvious what will get you in trouble.

> Procter & Gamble has several times had to fight rumors that its hundred-year-old "Man in the Moon" logo is a Satanist symbol.

> Lifesystems Company was occasionally confused with the then-notorious polluter Life Sciences Corporation.

I was careful to avoid the word *chemical* when naming Reaction Design Corp. The name we chose identified us to customers, who were technically sophisticated, but, we hoped, conveyed nothing ominous to the general public. Yet, as it turned out, we occasionally were asked if we had anything to do with nuclear reactors and radioactivity. Perhaps you can't win after all.

REM

On a more positive note, your name should convey to your customers at least a rough impression of what you sell. It's nice if you can make the name sound compatible with your company's style. If you're setting up a hot high-tech operation, naturally you should use technology buzzwords (but try not to overdo it). If you're selling sweaters to preppies, something that suggests yachting or duck hunting may be more appropriate.

Unfortunately, selecting a good name is becoming increasingly tough because so many clever ideas have already been used. When you come up with a dozen good possibilities and have your lawyer search them for previous trademarks, you're likely to be shocked at the results.

> NBC spent a small fortune having a new logo designed by prestigious consultants, only to find that an obscure independent TV station was already using the same design. NBC had to buy the rights.

In some cases your product needs a name too. If it does, the product name will be even more critical than your company name. Again, targeting the customer is the key.

> A rather ordinary candy caught on as a fad some years ago by calling itself "Spider Eggs"; somehow this caught the perverse fancy of the younger generation.

The personal computer business has seen two very good product names. One, of course, was "Apple"—conveying, as was intended, an image of simplicity and accessibility to the user. But though less appreciated, IBM's "PC" was an equally brilliant choice, conveying the image of the generic standard which the IBM PC in fact became.

We don't want to ruin your pleasure. Have fun selecting your company name, but recognize that your choice will impact your results in the market.

YEAH, BUT WHAT ABOUT . . . ?

There are counterexamples to this chapter. You can find small-business marketers who do none of the work and systematic analysis that we recommend yet are strikingly successful in the marketplace. Some entrepreneurs have an amazing talent for intuitive marketing. Somehow, by experience or by instinct, they automatically develop and follow a clear market strategy. These natural talents swim in the market like fish, doing all the right things without having to think about it. The rest of us have to use Aqua-lungs. Grinding through the detailed analysis is a lot of work—but it pays off.

CAUTIONARY TALE
The One About the Traveling Salesman

My first business venture began after I had become disenchanted with my lot at the Aluminum Company of Canada. I finally left, and then rummaged around New York for something to do. I was introduced to a company called Trig-A-Tape. Its product was a device that put price labels on items in retail stores. I bought 10 percent of the company for $10,000 and became General Manager.

The hand-operated labeling device was invented by a gentleman who had spent five or six years manufacturing the gadgets in his basement and selling them to local stores. At that time there were various existing ways to label cans and boxes and so on. Some stores used sticks with ink stamps on them. Others ordered preprinted labels, which a clerk would then stick on the items by hand. The Trig-A-Tape machine was a real advance; you could set a price on it, make pressure-sensitive labels on the spot, and conveniently extrude them onto the product. Our approach was to get into serious production of these devices and sell them into what appeared to be a very significant market.

We quickly ran into major manufacturing problems. Nobody had looked into the intricacies of manufacturing this gadget. Up to this time the machines had been put together, one at a time, by the inventor. He did it almost as a craftsman would assemble a fine piece of custom furniture, shaping and fitting each piece individually to make the final product work. When that same piece was put on a production line with fifteen or twenty people who had never seen it before, the result was a chaotic mess.

There were not only defects in assembly, in some cases there weren't even drawings for the parts. The inventor, who knew it all by heart after making these things for years, didn't need drawings. Neither my partners nor I had any specific manufacturing experience, and we didn't realize how difficult making this simple-looking device would be. So again and again, machines were shipped out and returned because they didn't work. It was a valuable lesson for me. Since then I've made it a rule that anything with more than two moving parts gets jobbed out.

But this was only the beginning of our troubles. Our real problem was selling the things. We had selected a distribution channel on the basis of the experience of one of my partners. He had had a very considerable success a few years earlier with a paint spray gun, using what are called specialty salesmen. The specialty salesman (few women in those days) was an independent rep, a freelancer. He drove around to retail stores with sample cases promoting various products; when he made a sale, the order was filled directly by the manufacturer. This had turned out to be very successful in selling spray guns, so we used it for our new gadget.

We advertised the availability of the project in great detail in a series of full-page ads in a magazine called (what else?) *Specialty Salesman*. We got a very good response; we "sold" the salesperson a sample kit for $20 or so, which included the device itself, some rolls of tape from which the labels were made, sales literature, order forms, and some nice impressive cards from the Trig-A-Tape Corporation of New York City.

What hadn't occurred to us in selecting this distribution channel was that we had the right customers, and salespeople who called on those customers, but *the customers did not buy this type of product from those salespeople*. The retail-store operator bought all sorts of things from the specialty salesman—hardware, dry goods, gadgets—but only items for resale. The Trig-A-Tape machine was not for resale but for use by the retailer—it was a *system* sale. The specialty salesman didn't want to make system sales and wasn't good at it. It involved convincing the retailers to abandon their old labeling methods and use a new one. This is not an on-the-spot decision; it takes repeat calls and working with the customer. The specialty salesman didn't do that sort of thing. He went to the customer, showed him something, and the decision was made in fifteen minutes. Of course, our quality control problems didn't exactly help the sale.

Worse yet, we had zero control over our sales force. We didn't even know who they were; each one was just a piece of paper and a check when he sent in his mail-order coupon from our ad. It might be an old hand, or it might be someone who'd never tried selling before and thought this was a good way to get rich quick.

So what happened was that these couple of hundred people got discouraged, sent their sample cases back, and demanded repayment.

By this time, between manufacturing and marketing costs, plus some considerable overhead, the company had run through its original invested capital, some $200,000, and—not to put too fine a point on it—was broke, or perhaps a little worse. At this juncture, my partners approached me with an offer to sell me the other 90 percent of the company for about $100,000, which was a superb piece of chutzpa. Happily, I had the wits to sit tight. My partners were already involved in starting a different venture and didn't like the idea of simultaneously going into bankruptcy with Trig-A-Tape; it would not have greatly enhanced their credibility with investors. So I acquired the company for $1.00, and they even paid off the outstanding debt.

Then I had to move fast. We had a monthly overhead of $35,000 and no income to speak of. I took over the business on a Thursday afternoon. By Saturday of the next week I had overhead down to $2,000 a month. I had to let go the entire staff. I stopped my own salary, of course. I sublet the loft where we had been "manufacturing" the gadget. I hired an engineer, offering him a piece of the company, and we moved what was left of the operation into his basement. The only other person we kept was the inventor, who still kept rolling out two or three gadgets a day by hand as he always had.

The engineer began redesigning the product from the ground up so that it could be manufactured more easily. First, however, we went out and met with people from some major chains like Sears and Woolworth. In short, we did a little market research, finding out what customers wanted in their price-labeling system and even going into the minor matter of what they would pay for it. Six months later we had some prototypes and took them out for testing.

About this time I was approached by some of the big names in pressure-sensitive labels—Dymo, 3M, and a couple of others. We had a patent not only on the machine itself but on the pressure-sensitive labels it produced, so if these devices got out in any volume, there would be a substantial effect on the demand for pressure-sensitive adhesives. We negotiated over a period of months and finally sold the company to Dymo.

There's a rather amusing anecdote attached to this sale. I had a very clear idea of what I wanted. Dymo had just gone public and was considered a hot stock (this was in the bull market of 1961). Dymo wanted to give me some cash and a royalty, but since I wasn't at all sure Dymo would ever actually get the product on the market, I was unwilling to take this deal. I wanted a nice piece of Dymo's stock. The negotiations went on for weeks. Dymo was on the West Coast, and periodically the chairman and president would come east to buy another company for $5 million or $10 million—and then come and diddle with me for less than $1 million. Finally, in some frustration, the president of Dymo told me that he had examined the finances of Trig-A-Tape—which of course he had in the course of his due diligence—and he'd also examined my own personal finances. He'd found them both very thin (which they were) and told me that his offer of cash and royalty was the last offer and I could take it or leave it.

I asked him if in his investigation of my background he had looked up my wife's maiden name. He looked at me blankly and said, "No. What does that have to do with anything?" I said, "Well, I'm married to Patricia Ann Rosenwald." Now, Rosenwald to anyone informed in business history is a name that bears some clout. Julius Rosenwald founded Sears Roebuck, and his heirs are not generally poverty-stricken. I went on to say, "I don't *need* to sell this company. If I don't get what I want for it, I'll just put it in a drawer." That did the trick, and I got my deal. As it happens, Patsy's father was James Benno Rosenwald, no relation at all to Julius Rosenwald.

So I ended up with a tidy sum in Dymo stock at $3 a share, which promptly rose to about $40 and made me what for that time was quite rich. It took Dymo about two years to get the product out on the market in volume. It became the industry standard and was used almost universally until, recently, computerized pricing systems began to displace it.

Overall, this venture was extremely instructive as well as lucrative. It taught me a lot of lessons that were helpful in later ventures (though I still had something to learn, as you'll recall from Chapter One's Cautionary Tale). The most important lesson concerned distribution channels. Manufacturing hassles, distracting though they were, presented fairly easy problems to solve. The company's big mistake lay in jumping into the market with the specialty salesmen, a totally inappropriate method of distribution. In the end, I was able to finesse this difficulty by selling out to a large company that already had its own distribution set up. You may not want to sell out, of course. But if you're having trouble with setting up distribution, consider ways of getting a big company to do it for you. Often it's a lot better than reinventing the marketing wheel yourself.

HDS

Seven

SALES TACTICS

With the money he had he was able to purchase a good supply of matches, and when it became light enough he began to vend them.

Hitherto he had not been very fortunate in the disposal of his wares, being timid and bashful; but then he was working for Mother Watson, and expected to derive very little advantage for himself from his labors. Now he was working for himself, and this seemed to put new spirit and courage into him.

Horatio Alger, Jr., *Mark the Match Boy*

Somebody has to sell!

It's amazing how many businesses succumb because they forget this simple truth. And not just new or small businesses either. Huge corporations, generations old, go bankrupt when they get complacent and take their sales for granted.

Somebody has to sell!

So, how do you feel about selling? Perhaps you are already an experienced sales professional. You know how to sell, you've done plenty of selling in the past, and you know your industry. If so, you may have problems, but probably making sales won't be one of them.

On the other hand, maybe you've never had to actually get out there and make a sale. You come from the laboratory or the office or the plant—or maybe straight out of school. Salesmanship appears to you as a sort of black art, one you're not quite sure you really want to learn.

In fact, perhaps you consider sales . . . not too respectable. When you think "salesman" you think of some character in a loud checked sports jacket with his foot stuck in the door, shouting out his spiel as

Dagwood tries to eject him. Your contacts with sales types—at least the ones you remember—have not been happy ones: the car salesman who got you to pay $1,500 more than you'd budgeted, and stuck you with a lemon too; the fraud who told you that you'd won a contest, then personally delivered a cheap "prize" and hit you with an aggressive sales talk; the obnoxious boiler-room squads who bombard you with telephone solicitations all evening. As far as you're concerned, Willy Loman had it coming.

Scientists and engineers are particularly prone to regard selling as a low-status occupation. The result is that many high-tech start-ups simply starve to death. Like a bevy of Victorian virgins trying to open a whorehouse, the founders just can't bring themselves to dirty their hands with such degrading labor.

Somebody has to sell!

Don't kid yourself that a good product will "sell itself." It won't. Don't think that brilliant advertising will "make it sell." It won't. Don't persuade yourself that a half-hearted, fastidious, arm's-length approach to selling will work. It won't. Somebody—some specific person or persons in your organization—must be responsible for moving the product. If you take direct responsibility for sales yourself, you must be committed to performing the task and performing it well. If you lack the talent or inclination to do so, you must delegate it to someone competent and motivated. And if you hold salespeople in contempt, you'd better learn to get over it, or at least hide it well—because you need them.

SELLING: A SURVIVAL SKILL

In any case, even if you employ a good team of experienced sales professionals, you as the founder of a small company will find that you spend a large part of your time doing selling. It goes with the territory, as they say. Just think of all the people you'll have to "sell":

• *Investors.* Before you even start your company you'll probably have to sell some investors. Unless you can finance your company out of your own pocket, you'll have to sell some company before you can sell your product. This is a sales job that doesn't go away. Growing companies always need capital, and the CEO must take the lead in raising it. If your company survives you'll be "selling" its prospects to venture capitalists, bankers, maybe even Wall Street analysts.

• *Cofounders and employees.* Don't forget your cofounders and your employees. You'll have to "sell" them on investing time and effort on your new, untried, and risky business concept. Once again, this is a task that won't go away. Whenever you conceive a new project, a special effort, a change in approach, you will have to "sell, not tell" your personnel if you want to engage their enthusiasm.

▪ *Customers.* Customers, of course, must be sold. In the early days of your start-up you'll be desperately shorthanded. Developing a reliable flow of sales, starting from scratch, is a terribly difficult job, and everybody is going to have to pitch in. When your company prospers and grows, the need will not go away. In successful concerns the CEO and other members of top management get plenty of customer contact. Their active participation is frequently essential to close unusually large or pioneering sales. They must be involved in the sales process in order to motivate—and monitor—the professional sales force. And finally, top management cannot understand or anticipate changes in the market unless it is in constant contact with customers.

This last point is so important it needs elaboration. You as CEO must balance conflicting claims from the segments of your organization in order to make crucial management decisions. The impact of the various factors on sales is a primary criterion. Production wants to reduce costs by restricting the number of different models; Sales wants even more variety. Finance wants to reduce inventory; Sales wants to increase it. R&D wants to develop a new product; Marketing wants to improve the old one. *You* must decide such issues. What will be the effect on sales? There's no substitute for getting out and making a few sales yourself. It gives you a real feel for the difficulties your sales force faces. It also makes it harder for the salespeople to give you a snow job.

EXERCISE
Sales Responsibility

A. Who is the person ultimately responsible for sales in your company? Who gets taken to the Tower and beheaded if sales projections are not met? _____

B. Nonsales types may have to pitch in to get your start-up sales going. What proportion of total working time do you expect each of the following team members to spend on sales? Has each one been informed of these expectations?

CEO	_____ %
VP of Sales	_____ %
VP of Marketing	_____ %
VP of Production	_____ %
VP of R&D	_____ %
VP of Administration and Finance	_____ %

THE SALES PROCESS: A FOUR-STAGE MODEL

Full-time selling is not for everyone, but anyone can learn the rudiments. It doesn't require mystical endowment or innate talent. Much of the vast array of books, seminars, and lectures on selling is disquieting to those of us who come from, say, a technical background. To hear the "experts" tell it, selling is a highly emotional fine art of psychological manipulation not much removed from hypnotism. And if you're selling underwater lots in Florida to elderly pensioners, perhaps it is. Most selling, however, involves offering a real value. And that makes selling a relatively straightforward exchange of information. The customer provides you with information about her needs and wants; you provide her with information about your product or service.

In the analysis that follows, the sales process is broken down into four stages. Other writers on this subject may divide it into three, or seven, but the process remains the same. The steps are simple. First, attract a customer, interest him, get him to consider buying. Second, exchange information with him and deal with his objections. Third, persuade him to buy—"close" the sale. Fourth, follow up, and thus renew the sales cycle.

Stage 1. Attract a Customer.   For most businesses the first stage, attracting a customer, is actually a marketing responsibility. We've already discussed it in some detail in Chapter Six. But it's worth some additional consideration, for one of the most common mistakes in selling is failure to recognize that this first step is *essential*. The mere fact that a customer happens to be in physical proximity to you doesn't mean he is ready to be sold. If you start at stage 2 without completing stage 1, the prospect will be confused at best, and possibly infuriated. On the other hand, by laying the foundation well when you develop initial interest, you make it easier to apply your sales presentation.

How should the customer be engaged in the sales process? To start with, he must become aware that he has a *need:*

> "Only seventeen shopping days till Christmas. Have you bought a present for your mother-in-law yet?"

Then he must realize that his need *can* be satisfied:

> "Don't despair! This year you can give her the perfect gift. . . ."

And finally, he must recognize that your product *might* satisfy his need:

> ". . . a vacation in sunny Ulan Bator. Special bargain price on one-way fares."

You should not jump into the sales instantly, but neither should you beat around the bush or stall. Beware Dale Carnegie! Not because the Carnegie approach to selling is bad—it's actually quite good—but because any approach is bad if you use it in an indiscriminate manner. The idea that you should establish a personal, friendly relationship with the customer before opening up your sales case is sometimes valid—and sometimes not. This approach works best if (1) the customer already knows, before you walk in the door, that you have come to peddle widgets and (2) the customer is expected to become a long-term account with you.

When selling, you make a serious mistake if you try to become "friends" with a customer who doesn't know what you're there for. "Hello, nice day. What a lovely house you have, Ma'am!"—this tends to arouse suspicion. Who is this stranger and why is he trying to act so friendly? What does he really want? Obviously he's a salesman, so why is he trying to hide it? Is he ashamed to mention what he's selling, trying to become "friends" so I won't kick him out when I find out?

Much more effective is "Hi, I'm selling a rug cleaner that will take out any stain you can imagine. Mind if I demonstrate on that mark in the hallway? You won't believe what this baby can do . . ." You show respect for your customer by recognizing that she doesn't need a friend—she has her own friends—she needs a solution to her carpet problems. And you demonstrate confidence in, and enthusiasm for, your product. If you believe in it, maybe she should too.

Several times I've sat in on meetings where a big sale was blown in the first few minutes by an attempt to establish a "personal" relationship. In one case, the salesman spotted a picture of the prospect's dog on the wall and immediately picked up on it, playing it by the book and very competently. The prospect later told me he had found this ploy disgustingly cynical and decided at that moment not to have any dealings with this guy.

Yes, establishing a personal relationship with the customer can make the sale. But, unless you are a *very* good actor, you'd better be sincere. This is one reason we stress the importance of going into a business where you like your customers.

REM

Whether the customer is retail or business, you can profit by not being too presumptuous. Your job as a sales professional is to solve the customer's problem with your product or service. If the customer wants someone to gossip with, or talk politics with, or tell dirty jokes with, she knows where she can find him; she doesn't need you for that.

Personal selling boils down to sensitivity to the customer. What does the customer need and want? What are the customer's problems? How does the customer want to be sold? The great danger for the beginning salesperson is canned, formula selling. No formula, no matter how popular it is, or how famous or successful its inventor, can be effective if applied blindly. You must constantly observe the customer to sell effectively.

As soon as you encounter a prospect, begin by determining whether she's considering a purchase. You'll probably encounter all kinds of prospects. At one end of the spectrum is the prepared buyer: "I need a personal computer to analyze my stock investments." At the other end, you might hear, "I'm curious about personal computers. What are they good for?" Please note that the latter may be just as likely to buy, ultimately, as the former! The object at this stage is not to cull out poor prospects and chase them away, but to find out *where you have to start* with this particular customer.

Stage 2. Handle Objections.   Once the prospect is ready to consider buying, you can begin stage 2. At this point, the prospect begins to produce objections to buying—otherwise known as sales resistance. You must find out what these objections are and answer them. *Answering objections is easy—it's finding out what they are that's hard.* Rarely will the prospect frankly state her objections. Instead, she may chatter about irrelevancies; or bring up a problem that actually doesn't bother her while avoiding mention of her real concerns; or perhaps just sit there, refusing either to buy or to state any reason why she won't. Don't be in a hurry to chase her out. Unless she has an obvious ulterior motive, like getting out of a rainstorm, she's probably hanging around in the hope that *you* will state her objection—and answer it.

How can you do this? There seem to be hundreds of possible obstacles to the purchase of a product. Most can be reduced to one of four basic objections.

Objection #1: "It Isn't What I Want."

The first key to dealing with this objection is to realize that it says "want" and not "need." Entrepreneurs tend to think in terms of satisfying human needs. They are prone to fall into the trap of telling the customer, "This is what you need." But you shouldn't take it for granted that he wants what he needs. If he doesn't, you may produce a list of irrefutable reasons why he needs your product—and get absolutely nowhere. You must find out what he *wants,* and convince him that your product will provide it.

How? Communicate. Get him talking, and listen. What are his motives, his likes, his dislikes? Your market research should have given you some hints. Now use them as a starting point to analyze this particular customer.

By *listening* to the customer, you obtain the key to dealing with this objection. Once you know what he wants—very specifically—you can present your product in a way that will attract him. Stress the features that he wants. Perhaps you can offer him a different model, a customized version, or a special service.

Objection #2: "I Can't Afford It."

This is the objection that separates the pros from the amateurs in the selling game. The mediocre salesperson is always pressing management for lower prices so he can sell more. But to give away your product, you don't need salespeople. When a salesperson comes to you with a request to drop prices, grasp him firmly by the shoulders, rotate him 180 degrees, and send him out again, with the following advice: Handle this objection by determining which of two forms it takes. Listen carefully to the customer. What is her real meaning?

■ *"It's not worth the price. I could pay this price, but I don't like it that much."* If this is the obstacle, don't talk price, talk value. Your task is to make the customer like it more. Here is one technique: The question of price and value can lead easily into a discussion of the "good old days" and from there to the customer's previous purchase of a similar product. Get her talking about the old one that she really liked. Then point out to her the similar features of your product. The association with her memories will make your product's advantages real to her. What if her last purchase was a lemon? Then, of course, you use the contrast.

■ *"I love it, but I just don't have the money."* If this is the case, don't waste your breath trying to make the product seem even more desirable. Deal with the cost problem. Perhaps she could manage it on credit. Perhaps part of the purchase price is tax-deductible, so it doesn't really cost as much as it seems. Perhaps she could manage a cheaper, stripped-down version and upgrade it later.

Objection #3: "It's Not the Best Value."   If your salespeople complain about Objection #2, be very skeptical. Complaints about Objection #3, however, raise the specter of effective competition, so give close attention.

Even seasoned sales professionals get defensive when this objection surfaces—and that's a serious mistake. If you start to counterattack by, say, bad-mouthing the competition, the customer may well clam up. Then you may lose the sale; worse, you will certainly lose some extremely valuable information. If a customer is willing to tell you why he prefers the competition—*listen!* Even if he's wrong, ridiculous, stupid, bite your tongue and hear him out. When he's done, still don't respond. Instead, ask probing questions. Make sure you understand what his objections are, and that you've heard them all. Don't hesitate to give up the sale if necessary to get frankness from him. You're getting priceless information that can pay off handsomely in future sales.

Keep listening until the objection *makes sense.* Even if the customer is wrong, he has a reason for his opinion. You haven't listened enough until you understand why he feels the way he does. Then restate his objections, check each one to make sure you've understood him correctly, and deal with it tactfully.

How? There are basically two responses. One is, "So sorry, you're wrong." Obviously, you use this when the customer is mistaken in his *facts*—not his evaluations. (And only then, or he'll get mad. So listen carefully.) With this response, you must bend over backward to be tactful. "I'm sorry, sir, I should have mentioned that this system *does* translate office memos from English to Sanskrit and vice versa." (Even though it was clearly stated in the ad, not to mention your original sales pitch.) The other response is, "Yes, but." If he's got a point, concede it—frankly and freely. This will enhance your credibility. Then counter in an area of concern to him where you have the advantage. Suppose, for instance, that he has previously expressed concern about reliability. When he brings up a competitor's superior convenience, quickly return to favorable ground: "It's true that the five-inch diskettes are more widely used still, and I have to admit that it's a nuisance to transfer data to a different medium. But we've found that there are a lot fewer errors with the 3.5-inch diskettes."

It's usually a poor idea to criticize competitors. You'll be more credible if you imply, "They're good, but we're better, at least for *your* particular needs." Remember that the customer sees you—quite correctly—as a biased party and that anything you say about the competition will be heavily discounted. Comments about your competitors should be confined to noncontroversial statements of fact; leave evaluations to the customer.

Objection #4 "I Don't Trust You." This is an objection you'll almost never hear made explicit, but it's the deadliest of them all. Even when the product is terrific, the price is right, and you're head and shoulders above the competition, the customer may balk because he suspects he's being taken.

This objection is best handled with prophylactic measures. Once trust has been lost, it's hard to retrieve it. There are four common ways of inspiring mistrust in customers:

1. *Misbehavior of sales or service personnel.* When the pressure is on to meet quota, a salesperson can be awfully tempted to cut corners. Common sins include making exaggerated claims or promises, understating the price and hitting the customer with hidden costs, and bait-and-switch tactics. You should set up systems to monitor the sales force. And emphasize attitude. Never let your salespeople speak contemptuously of customers, even in private. Make it known that customers are to be referred to with respect; they aren't "marks" or "suckers" or "fish" to be "landed."

Be sure that customer service, returns, and the complaint desk get top-management attention. Remember, turning a dissatisfied customer into a satisfied one is the *second* most important thing these people do. Their most important function is to let top management know that there *are* dissatisfied customers—and why.

A number of CEOs—some with large companies—make it a practice to spend one day a month dealing personally with customer complaints.

2. *Bad reputation of company or industry.* If your company has a bad reputation, you can—and must—do something about it. But what if your whole industry is held in low esteem by the public? Well, it becomes important then not only to differentiate your product from competitive products, but to differentiate your company from competitive companies. Change the terminology if you can get away with it; you're not selling used cars, you're selling "pre-owned vehicles."

3. *The deal is too good.* There's a tendency to be suspicious of the bargain that's too good to be true—to ask: "What's the catch?" If your customers are showing this reaction, there can only be two possibilities. One is that there *is* a catch. If so, maybe your salespeople should be a bit more frank about it. Or maybe there really is no catch. In that case, consider raising your price.

4. *Hard sell.* Think back to something you've bought that gave you real satisfaction—high quality, just what you wanted, bargain price. How was it sold to you? Not aggressively, was it? In fact, chances are you had to search it out. In selling, as in courtship, it's a mistake to come on too strong. The customer has a natural tendency to think that a really good product doesn't need aggressive selling. So the salesperson who appears overeager, pushy, high-pressure, will arouse suspicion. *We* know that a better mousetrap does not sell itself. But customers almost invariably believe that it *does*.

How to sell effectively without seeming overaggressive? Your best bet is to cultivate an air of serene confidence in the product, combined with eager attention to the needs of the customer. If the customer seems to be feeling pressured, back off. Leave him an exit. All high-pressure tactics are based on imprisoning the customer: Get him where he can't get away—the "closing room" if you're selling cars, his own living room if you're selling encyclopedias, a resort if you're selling desert lots. Then keep after him until he signs. Don't let him leave and don't let him stop to think. This tactic—or even the appearance of it—can backfire badly. You may lose not just this customer, but the others he warns about you.

The key to dealing with any objection is listening. Let the customer talk. Some objections will come out quickly and explicitly. But many will not. Customers can be amazingly shy. She may be embarrassed to admit that she can't afford your premium model. She may feel it would be impolite to tell you she likes a competitor's product better. If you get the impression that she has a hidden objection, try running down a list of plausible objections with her. (You, of course, have a prepared answer to each one.) If even this doesn't smoke her out, you're probably facing a #4—suspicion.

Finally, be willing to take your time. There's a saying on Wall Street that's relevant here: "If you want a fast answer, you have one: No."

EXERCISE
Sales Presentation Modules

You want to present your product to the customer in an organized way, rather than rambling on at random. The first step is to break up your sales presentation into modules. You can then adapt your sales pitch to each customer, without becoming disorganized, by assembling a set of modules suited to the customer at hand.

Start with the list of benefits (not features) of your product. Write down a short sales pitch—no more than 250 words—for each benefit. Be sure the first sentence describes the benefit to the customer. Then go on to tell the customer exactly what he will get— that is, describe the features relevant to that benefit. Briefly back up your claim by citing proof (such as tests) or endorsements. Rephrase and restate the benefit to close.

Now read the pitch out loud; imagine you are speaking to a customer. Ask a friend to listen, or tape-record it. Does it sound too stilted or formal? How effective is it? Revise it until it sounds natural when spoken.

As you get actual experience in the market, customer feedback should give you more ammunition. Collect stories of happy customers, for instance. Be constantly alert for arguments, offers, or buzzwords that produce sales, and add them to your arsenal.

For many products, the most powerful selling technique is the demonstration. That way the customer can actually see or feel or experience the benefits. But a demonstration can be very demanding; don't just wander through the features—plan exactly how you will show them and in what order.

Stage 3. Close the Sale.   Once you feel you have elicited and answered the customer's objections, you're ready for the third step: *closing the sale.* To close a sale is simply to induce the prospect to make a commitment to buy. It can take several forms: giving you a purchase order; signing a contract; handing over cash or a check.

Amateurs see closing as automatic; answer all the objections, and the customer will go ahead and buy. The sales professional knows better. As the close approaches, the customer and the salesperson both experience increasing tension. This tension frightens the inexperienced salesperson; she tends to back off, to give up the close attempt, hoping the customer will somehow take the initiative and close the sale by himself. She's usually disappointed, for the tension also causes the customer to hesitate, and perhaps withdraw.

There are all sorts of specific sales close techniques. Some are more effective than others for particular products, or particular customers, or particular salespeople. Every experienced salesperson has her favorite close. However, you should try to master and apply as many different closes as possible.

We'll divide sales closes, a bit arbitrarily, into four basic types: request, pressure, negotiative, and assumptive.

The Request Close.   The *request close* is quite straightforward: You simply ask the customer for the sale. Scarcely subtle, but it is used quite effectively every day to sell products ranging from Girl Scout cookies to the services of prostitutes. This forthright approach saves time and often prods a hesitant prospect to decide. It's easy to master even for beginning salespeople.

The big disadvantage to the request close is that if it fails you'll find it hard to retrieve the sale. You've more or less demanded that the customer commit himself, and if he says no it's hard to get a second chance. You have put him in a position where, in order to buy, he must reverse himself. Nobody likes to be caught waffling, or be thought lacking in sales resistance.

The request close is best suited to small purchases. The customer is more likely to respond positively if the amount at stake is not too large. Also, it's not economical to spend a lot of time making a small sale. The request close is nothing if not fast.

The most valuable use for the request close, however, is the subsidiary sale. After you've closed the main sale, use the request close to add value to the transaction. The classic example is the gas-station close: "Fill 'er up?" See if the customer will buy more—or buy accessories, extra features, even an additional main product. This can be especially productive when you've just closed a big-ticket item.

Often the customer assumes a go-for-broke attitude and readily buys add-ons that she wouldn't even have considered before she committed to the big purchase. Sales resistance, once neutralized, may be slow to recover. So when you make a big sale, don't take a break; push ahead and exploit your success.

The Pressure Close.   Next we come to the *pressure close.* Like all closes, this approach is intended either to force a commitment or to make the prospect expose her objections. As the name implies, the pressure close utilizes direct pressure on the prospect. There are several varieties.

The *negative time-limit close* tells the customer that if she doesn't buy now, the deal will get worse, or even disappear. Examples: "This is the last day at this price—it's going up 20 percent tomorrow." "This is the last one we have in stock." "They say interest rates are going up, so you should finance it now to keep your payments low."

The closely related *positive time-limit close* offers the prospect an inducement to act promptly. Examples: "We're having a special sale on it today." "You get a set of batteries free if you buy before Friday." "The author is here today autographing copies."

The famous *Franklin Ledger* is a highly effective pressure close. To use this, you sit down with the customer and list the positive and negative factors of the purchase on a sheet of paper. It's the openness and fairness of this objective, judicial procedure that puts pressure on the reluctant prospect. He is faced with the choice between admitting that the positives outweigh the negatives (at which point he has no excuse not to buy) or bringing out his hidden objections and writing them on the negative side (which gives you the chance to deal with them). It takes practice to handle this technique smoothly, but the results can be well worth it.

The Negotiative Close.   The *negotiative close* operates rather more subtly. Instead of applying pressure on the prospect, you suddenly remove it, so that her own momentum carries her into commitment. How? The key idea is to open a negotiation—to say, in effect, "What should I offer you to induce you to buy?"

One very powerful negotiative close is the *judo close*. To apply this technique, you must identify the customer's major objection. Deal with the less important objections normally, but withhold your answer to the major item. Instead, encourage the prospect to elaborate on it, to emphasize it. Then, state it back to her for confirmation. Get her agreement that this is her real objection—and finally, come back with a complete answer. The sudden disappearance of the problem that she herself emphasized will leave her with little alternative but to buy.

Another variety is the *subjunctive close*. Again, you must start with a key objection. Use this to ask the customer for a conditional commitment. Example: "Would you buy if I could get you one with chartreuse ventricles?" Note that this is most effective if kept in the subjunctive, even though you of course know that you can perform. Much less effective is: "I can get you one with chartreuse ventricles. Will you buy?"

Most subtle and powerful of the negotiative closes is the *Clarkson close*. To use this, you must get the prospect asking questions. Then respond with an offer phrased as a question. Example: Customer: "Could I get it in pink?" Salesperson: "Do you want it in pink?" Chances are he'll answer yes—and you've closed.

The whole point of the negotiative close is to give the prospect the initiative. Once he is induced to *make a demand,* he can frequently be closed simply by granting the demand.

The Assumptive Close.   Most subtle of all is the *assumptive close*. The idea here is to make buying the path of least resistance. You simply assume that the prospect will buy; in order to refuse, he must then actively object. And to object, he must bring out his hidden objections.

One approach is the *implied-consent close*. Here you simply ask a question that assumes that the prospect will buy. If he doesn't object, you've closed. Examples: "Should I ship this to your Stockton plant?" "Will you be using your credit card to pay for this?"

The *agreement close* works well for big-ticket items. When you start your close attempt, pull out a blank "agreement" form. As you discuss the customer's wants, fill in the blanks. When everything is specified, slide it in front of her and ask, "Would you check to see that I have everything correct? Yes? If you'll just sign right here. . . ."

Especially in consumer sales, it's much better to use an "agreement" than a "contract." An "agreement" using ordinary English is just as legal and binding as a "contract" strewn with whereases and heretofores. In fact, it may be more binding, because clear language makes it hard for the customer to claim she didn't know what she was signing. But an "agreement" doesn't sound as intimidating as a "contract."

The assumptive closes sound easy, but in practice they are the hardest to carry off. You need to develop perfect confidence in yourself and your product.

It's important not to get into a rut. Try to practice a variety of closes. A big sale is seldom closed on the first attempt. If the customer balks, you must back up and try something different. You need to know a number of techniques so you don't have to repeat yourself.

Above all, don't drop the sale because a close fails. Remember that a close has *two* purposes: either to get a purchase commitment or to make the prospect expose an objection. If either of these objectives is attained, the close has served its purpose. Simply keep trying closes until the customer runs out of objections.

CHECKLIST
Sales Closes

Have you and each member of your sales team mastered all of the following closing techniques? Are they all covered in your sales training program?

- ☐ Request close
- ☐ Negative time-limit close
- ☐ Positive time-limit close
- ☐ Franklin Ledger
- ☐ Judo close
- ☐ Subjunctive close
- ☐ Clarkson close
- ☐ Implied-consent close
- ☐ Agreement close

Stage 4. The Follow-Up. We now come to the fourth, and most often neglected, phase of the sales process. After you've closed the sale, *follow up*. Every customer should be regarded as an asset to be cherished—not a throwaway disposable.

It's very common, after a purchase has been made—especially if it's a big-ticket item—for the buyer to have second thoughts. Once he's got what he wanted, it may not look as enticing. And once he's committed to pay, the money tends to look larger. You can give sales a real boost by dealing with this "buyer remorse" effectively.

Begin by following up your successful close with reinforcement. Congratulate the customer on his ownership of such a fine product. Remind him about the features he particularly liked. Above all, get it into his hands and operational as fast as possible—the longer he has to wait for delivery, the more opportunity he has for second thoughts. And, until he actually takes possession, he may feel that the sale isn't complete—regardless of the legalities—and may try to cancel.

Of course, thank him. Consider augmenting your verbal thanks at the time of the sale with a written note or phone call a few days later. Better yet, provide the customer with an unexpected bonus.

We bought our first house from an excellent broker. By the time moving day arrived, some of the euphoria had worn off. We started early in the morning, and it was exhausting (190 shelf feet of books, among other things). Around noon we had just started to wonder what to do about lunch, when Juanita, our broker, arrived with a box of fried chicken.

REM

Another important factor in follow-up is *service*. This is especially critical if you're selling an innovative product—first, because it may not be completely debugged; and second, because the customer may not know how to use it effectively. Here is a key point: Salespeople must be involved in service work.

At first they may not like it. Salespeople tend to see service work as a diversion from selling. But there are very good reasons to discourage them from washing their hands of past customers.

1. *The salesperson knows the customer and her concerns.* If a problem arises, a nonsales service person will have to gather all this information starting from scratch—and every minute he spends on it not only costs you money but makes the customer more irritated. Often the salesperson can solve in thirty seconds a problem that could tie up an expensive technician for hours.

2. *Service increases the salesperson's knowledge of the product.* He gets feedback on its strengths and its weaknesses. It also teaches him a lot about his customers that he might not otherwise learn. And, unlike service technicians, the salesperson has a strong, direct personal incentive to prevent or correct quality defects or other problems. If your salespeople have to deal with complaints, you can be sure management will hear about problems—quickly.

3. *The customer doesn't like to be shuttled around.* There's nothing she hates more than being bounced from one anonymous telephone voice to another, each one saying, "It's not my department, but if you'll hold, I'll transfer you to . . ." From her point of view, the ideal situation is that she deals with only one person in your organiza-

tion—she wants one specific, accessible, competent, and motivated person to be responsible for keeping her happy. And she already knows the salesperson.

Speaking of telephone contacts: We strongly recommend that you *not* set up a voicemail system on any line that is used by customers. Yes, yes, we've heard all the explanations, excuses, and rationalizations that your voicemail vendor used to comfort you. The fact remains that you do not make any points with your customers by telling them that they're not important enough to justify hiring a real human being to answer their calls.

4. *Past customers are your best source of new sales.* Usually, you can make a new sale to an established customer with a tiny fraction of the time and effort it would require to develop a new one. What's more, your best source of new customers is referrals from your current customers.

Push follow-up. You'll be surprised what an edge it can give you over the competition. Your salespeople will become enthusiastic about it once they've seen the results—especially the reduced need for cold calls! Just be sure you're not paying them *not* to do follow-up. Look at your sales compensation system, and modify it if necessary.

YOUR SALES ARMY

An oft-used analogy compares selling to fighting a war. Marketing is the general, sitting in headquarters mapping strategy. The sales managers are the field-grade officers, directing and inspiring the units in contact with the enemy. The salespeople are the grunts who actually do the fighting. We're not sure this simile is really edifying. (Are customers the "enemy"? Or just the "ground" being fought over? Neither is very flattering.) But it does suggest the special importance of morale in dealing with the sales force.

It is hard to find a business activity more repulsive than making cold calls. As one sales trainer puts it, most people would find it more pleasant to stand in a cold shower and rip up ten-dollar bills. It takes real determination to make that first call, and even more fortitude to keep it up after a dozen or so rejections.

As stated earlier, every entrepreneur needs to be a salesperson at least occasionally, and anyone can learn enough salesmanship to handle this need. But to sell full time, day in and day out, is *not* for everyone. The professional salesperson, like the professional soldier, needs a special aptitude. He also needs a lot of support from above.

To nonsales types, the hoopla that surrounds selling activities can seem very childish. However, pep rallies, slogans, bonus parties, awards, contests, and so on can be valuable tools to keep your sales forces turning out to face another day of turn-downs and put-downs.

What do your salespeople need from you in order to function effectively? First, confidence in your product. Second, backup and support. Third, morale stroking. Let's take these in turn.

Salespeople, like soldiers, fight poorly for a cause they do not believe in. To convince customers that your product is good, your salespeople must believe in it themselves. So your first task is to sell your salespeople on the virtues of your product, your service, and your company. Begin with training. All salespeople should know the product thoroughly. This not only equips them to deal with customer objections, it gives them self-confidence. Your training should include a strong grounding not only in the features, operation, and applications of your product but also in your company's sales and service procedures. Don't neglect to pass on the results of your market research; the more your salespeople know about your customers, their needs, and their habits, the better they'll be able to sell. The sales force may also give you some valuable real-world feedback that could correct any misperceptions developed by your marketing group.

The salespeople's specific duties are closing sales, maintaining customer satisfaction, and providing market intelligence. That's plenty. Don't ask them to do anything else, and help them as much as possible to make the essential tasks easy. Minimize their paperwork, and make that unavoidable minimum simple and convenient to fill out. Make sure sales administration is performed by clerical personnel— not by the salespeople. And make sure it runs smoothly; quotations, price lists, credit OKs, specification changes should be provided quickly, conveniently, and reliably. If there's any foul-up or delay on an order, inform the salesperson at once so that she can cover herself with the customer. Above all, make it clear throughout the company that sales problems have priority in the use of administrative resources. The controller's important memo about paper-clip consumption can get typed *after* the quotation requested by a new customer.

The sales clerk was just about to close the customer on an expensive camera—when the phone rang. A delivery-truck driver needed directions to get to the shop, in detail, and got them, while the customer fumed. No matter how shorthanded you are, make a special effort to shield your salespeople from interruption while they're selling. The telephone is a particularly obnoxious of-

fender. If you have a sales floor, consider laying it out
without telephones—or, if you must have them, disabling
the bells so it's impossible to call in.

Even with all this, salespeople still need to be stroked, praised,
and encouraged. Here again, it's a real advantage to ride along with a
salesperson regularly. You'll be reminded of the difficulties and dis-
couragements she has to face every working day. She'll realize that
top management really understands and cares about her problems.

Compensating and Motivating Your Sales Force. Because of
the special importance of motivation, compensation of sales personnel
presents unusual problems. Unfortunately, one cannot lay down exact
rules in advance; each industry has its own needs, and you'll have to
be guided by the usual approach in your industry in setting commissions, quotas, bonuses, and other incentives. Be wary of innovations;
it's the salesperson's bread and butter you're tampering with. Try to
work within the familiar structure if possible; if not, make the new
incentives augment rather than replace the traditional payments.

In structuring sales compensation, it is exceptionally important to
tie incentives properly to objectives. A straight commission based on
sales volume may motivate neglect of high-profit items for other
products that offer easy volume. It's common to offer bonuses for
specific goals such as signing new customers, selling some of a specific
item every month, or achieving a sales goal before a given deadline.
Such objectives may be valid, but consider possible pitfalls carefully
before imposing them. The danger is that this type of incentive may
work too well. Remember that concentrating effort in one area almost
invariably reduces it somewhere else.

Consider the examples given. Salespeople, if paid to sign new
customers, may neglect the old ones—and the new ones may not last
long if they were given one-time incentives to get that single sale. The
"sell some *X* every month" bonus may just result in a large order
being chopped into several smaller ones. Contests or bonuses with a
time limit may cause sales to be "borrowed" from the future. Structure
special incentives very carefully, and try them on an experimental
basis before full implementation.

A final but by no means minor point in sales tactics is deploying
your troops efficiently.

You can observe the effects of mismanaged sales incentives by trying the following experiment. Go to any de-

partment store. Walk into the men's suits section, pick a sleeve at random, and feel the fabric. Suddenly the stillness of this deserted area will be broken as half a dozen salesmen descend on you simultaneously, like piranha attacking a lump of meat. Then, if you can break away, go over to the shoe department. You'll find the chairs filled with impatient customers, and one frantic clerk rushing back and forth trying to fit them all.

CHECKLIST
Sales Planning

☐ Have you designated one specific person as responsible for sales?

☐ Have you made it clear to that person that sales must have priority over any other duties?

☐ Have you arranged for at least rudimentary sales training for all employees who have customer contact?

☐ Have you got a list of common customer objections?

☐ Have you developed a complete set of sales modules for your product, and trained your sales personnel in their use?

☐ Does each salesperson have the ability to use at least six different closes to sell your product?

☐ Have you made sure that each and every customer will be thanked for his or her purchase?

☐ Have you made every conceivable effort to get your product into the customer's hands as quickly as possible?

☐ Have you thought about a special, unexpected bonus you can add to each sale?

☐ Do all your salespeople clearly understand that they have primary responsibility for service to their customers?

☐ Do you have systems in place to ensure that every salesperson is thoroughly familiar with your product?

☐ Have you definitely eliminated all superfluous paperwork for your salespeople?

☐ Have you made it clear to all administrative people that sales jobs have priority?

☐ Have you taken precautions to prevent interruptions of sales work?

☐ Have you set up a program to provide regular sales contact for each member of top management?

☐ Have you developed a procedure to test your sales incentives and monitor their effectiveness?

☐ Do you have a system to ensure that salespeople are moved to areas where they are most productive?

CAUTIONARY TALE
Printing Money

After the FOTO COMP disaster (see Chapter One), I founded another venture aimed at the publishing industry which was much more successful. At the time, typesetting was done manually, whether using the traditional Linotype or more modern machinery. One could of course do photo-offset from computer printout, but this was considered unacceptable because computer printers in those days produced a distinctive, and ugly, typeface.

So there was a great deal of interest when a machine became available that would do true computer typesetting. Several companies bought these machines and went into the business of providing computer typesetting services to publishers. Sedgwick Printout Systems was one of them. I set up this company in partnership with the Courier Journal Louisville Times Co.

Now, we had nothing proprietary; we didn't make the machines, we bought them, and anyone else who had the money could buy one too. And we were, if anything, *less* proficient in the technology than some of our competitors. We competed and won by understanding the market and being better salespeople.

In the 1960s it was already clear that computerization was the future of the publishing industry—and publishers were scared to death. There was a lot of talk about the new methods, but nobody wanted to be first. The first high-speed typesetter was a tremendous technological advance. But it was much more expensive than the old machines, and the output was not quite as good-looking. Above all, though one could spew print out of the computer very rapidly indeed, one still had to get the material *into* the computer. So as a typesetting device, the machine was really no more than a souped-up Linotype. You still had an operator at one end keying the stuff into the machine, and type coming out the other end; only the machinery in between was different. So why should publishers pay the extra cost and take the risk involved in switching?

Our competitors' answer was: "This is hot, new, state-of-the-art technology! Look at our gleaming gadgetry! Look at the beards on our programmers! Isn't all this just too exciting for words?" This approach was not just unproductive, it was counterproductive. The more publishers heard about complex new technology, the more nervous they got.   .

Sedgwick Printout took an entirely different tack. I perceived the one critical advance provided by the high-speed typesetter: *While the text was in the computer it could be revised.* This was unimportant to most publishers; they set type, print the book, and throw away the type. But database publishers— those who publish directories, dictionaries, encyclopedias, reference works, and so on—have to make revisions in every edition.

Consider, for instance, how a dictionary was handled in those days. Each entry was kept on a three-by-five card. For a new edition, these thousands upon thousands of cards would be spread out on long tables, and the staff would go through them by hand, putting in new cards and removing old ones. Then it was off to the warehouse, where the lead type of the previous edition was stored. For each obsolete entry, the entire plug line had to be removed. Meanwhile, the new entries, hot off the Linotype, had to be inserted. Of course, this would throw off all the pagination, so they then had to go through all the type and rearrange it by hand. Obviously these people, unlike the typical book publisher, had a real need for our services. We could put their whole database on the computer and store it. They could revise it easily at any time, and even pull out segments for separate printing if they wanted. So we concentrated entirely on database publishers.

This targeted market focus was a major key to our success. Still, we couldn't have made it if we hadn't applied some highly effective sales tactics.

First, we had to realize that the publisher that bought our service would be changing its whole method of operation. We therefore had to concentrate on selling the top people in the company. It would have been a waste of time to approach the production people in the publishing house, as our competitors were doing; they didn't have the authority to make such sweeping changes. So I made it a rule to go straight to the top. Our location in Manhattan, the heart of the publishing industry, helped a lot.

Second, I plugged away continually on making everyone in our company sales-oriented. Every member of the staff had to be qualified for customer contact. This included the technical people. In the nature of the business, our programmers and other technicians had to work intimately with the customers to adapt their procedures to the new technology. I made it a personal crusade to stamp out computer jargon in these communications and force our technical wizards to speak English to the customers.

Third, I realized that we were selling a rather intangible service, and that our customers—publishers—were accustomed by the nature of their business to put a lot of emphasis on appearance. I insisted that our entire operation present a class look in every way. I wanted a quality appearance to our office, our personnel, and most particularly our printed literature and brochures, which would be going into the hands of real pros.

Along with this, I worked to develop a reputation as a significant expert in this field. There was a lot of interest in the new methods in the publishing industry, and it wasn't hard to get a high profile. I gave speeches, participated in workshops, and wrote articles on high-speed typesetting. The aura of expertise thus attached to my name rubbed off on the company, which had the same name.

We had to educate our market—something that is necessary with almost any new product. You can regard this either as a terrible hassle or as an opportunity to get your company a good reputation with your customers. We took the latter tack. I got off to a good start at a major meeting of publishers and printers with a very dramatic presentation that attracted a lot of attention. (One trade journal's description: ". . . and then the microphone was given to Harry Sedgwick of Sedgwick Printout Systems, who, like a windstorm in a wheat field . . .")

But in personal sales calls I took a low-key, soft-sell approach. All of our competitors were making exaggerated claims, glossing over the problems, and offering wildly optimistic estimates of the time and money needed to convert. I, on the other hand, would spend a great deal of time explaining to a publishing-company president what the problems would be. The editors would be dealing with an entirely different medium. They would be using computer printout and editing voluminous information. Mistakes would be made in converting from manual files to computer files, and careful proofreading would be required. It would cost far more than the initial estimates, which were always too optimistic. It would take far longer than anybody anticipated, because human factors would get in the way, and they should prepare for that and plan for it. By explaining it this way, I lowered their expectation, and they got a growing confidence that my concern was to convey to them the truth about this new technology and not to wow them with high-tech phrases. This gave us a major advantage in credibility compared to our competition.

Basically, we presented the contract as a capital expenditure. There would be a lot of expense and hassle up front, but a big payoff once the system was in place.

We made it a point to refrain from announcing new contracts. Our competitors blew a loud fanfare every time they landed a sale—followed by an embarrassed silence as they ran into the inevitable problems getting the system set up. We didn't say a word until we finished and everything was running smoothly. *Then* we announced that Sedgwick Printout had installed another successful system—and, with the satisfied customer's assistance, we put out a glossy brochure showing what we had accomplished and circulated it to new prospects. Since the customers had names like Standard & Poor's and The New York Times Index, these brochures developed a lot of credibility.

Although we focused primarily on the top people when making a sale, we had to take into account some of the others. The art director was usually an enemy. Our output, if one looked closely, was not quite as sharp as conventional methods could produce; one art director brought in photomicrographs to prove it. On the other hand, the marketing people freaked out when we explained the options that would now be available. For years they had dreamed of being able to, say, pull out all the names in Arizona from the database and make up a separate directory for local sales. They'd always been told by the production people that this would be impossibly expensive. Now, we pointed out, this and similar projects would become absurdly easy. In this way we developed some powerful allies in each company.

My objective was to jump into the buyer's head and try to see his problems and his point of view. If he didn't really need our service, I went away. Why waste his time, not to mention mine? But if he did need our service, he couldn't get me off with a barnacle remover. I would cling to him relentlessly until I got that sale. All very low-key, of course. An occasional phone call, a copy of an article, a brochure—but it just wouldn't stop until he signed on. This Chinese water torture would usually bring results in the end.

I had a brilliant idea for breaking into the market, but it almost backfired. We were aiming at database publishers, so I chose as our initial target one that was totally conspicuous in the publishing industry: R. R. Bowker, publishers of *Books in Print*. Of course, everybody in the book business knows them, so if they signed up it would be a highly visible feather in our cap.

Well, they did sign up. But perhaps I wasn't quite low-key enough, because they were more optimistic that we were. They had appeared at the Frankfurt Book Fair for decades, and this year they wanted to show up with their latest edition done by the new computer typesetting. I told them there wasn't enough time, but they brushed it off. Of course, we didn't make it, which was embarrassing. If only that had been all. We also left out two whole letters of the alphabet—L and N—and it wasn't caught until the books had been bound.

What could I say? There was nothing for it but to put the best face on it we could. I wrote up a press release describing the heroic efforts of Sedgwick Printout and R. R. Bowker to make the switch to this revolutionary new technology in a thrilling race against a tight deadline. Then I frankly conceded that we'd fluffed it, and explained that R. R. Bowker had set up an 800 number that people could call if they wanted to know about a book that began with L or N. They quickly got out a supplement, of course. Oddly enough, this incident seemed to work in our favor. Publishers were a bit fed up with the hype and broken promises of our competitors, so we looked refreshingly honest. Probably the fact that Bowker was also at fault (they really should have caught the omission in proofreading, though of course we carefully didn't say so) helped a bit too.

Sedgwick Printout did extremely well. After a few years I decided I was ready for something new, and I sold out my interest to the partner for a tidy sum.

It was a very valuable experience in effective selling. Unfortunately, the sales training that most people get in this country is the full-speed-ahead, high-pressure, take-it-to-them approach. Managers don't even get that; face-to-face selling is not taught in any business school I know of. That is considered to be an activity beneath the dignity of the exalted executive-to-be. But the fact is that we must sell all the time—whether it's a bar of soap or a major financial deal. The higher you rise in business, the bigger and more critical the sales you have to make. And the need to identify with those to whom you are selling is absolutely critical to the transaction.

I think the thing to be kept in mind in selling almost anything is that your customer is ultimately your partner. You must look beyond the first transaction and make sure that this partner is satisfied in the long term; otherwise you haven't got a business.

HDS

Eight

PRODUCTION

Where there's muck, there's money.

English saying

The word *production* conjures up images of manufacturing—machine tools, riveters, assembly lines. But we use the word here in its most general sense. Every business has some sort of production function, because every business must create value for the customer. In a manufacturing company the production process is obvious. But in a service company the performance of the service is production (though it's usually called "operations"). In any company, somebody has to make, or do, something for the customer—and that process, whatever it may be, is production.

These days a lot of entrepreneurs turn up their noses at those gritty, smelly, noisy manufacturing businesses. And it's true that the American business climate, especially in the regulatory sphere, is increasingly unfavorable to manufacturing. But as the epigraph to this chapter suggests, there are real profit opportunities for those who aren't afraid of a little muck.

WHERE EXPERIENCE COUNTS

In production, more than in any other aspect of business, experience is important. A marketer who's never sold a widget before can learn how to peddle one without difficulty. An engineer who's never designed a widget before can develop an excellent prototype (often bringing valuable fresh ideas to his work). But if you've never manufactured a widget before, you are likely to get into big trouble. Successful production is highly dependent on know-how. This is true almost regardless of the industry.

> The chemical producer should know how to prevent air pollution by running certain processes under a partial vacuum. This and a thousand other hard-learned tricks make the difference between a clean, efficient chemical plant and a dangerous one.

> The restaurateur must know where to buy good fresh meat and vegetables—and how to select them. It's a skill that can't be learned from books.

> The warehouse manager must know not only what type of forklift to buy but also how to handle employees so as to minimize pilferage.

In each industry, a number of vital production skills virtually demand hands-on experience. It's like training a physician—after all the lectures, textbook illustrations, and demonstrations, the experienced doctor must still take the intern into the wards, place her hands on some patients, and explain: "If it feels like this it's a tumor, but if it feels like this one it's only a cyst." Production experience in your chosen industry is imperative. If you don't have it, be sure you get a cofounder, or at minimum hire a key employee, who does.

The Learning Curve.   The importance of experience in production is expressed in the theory of the learning curve. Simply stated, this theory asserts that among companies competing to make a certain product, the most efficient producer will be the one with the most experience—that is, the one with the highest cumulative unit output. The idea is that productivity rises with increasing experience; therefore, marketing policy should emphasize rapid acquisition of market share and sale of large volumes so as to move down the learning curve faster than competitors do.

The problem with the learning curve theory is that it is based on studies of large companies, where dozens or hundreds of individuals are involved in production management and the effects of their varied talents average out. In a small company, this statistical blur disappears. Your progress down the learning curve depends less on how many units you've shipped than on how hard you've worked at learning from that experience. In reality, production expertise is not an automatic consequence of experience; learning from experience requires effort and ingenuity.

GOALS FOR PRODUCTION

The management of production has three objectives. First, the production process should be reliable—the product should be finished at the predicted time. Second, the product should be of high quality. Third, production costs should be low.

Traditionally, production management has been perceived as a matter of optimizing the trade-off among these three goals. The modern approach, imported from Japan, is to view these apparently conflicting objectives as complementary. Over the long run, they are. A smooth-running and reliable production process lowers costs—partly because it minimizes downtime and partly because its predictability facilitates planning and inexpensive purchasing. Attention to quality improves reliability, since rework interferes with production schedules—and it reduces costs, because scrap and rework are expensive. And, ironically, cost cutting can contribute to higher quality, for money saved by eliminating waste can be applied to buying improved raw materials.

Ensuring Production Reliability. The hardest task for a new manufacturing business (and many service businesses also) is to develop a reliable production process. Nothing is more embarrassing than announcing a new product, accepting purchase orders, and then running into production problems—postponing delivery dates again and again as your salespeople phone irritated customers with increasingly weak excuses. This kind of snafu is the bane of new companies. Your customers, who may have gone out on a limb to give your start-up a break, will hear from their friends, their colleagues—and their bosses—"See? I told you so. You should have gone with IBM." Broken delivery promises inflict long-lasting damage to your reputation and may even sink you before you begin.

Job It Out. A valuable expedient for start-ups is jobbing out parts of the production process. Many young ventures make the mistake of trying to cut costs by vertical integration. "We'll smelt our own steel, roll it, draw it into wire, and wind the coils for the frammistan. Think of the money we'll save—iron ore is really cheap." This is a poor idea. By the time you master the intricacies of all those extra production steps, there will be cobwebs on your customers. Your savings on the cheap raw materials are eaten up and more by your losses on production hang-ups. Today, even the industrial giants are getting smart. They are breaking up their vertically integrated operations, selling off the layers where they have no strategic advantage. You should do the same: *Focus on the key step of production.*

By "key step" we mean the step that is *your* company's contribution. The ultimate justification for being in business at all is your ability to produce something better than anyone else. Somewhere along the long line between the iron ore and the completed widget there is presumably one step that your company can handle better than any other. Identify it. That is the step you should perform, and ideally it should be the *only* step you perform, especially at the start. Job out everything else. In this way you get to market quickly and minimize the difficulty of your production task. It's true that more highly finished materials and outside services will cost you more—but this is really only appearance. Performing unfamiliar operations in-house almost always costs more than jobbing them out; the experts are usually so much more efficient that they can cover their costs and make a profit and still be cheaper. That's why *they* are in business.

One important caveat: This principle of farming out as much work as you can doesn't necessarily apply to do-it-yourself projects in setting up or improving your company's facility. Often building your own machinery or installing your own plumbing can save critical cash in your start-up phase. Always be alert to chances to save money; use "sweat equity" to acquire capital assets in these one-shot projects. But don't do any more of the *production process* than you absolutely have to.

Keep It Simple.   It will also simplify your life if you minimize your product variety. Ideally a start-up should have only one product. Once it's running, add a new item to the line only when production of the old ones has been thoroughly debugged. However, this is not really under the control of Production. The production manager can and should argue the point with Marketing, but if the market does demand a variety of models, he will have to find a way to make them. What he can do is ask that the new products be as similar as possible to the old ones in design, materials, and manufacturing process. By working closely with Marketing and R&D, he should be able to come up with a reasonable if not perfect solution.

In short, when it comes to production, simplify to the max. Your best chance to achieve excellence, and thus a competitive advantage, is to focus your efforts as tightly as possible.

Three further maxims will do much to increase the reliability of your production if you apply them religiously.

1. *Correct problems as they come up—permanently.* Give yourself a black mark for any problem that occurs twice. Yes, this sounds trivial and obvious, but very few organizations actually put it into practice. Each fire is forgotten as soon as it's under control—there are too many other problems to worry about. But most of those distracting problems represent previous fires that were not quite put out, but were allowed to smolder until they broke out again. If you make it a policy to concentrate on the immediate problem and don't leave it until you fix it for good, after a while you'll find there are a lot fewer problems.

Of course it's easy to say, "Fix it permanently." The reason that axiom is often neglected in practice is that it isn't easy to find lasting solutions. It takes a determined effort to discover the root cause and develop an understanding of the problem. If you don't understand how your process works and what has gone wrong, your efforts at correction will be confined to trial and error—a method notoriously slow, inefficient, and unreliable.

Instead of trying changes at random, based on guesswork, conduct a systematic investigation of the source of the problem. You don't need genius for this—just guts. When you're under heavy pressure to get the line running again it's tempting to opt for trial and error, which offers at least the possibility of a quick solution. ("We're resetting the spring tension—if it works, we'll be up again tomorrow.") The systematic approach requires you to make an unavoidable investment of downtime. ("We'll disassemble unit 3 and test each roller at different speeds until we find the problem. It will take at least two weeks.") But this investment tends to pay off in the long run, and often even in the short run.

In manufacturing a complex catalyst, a serious problem developed when an intermediate turned out to be impure. We isolated the impurity and sent it out for analysis—which required two weeks, two weeks lost while customers screamed about their orders. But from the analysis, when it arrived, it was immediately clear that the intermediate, contrary to its reported chemistry, had reacted with the solvent. A simple modification of the procedure quickly and permanently eliminated the problem. Since it was "known" that no such reaction could occur, we might never have hit on the solution by trial and error.

REM

Production will solve process problems much more quickly if there is a permanent troubleshooting team from R&D on call. The team's assistance will be greatly amplified if it is provided with adequate production records. Troubleshooting boils down to an effort to connect cause and effect by making comparisons between various results.

Another chemical process gave intermittent problems over a period of years. Usually it worked, but sometimes one of the intermediates turned into a useless, sticky gum. In this case the critical information turned out to be the dates; all of the bad batches occurred during July or August. The intermediate in question was known to be sensitive to water, and summer in New Jersey is like living in a Turkish bath. We had merely to improve our precautions for protecting the material from atmospheric moisture.

REM

2. *Keep complete and detailed records.* This is a nuisance. Production personnel invariably resist it; they want to crank out product, not waste time on paperwork. But this is another investment in time that pays off dramatically when you get into trouble. Follow a simple principle: If you know it, record it. If you don't know it, find out, then record it. Many important things are obvious: the supplier and lot number for raw materials; the name of the operator; any unusual events during the production run. But the toughest production problems result from factors that nobody kept track of because they were "obviously irrelevant."

There is a story, possibly apocryphal, of an electronic gadget that developed quality problems suddenly, for no apparent reason. After tearing their hair for weeks, the engineers working on the problem accidentally found the cause: One of the women working on the assembly line had changed her brand of lipstick. Experiments established that unless the person working at that particular position wore a certain brand of lipstick, the gadgets coming off the line wouldn't work properly.

Obviously you can't record every conceivable detail; you have to draw the line somewhere. But draw it as low as possible, and draw it especially low around production steps that exhibit frequent problems. You'll want to design your information-gathering procedures carefully to make it as convenient as possible for your people to record the data.

3. *Don't skip preventive maintenance, a major factor in production reliability.* This is where established concerns have an advantage

over most start-ups. They've learned from bitter experience that the policy "if it ain't broke, don't fix it" means in practice that it will break just when you don't have time to fix it. Skipping preventive maintenance is enormously tempting in the early days of your company. When you're desperately busy with jobs that clearly *have* to be done, wasting time on do-it-once-a-week-whether-it-needs-it-or-not chores seems hopelessly illogical. The benefits of preventive maintenance—the breakdowns that *don't* occur—are invisible but nonetheless invaluable.

Ensuring Product Quality. The Japanese have taught us an important lesson about *quality control*. American managers have usually regarded lowering quality as a means of lowering costs. Japanese managers have learned to regard low quality as a production problem. Low quality is an indication that something is wrong in the production process and should be fixed. Fixing it doesn't necessarily raise costs; usually it lowers them.

Quality control is by no means restricted to manufactured goods. Whatever you sell—services, information, entertainment—quality can be defined, measured, and controlled.

> How on earth can you develop quantitative, measurable criteria of entertainment? Disneyland does it—managers come from all over the world, including Japan, to observe and learn. A fun day with the kids can actually, to a surprising extent, be reduced to numbers—from how many minutes one has to wait in line for a popular ride to how many pieces of trash per square yard of sidewalk.

Much of the immense and rapidly growing literature on quality is of limited relevance to small business, unfortunately. It deals with rather elaborate statistical methods that are hard to apply to a small operation—partly because the procedures are too complex, but also because sample sizes are too small to produce reliable conclusions. We give this area only a brief summary and refer you to the Reading List for more detailed treatment.

The first step is to define what quality means with regard to your product. Of course, quality is ultimately judged by your customers, and their criteria may be unusual, and even downright peculiar.

> American auto buyers traditionally judge the soundness of a car's construction literally by sound—the sound

made when the door is slammed. Detroit long ago learned that a certain sound gives the optimum impression—although technically it has no connection with actual quality—and designed car doors accordingly.

Market research should tell you what your customers value. Then you must try to quantify it. This is tricky, but it can usually be done. Most quality criteria fit into one of four categories: performance, reliability, durability, and appearance. For manufactured goods, it is usually not difficult to devise quantitative definitions for the first three. Appearance, though, may be tougher. For, say, a service business, such definitions may be less obvious, but they can be found. For instance, a Chinese restaurant might define performance with numbers such as the average time customers must wait for their order; reliability by the number of complaints per thousand customers; and durability by the average time that elapses until a customer gets hungry again.

Once defined, quality must be continuously and systematically measured. To the typical business, quality measurement equals "final inspection," and the big question is whether to do 100 percent testing or sample each batch. But this one-point measurement approach misses important opportunities. You should make quality measurement a process that operates all the way through the production cycle—and beyond.

Obviously you should begin by concerning yourself with the quality of your raw materials. These days, customers often show a surprising interest in this issue. Look how ads for sweaters emphasize the wool comes from premium sheep.

> Perrier learned a very expensive lesson about customer perceptions of quality when minuscule amounts of benzene showed up in its bottled water. When it became clear that this did not represent a processing problem, that the benzene was actually present in their raw material—the famous spring water—the effect on its market image was devastating.

Go on to monitor quality throughout your production process. Break down your quality definitions into criteria for the various segments of your product. Then set up regular measurements all the way through the production process; check quality at each stage. This has two advantages. First, when a problem arises, you don't have to do much detective work to find out when and where the mistake was made; it's obviously at or before the stage where defects began to appear. Second, you cut waste dramatically by stopping defective units immediately instead of finishing them and then having to scrap or rework.

Even more neglected is quality follow-up after sale. Often, a quality problem will not show up until the product has been used for months or years. Defects may be missed even by "torture testing." Use your Service Department aggressively to acquire data on how your product fails in use—and when—and how often. Ask Market Research to survey your customer also. And, as time goes by, send someone to the scrapyards to pick up worn-out widgets from your earlier production. Bring 'em in and analyze how they failed.

Controlling Production Costs.

Achieving lower costs—the third responsibility of Production—begins with knowing what your costs are. As soon as you pronounce this question, your office window will shatter and there, flying through a spray of broken glass, cape flowing in the wind, will appear . . . your accountant. She can solve all your cost-control problems, it seems—tell you exactly how profitable each of your products is, determine where your inventory costs are worst, locate wasted materials, evaluate operator efficiency. Of course, she'll need more complete data from you, a little more record-keeping. To start with, each of your production workers should keep a log, and stop work and make entries every five minutes . . .

Cost Accounting.

Cost accounting has a long and honorable history. But one of the major problems of modern business management is that cost accounting is obsolete, and there is no well-accepted replacement for it.

Cost accounting reached its zenith in the nineteenth century. Imagine a factory in 1890, making, let's say, paper clips and staples. It employs 200 people: 195 production workers, 2 clerks, 2 salesmen, and the president. The owner wishes to know how profitable each of his two products is. Cost accounting is quite straightforward: The accountant simply makes up a little chart as shown in Exhibit 2.

The 1890 company has $225,000 in direct costs, which can be easily assigned to one product or the other. Overhead, at $15,000 annually, amounts to 6.25 percent of total costs, and it can be handled quite simply by allocating it between the two products in the same proportion as the direct costs.

Consider now the modern equivalent company. It is highly automated. It employs 200 people: 15 production workers, 10 maintenance people, 35 clerks and secretaries, 50 salespeople, 15 R&D personnel,

Exhibit 2. Smith & Co. Clips and Staples—statement of annual
costs.

Cost Item		Clips	Staples
Raw materials		$ 80,000	$40,000
Direct labor		50,000	30,000
Depreciation (machinery)		20,000	5,000
Total direct costs		$150,000	$75,000
		(67%)	(33%)
Office salaries	$ 8,000		
Depreciation (G&A)	7,000		
Overhead	$15,000		
allocated 67:33		$ 10,000	$ 5,000
TOTAL COSTS		$160,000	$80,000

25 line managers, 40 people in Accounting, Payroll, and Human Resources, 9 vice-presidents, and the president. It has a rather different
cost breakdown, as shown in Exhibit 3.

The 1990 company's costs are 84 percent overhead, and this is
allocated based on 16 percent direct costs. Cost accounting has simply
broken down; the direct-cost tail is wagging the overhead dog.

What to do? Much of modern accounting theory is devoted to
methods of turning back the clock to the days when costs could be
assigned to products in a simple way. Much overhead can be reas-
signed as direct cost if sufficiently detailed reports are obtained.
(Secretary X spends 34 percent of her time on correspondence relating
to staples, and we therefore allocate 34 percent of her salary. . . .) But
to obtain the necessary data at such a fine level of detail is difficult,
inefficient, and irritating. Even in a large company, demands for cost
breakdowns of this sort are so onerous that they provoke rebellion,
open or covert. In a small company, modern cost accounting can
constitute a crushing burden.

The best way out of this dilemma is to abandon traditional cost
accounting as an analytical tool (which may result in your CFO having
a conniption, but it can't be helped). Briefly, the idea involved is this:
Traditional cost accounting breaks down primarily because "direct
costs" are now a small proportion of total costs in an average business,
whereas "overhead" is the major item. It therefore makes sense to
abandon the direct/indirect dichotomy, which is based on a theoretical

Exhibit 3. Twentieth Century Office Technology, Inc.—statement of annual costs.

Cost Item		Clips	Staples
Raw materials		$ 100,000	$ 80,000
Direct labor		200,000	100,000
Depreciation (machinery)		150,000	120,000
Total direct costs		$ 450,000	$ 300,000
		(60%)	(40%)
Office salaries	$3,700,000		
Depreciation (G&A)	300,000		
Overhead	$4,000,000		
allocated 60:40		$2,400,000	$1,600,000
TOTAL COSTS		$2,850,000	$1,900,000

model of the company dating back a couple of centuries, and instead determine where your costs actually are.

To do this, cut yourself loose from the financial statement, which *defines* certain items as "overhead" and so on, and directly analyze the costs of your operation. Identify the biggest costs and assign them to cost centers. Then use them to allocate the rest of the costs. Do this without regard to traditional classifications of "direct" and "indirect" costs.

> In a company doing small-scale "custom synthesis" chemical manufacturing, it turned out that the major cost was process testing and setup. Raw materials and "direct labor" were minor items. Thus the cost of a batch was calculated by costing the setup time and allocating raw materials and labor accordingly. You may ask (if you don't your accountant will), why not just use the actual values for these items rather than allocate? Because each chemist was running three to four batches at a time and could only guess at how much time she was devoting to each. Raw materials were partly dedicated and partly drawn from common stock, raising other difficulties. This particular example was a chemical company, but a similar costing problem occurs in many job-shop operations,

ranging from machine-tool companies to Chinese restaurants, and a similar solution can be applied.

Direct-marketing companies with small average sale sizes provide another example. Often it costs such companies more to *process the order* than it does to pay for the goods themselves. So it makes sense to base costing calculations on these "overhead" costs rather than the "cost of goods."

Our discussion here summarizes the ideas developed at more length in Peter Drucker's book *Managing for Results*. We're not pushing for some particular method of cost calculation. What we do want to emphasize is the importance of taking a fresh look at costs rather than blindly following tradition.

The Strategy of Cost Cutting. Once you identify your costs and understand their relationship to your output, you can implement cost cutting. All companies attempt to do cost cutting, and they mostly fail. Successful cost cutting requires you to follow three simple—but painful—rules.

1. *Make cost cutting a continuous activity.* Most companies have cost-cutting drives at intervals of several years—generally during recessions. In between, a token effort at most is made to run economically. You can win big by making sure your production manager *works on cost cutting every day.* Require a written report on his progress on cost reduction at least quarterly. This not only reduces problems in bad economic times but will substantially increase your cash flow during the booms. The resulting edge over the competition can be decisive. What's more, this is a much more efficient way to cut costs. Crash programs tend to result in process hang-ups and quality problems because the measures taken are not well thought out and are implemented hurriedly. Continous cost cutting gives you the opportunity to carefully test results and avoid false economies.

2. *Cut the major costs first.* Traditional cost accounting tends to lead to irrational economies. Certain items are defined as being "overhead" and are automatically considered better candidates for cutbacks than "direct" costs; overhead is allegedly "nonproductive," so naturally it should be cut first, right? But those small, seemingly useless expenditures may have a high leverage. Clear your mind of preconceived notions and examine your costs in order of size. Ask what you're getting for the money.

3. *Cut costs by eliminating, not reducing, activities wherever you can.* As you examine each cost center, the first question you should ask is, "Can we get rid of this entirely?" The answer of course will be no, but you can jar your people out of the rut by rephrasing it like this: "Okay, suppose we were *forced* somehow to stop doing it. What would we do instead? And would it be cheaper?" Don't even consider your options for reducing the cost of an activity until you have convincing evidence that it is impossible to eliminate it.

There are many different ways of analyzing costs, which depend on how the company's cost structure is broken down. You can divide up costs by product, as we did above. This may result in a decision to drop the least profitable items. Alternatively, you can divide costs along the process axis: raw materials, labor, shipping, and so on. This may lead you to the conclusion that certain process steps should be jobbed out. A less common but often instructive approach is to use the product-lifetime axis: Analyze costs as a function of product age. You might find from this, for instance, that older products don't yield good profits for you and adopt a policy of licensing products after they mature. There is, of course, functional analysis: How much does it cost to run each department? You might decide, for example, to eliminate your payroll operation and hire a service agency to do it.

Break-Even Analysis. Of course, one of the most useful breakdowns for cost analysis, and the one most traditional for pre–start-up calculation, is the distinction between fixed and variable costs. Break-even analysis is easy to do and instructive, although it has its limitations.

To perform break-even analysis, begin by dividing all your costs into fixed and variable items. You must specify your maximum production capacity. Then, within that capacity, costs that don't depend on production rate are considered fixed. Costs that change with the production rate are considered variable. Certain assumptions are usually made:

- *That fixed costs are really constant.* In reality, some (e.g., rent) are; some (e.g., maintenance costs) aren't.
- *That variable costs are proportional to output.* In reality, this is seldom exactly true. For instance, at high output you may get a better price on raw materials, since you're buying larger quantities; on the other hand, you may pay more for labor, due to overtime.

- *That revenues are proportional to output.* In reality, your price may not be independent of output level—particularly if (as you may hope to be the case) your company is a significant factor in the market.

Generally, it is not a serious omission to ignore these complicating factors in your pre–start-up break-even analysis; often they will more or less cancel out.

Exhibit 4 shows a typical break-even graph. The horizontal line represents fixed costs, which, by assumption, are the same at any capacity utilization. To this we add the variable costs to get a diagonal representing the total cost. Another line represents revenues, which start at zero when there is no production. The intersection of the cost and revenue lines marks the break-even point. The vertical distance between the cost and revenue diagonals represents the profit (to the right of break-even) or loss (to the left of break-even).

The obvious value of break-even analysis is that it allows you to predict how high your sales must be for the business to break even. In addition, it provides you with an estimate of the magnitude of your profit (or loss) at any sales level. It provides useful guidelines for planning, but always keep in mind that a break-even chart is only an approximation. When you actually get into production, your mileage may differ.

Exhibit 4. Typical break-even chart.

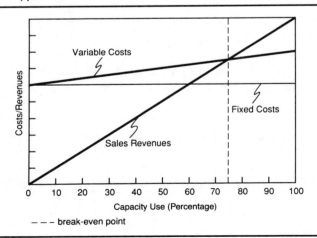

CAUTIONARY TALE
Ma and Pa Kettle Get Clobbered

I found it very disconcerting when I developed an interest—indeed, an obsession—with entrepreneurship. I had considered myself a dedicated academic type, and, as a research scientist, thought of businesspeople as necessary but grubby creatures. But in my first months as an employee of Lifesystems Company, I discovered how fascinating a small venture could be. I began to read everything I could find on small business. When I had cleaned out the bookstores and the libraries, I turned to MIT, my alma mater, conveniently located in Cambridge, Massachusetts, and was directed to the Enterprise Forum, which was then just getting started. The more I learned, the more skeptical I became about the prospects for Lifesystems. What would I do if the company went under? (Which in fact it later did; see Chapter Five for the full story.) This was 1978, and Ph.D. chemists were not in heavy demand. I began to toy with the idea of starting my own business.

My plans began to crystallize when an old college friend, Dave, came to visit. His job in marketing used only about 30 percent of his capacity, which bored him. He was ripe for a challenge. The opportunity to have his marketing talent on board was too good to pass up. We decided to go ahead with what was to become Reaction Design Corporation.

Briefly, the idea was this. The chemical industry suffers from pollution restrictions and high capital costs. Pollution results from inefficient chemical reactions, which produce wastes and by-products in addition to the desired products. High capital costs are due primarily to the violent conditions necessary to conduct much chemical synthesis: high temperatures, high pressures, corrosive reagents—these require costly equipment to handle them safely.

We believed these problems could be attacked by developing improved catalysts for chemical processes. (A catalyst is a molecule that causes other molecules to undergo a chemical reaction but is unchanged itself in the process.) A number of major advances in recent years had resulted in revolutionary new types of high-selectivity catalysts. Yet these improvements were not being brought out of the lab and into the plant as—in my opinion—they should have been. Using properly designed catalysts, one could run chemical processes under mild conditions and very selectively (no by-products = no pollution).

To attempt to revolutionize the entire chemical industry at once would be to bite off more than we could chew, so we decided to concentrate on a particular high-value-added sector. Some molecules are "chiral"—that is, they come in right- and left-handed forms. The two forms are identical in their chemical properties, so ordinary chemical processes produce a 50:50 mixture. However, the right- and left-hand forms differ in their biological properties. This has important consequences; the infamous drug thalidomide, for instance, was perfectly safe in its right-hand form—but the left-hand form, 50 percent of the mixture as it was sold, caused birth defects.

Separating the two forms is very inconvenient and expensive—imagine sorting right-handed from left-handed gloves that are too small to see. But it is possible to design a catalyst that will work to make only one of the two forms. In fact, a number of such catalysts were already known in 1978. They were not yet commercially available, and we figured drug companies would jump at the chance to buy them.

We spent over a year developing our business plan. I studied not only general topics in small-business management but also the specialized chemical techniques needed to make the chiral catalysts. Dave conducted a market research study. We wrote a pretty good business plan, considering that it was a maiden effort. We raised almost $120,000 in first-round capital from private investors, mostly technical types who could understand the concept and its potential.

Our original intention was to bring on a third cofounder to be CEO and handle administration and production. I would be vice-president of R&D and Dave would be vice-president of Marketing. I was painfully conscious of my limited business experience, and I also wanted somebody on board who was familiar with large-scale chemical processes; I, at that time, was not. We interviewed several candidates for this slot; none were satisfactory. Since Dave and several of the investors wanted me to be CEO, we ended up dropping the idea of a third cofounder, in spite of my misgivings.

When we finished our business plan I asked several colleagues in the Enterprise Forum to give us an informal critique. Their major criticism was one we had not expected. We had planned for Dave to stay with his present employer and not join the company full time until it was running well and could support his salary. To us this seemed a sensible way to conserve cash. Our advisers, however, insisted that he come on board right at the start—advice we could not understand and did not take.

Dave's market study had shown that the market for chiral catalysts was currently restricted to research quantities—only about $20,000 per year— though it would expand dramatically later as customers brought new processes on stream and bought production quantities of the catalysts. Obviously we needed some other products initially to provide an adequate sales level. We were considering various possibilities when our schedule was disrupted—I lost my job at Lifesystems.

It hardly seemed practical or worthwhile to seek a new job that I would hold for only a few months. So we accelerated our plans for Reaction Design. We incorporated, found premises in New Jersey (home of a plurality of the big pharmaceutical companies), assembled a lab, and were in business within a few months.

It proved even more difficult than we had expected to make the chiral catalysts on a practical basis, and I threw myself into the problem of improving the technology. After a few months we began to make some pretty good progress on the production front. Fortunately—from the production point of view—the small research quantities needed could be made using ordinary lab glassware rather than the much larger "kettles" needed for plant- or even pilot-scale production. I was already familiar with the techniques involved in using these small kettles—and larger equipment tends to be *much* more expensive.

However, things weren't so good from a sales point of view. Dave's market research turned out to be distressingly accurate; sales of chiral catalysts leveled off at about $15,000 per year. We owned the market, but it wasn't enough.

At this point another chicken came home to roost—at the worst possible time, as they always do. Dave's company moved to another state. Reaction Design was not doing nearly well enough to pay him, so he had to find another job. He did—a demanding one that left him almost no time for Reaction Design.

The company faced a tough marketing problem, and we lacked the needed sales talent. We had to find additional products to sell that could be brought on stream quickly and that had very high value—thousands of dollars a kilogram, because we couldn't make batches larger than one kilogram.

The trouble was, there aren't many such products. Our best bet was insect pheromones (a kind of nontoxic pest-control agent), but we were never able to do much with this. It's a tricky business, subject to the vagaries of the bugs and the EPA. Several much larger companies got bloody noses in pheromones, and so did we.

We took a shot at adding other research chemicals to our line of chiral catalysts. But retailing research chemicals is very different from chemical manufacturing. What's needed is not so much technical expertise as shrewd inventory control; one needs to have a large catalog and stock a complete inventory. This takes a lot of working capital—which we didn't have.

Another possibility seemed a natural: contract research. We actually did land one contract. But this, again, is a specialized business. Success depends on developing a good track record; having some big names helps. It's not easy to get a contract-research company going quickly.

Several times sales seemed to take off and it looked as if we were going to make it. But each time they petered out again. For three years, I methodically tried one approach after another, looking for the way out. There *was* no way out. The mistake was not a wrong turn in the maze, but entering the wrong maze.

In the end, the company simply starved to death. The money ran out and we liquidated. We were able to last so long only because I was taking a salary of $1,000 per year. (How? We had no children then, and my wife was working. Reaction Design put a serious strain on our finances and our marriage, but that's another story.)

With hindsight, I can see a number of mistakes. One, of course, was not making sure, by hook or by crook, that we had full-time professional sales skills working for us right from the start. My amateurish efforts to get out and sell were totally inadequate. Also worth mentioning are lack of proper planning, incomplete market research, an unfocused approach to the market, and over-optimistic estimates of R&D costs.

A minor but significant error was in concentrating our sales effort on the pharmaceutical giants. Their patented drugs are proprietary and sell at what the market will bear, so these companies are not particularly cost conscious—and making the active ingredient represents only a tiny fraction of their costs in any case. Our powerful cost-cutting technology would have found a much more receptive market in the viciously price-competitive generic drug industry.

But the truly critical mistake was entering a business in which I lacked the necessary production know-how. More than all the other problems put together, what beat Reaction Design was our inability to produce on a reasonably large scale. Our tiny "Ma-and-Pa" kettles were utterly inadequate to get us into the market on a scale where viable products existed. Of course, to have a real production capability, we would have needed someone who had the skills; we would have had to find a different location; and we would have needed a much higher capitalization. It isn't the sort of change that can be made in midstream; it would have had to be planned differently from the start.

All this is obvious—now. If I hadn't been through the experience, I wouldn't have believed that I could miss these simple conclusions every day for three and a half years.

REM

Nine

RESEARCH AND DEVELOPMENT

Science is a first-rate piece of furniture for a man's upper chamber, if he has common sense on the ground floor.

Oliver Wendell Holmes, *The Poet at the Breakfast Table*

Who needs R&D? Not every company, though many nontechnology companies do research. Who needs R&D but neglects it? Ironically, most commonly high-tech companies. Once the first product hits the market, they often ease up in the lab, thinking their job is done. Then they get clobbered by a competitor that brings out an even better product. You may not need R&D; but if you do, you need it forever. There's no getting off the tiger.

THE TAX ADVANTAGE OF R&D

It is not sufficiently recognized that R&D offers one of the few remaining tax shelters in the United States. It works like this: Suppose you buy a piece of production machinery that costs $100,000 and doubles your output. On your corporate tax return you try to deduct $100,000 as a business expense. The IRS says, "No way! You've expended $100,000 in cash, but you now have $100,000 worth of machine. You'll have to depreciate it [that is, expense it gradually] over its useful life." But now suppose you spend $100,000 on research and you come up with a process improvement that doubles your output. You deduct this $100,000 on your tax return—and the IRS doesn't let out a peep! It's perfectly legitimate to "expense" R&D costs as you incur them. Putting it another way, purchases of capital equipment come out of after-tax profits; expenditures on R&D come out of before-tax profits.

Some companies try to "capitalize" their R&D, usually because they want to inflate their net worth on the books. The IRS is generally willing to go along, of course, since it gets to collect more tax. However, accountants tend to disapprove, because of the difficulty of assessing the monetary value of know-how or scientific information.

Of course, if your company isn't making any profit for the R&D expenses to shelter, the tax advantage does you little good. One option then is to strip off the tax benefits and sell them to someone who does have income that can be set against them. This is the principle behind the "R&D limited partnership"; unfortunately, changes in tax law have made it much harder to use this technique.

MANAGING R&D

No aspect of business management is so badly neglected as research and development. A plethora of textbooks, audiotape courses, and seminars offer instruction in management of the marketing, financial, and production functions. Guidance and training are readily available for traffic managers and waste-disposal managers, for CEOs and for executive secretaries. But if your job is to manage research, the huge management-training industry falls silent.

Part of the problem is that scientists and engineers resist being managed; indeed, many of them hold it as an article of faith that research is impossible to manage. "Breakthroughs," they say, "are impossible to predict. The purpose of research is to discover new and unexpected phenomena; how can it be planned?"

Another factor is that in most companies scientists are systematically excluded from management. They are routinely regarded as having their heads in the clouds and no respect for the bottom line. Since scientists cannot be promoted, nobody in the upper echelons understands research or has a clear idea of how results can be measured or objectives set. As a result, the typical R&D Department is an amorphous blob that produces results—if any—on unpredictable occasions and with very low efficiency.

Yet the fact is that research *can* be managed. An R&D project can be planned; it can be scheduled; it can be budgeted; and it can be performed efficiently.

Begin by setting aside all the literature on the importance of "creativity" and "nurturing innovation" and so on. Ignore all the noise about the psychology of invention and the scientific temperament. The key to success in research is not hiring geniuses and pampering them in just the right environment. It's plain old ordinary day-to-day management skills—what Ross Perot calls "blocking and tackling."

If you want to understand research, talk to a successful gardener— a really good one. You probably won't hear her talking a lot about how beautiful flowers can be and how important it is to get the blooms that show the finest colors. Rather, she will be interested in such mundane matters as this year's rainfall, how to deal with aphids, and where to buy the best manure. Successful scientists and engineers are equally down-to-earth. Ideas are like flowers; you seldom find good ones produced by people who don't like to get their hands dirty.

THE NATURE OF RESEARCH

Most small companies (most big companies also) do no basic research. They concern themselves strictly with applied research. The main focus differs, of course. In some companies the primary concern is *product development,* the design and testing of new or significantly improved products. Elsewhere, the most important work may be *process research,* aimed at developing new or improved ways to manufacture the product. Even companies that do little innovation may need *troubleshooting,* research aimed at solving production problems as they come up.

> Troubleshooting sounds mundane but in fact may involve some very sophisticated research. Consider an example from the electronics industry. Production of DRAM chips at one company was plagued by low yields (that is, most of the chips came out bad). Careful examination of the wafers with an electron microscope indicated that 0.2-micron particles were shorting circuits on the chip. X-ray analysis of the particles, followed by electron diffraction studies, showed that they were composed of metallic silver. Where was it coming from? After further work, the problem was traced to a silver-plated screen that supported one of the gas-line filters.

Whatever kind of research your company conducts, you must understand its purpose in order to run it effectively. Management outside R&D tends to focus—understandably and correctly—on end results: a new product, a reduction in manufacturing cost, elimination of a quality control problem. Such objectives are valid, but they are not in the correct format, so to speak, to lead to effective research.

The real purpose of research is to acquire new knowledge. *Research is manufacturing information.* A research project cannot be effectively planned or organized until it is formatted into information objectives.

The most fundamental task of the R&D manager is to connect the company's needs with its scientists' talents by formulating R&D objectives in a "knowledge-needed" format. Thus top management may assign a task: "Design a mushroom-cutting machine using the hot-wire technique which meets the following specifications demanded by our customers. . . ." Or a scientist or engineer may come up with an exciting possibility: "We could cut three steps out of the manufacturing process if we shaped the ventricles with an exponential smoother." Whatever the genesis of the project, R&D management must relate the practical results desired to the specific knowledge required to achieve them.

The rational planning of a research project begins with a set of questions. For instance, the example given above might generate questions like: (1) What is the optimum temperature to cauterize the mushroom without excessive charring? (2) To what extent and in what way does the operating life of an incandescent wire depend on its thickness? (3) What commercially available alloy oxidizes most slowly at the optimum temperature? And so on.

Note how the project is now being broken down into a series of clearly defined tasks. Note also that research, conceptualized in this way, *can* "guarantee results." It can't guarantee that the new product will work or that it will be a profitable item—but R&D can guarantee that answers to the relevant questions will be produced.

RESEARCH PLANNING

In the next step, break down each task into two parts: setup and experiments. The experiment is the raw material of R&D. Bright ideas, and even serendipitous accidents, do play their part. But the good luck, and frequently the good ideas, come to those who do the right experiments and do them properly.

> H. C. Brown discovered the hydroboration reaction—and won the Nobel Prize—not by any brilliant theoretical

insight but by insisting on checking an anomalous result
that appeared to be due to an impure sample.

Each question the project must answer implies a set of experiments. First there is generally a setup period: building, calibrating, and testing the experimental apparatus; buying materials; developing analytical or test methods. When everything is ready, the experiments are run. Plan each experimental series for completion without interruption, over as short a time as possible, and by the same personnel, to ensure consistent procedure.

One of the greatest impediments to a productive research operation is flexible equipment. In research as in production, setup time is dead time, so time spent searching for, assembling, testing, or tinkering with research equipment is wasted. Rather than buy one instrument that can be used for two types of work, consider buying two dedicated instruments. Calculate the savings in setup time; you'll frequently find that the payback period for the second instrument is less than a year.

SCHEDULING THE PROJECT

Many start-ups face a major R&D project right up front: developing the first product. Quite a few go under without ever making a sale, because they underestimate the time required to finish this first project and run out of money. It pays to develop a realistic estimate of your project requirements. This involves assembling the various tasks and allocating personnel and other resources. For large projects this can be extremely complicated, but effective methods are known. PERT (Program Evaluation and Review Technique) and CPM (Critical Path Method) are the most popular. Now, the reality is that, unless you are a real pro at project planning, you are not going to get accurate estimates of the schedule no matter how many computerized flowcharts you generate. The value of these techniques lies in the way they force you to work out all the requirements in advance, using an objective methodology.

Here's a simplified guide to project planning. To begin, write down a list of things you don't know, yet need to know, in order to build your product (or improve your process, or whatever you wish to accomplish). *Be specific.* Next, list the conjectures or hypotheses you must test in order to answer the questions you are asking. Then enumerate the experiments you will have to do to test your hypotheses.

Now you need a number for how many scientist-hours it will take to do an experiment. Do *not* make a guess. Most areas of research have some sort of rule of thumb you can use. When it comes to writing software, for instance, a seasoned manager knows that so many lines of code per day is a reasonable expectation for a programmer. If there's no industry-standard number, generate your own by going over records of similar projects. How long did it take to do similar experiments in the past?

In my branch of chemistry—organic synthesis—an "experiment" generally consists of running a reaction. By analyzing the lab notebooks of chemists who have worked for me, I found that the average chemist, under certain defined conditions, ran around 2.5 experiments per week and needed to run a reaction, typically, about 5 times before it would be ready for scale-up. I could thus estimate that a sequence of four steps, say, would require two chemist-months to complete—in addition to setup time. Frequently I have found that the project schedule calculated by this method exceeds my off-hand estimate by an order of magnitude.

REM

Don't forget setup time. How long will it take to purchase materials, build test equipment, and so on?

Now you have gathered the raw material for your project schedule. Unfortunately, you usually cannot simply divide the number of experiments needed by the rate at which your team can run them. As the saying goes, nine women cannot produce a baby in one month. You have to take into account the sequence of work. What's more, in most cases you have to plan branch points into your project: "If the shape of the dinglebork loop turns out not to be a catenary, we'll have to investigate using nickel wire instead of chromium."

WHEN YOU HIT A SNAG

What about unforeseen problems? Well, what about them? In research, as in marketing or production, sometimes you have to go back to the drawing board when your plan is made obsolete by new knowledge. This does not invalidate planning. Follow your plan; if it fails, revise it and follow the revised plan.

The fact is, though, that when a research project gets off track, the cause is almost invariably just plain sloppy work. Even very complex projects can usually be brought in ahead of schedule and under budget if the work is done fastidiously. This means more than simply cleanliness and care. It means a policy of systematic, thorough experimentation. The unproductive scientists are usually those who habitually try to "run a quick-and-dirty experiment" to "just take a look" at a question.

Often it's higher management that is at fault. Top managers have a tendency to come to R&D with new projects whenever the fancy strikes them. That's not so bad; the trouble is that this is commonly combined with a passionate aversion to setting priorities—or a habit of imposing a new set of priorities every week or so. It is the responsibility of R&D management to insist that the company's limited technical resources be allocated to a minimal number of projects, each selected based on explicit and objective criteria. Then every project should be taken, if not to completion, at least to a logical stopping place.

The Seven Deadly Sins of Research

1. *Reinventing the wheel.* There's nothing like skimping on time in the library to get you into embarrassing situations—like finding out, *after* you've completed the project, that your competition has already patented your brilliant invention.

Don't stop after checking out the major background studies. Dig into the whole subject deeply. Compile and organize every bit of information you can find that could bear on your problem. Then set up a mechanism to keep this file up-to-date by continually monitoring the literature. Be constantly on the watch for those little tidbits of know-how that so often save weeks of work. You're more likely to find them in the older literature, before 1960 or so, when journals provided space for extensive experimental sections. These days such jewels may occasionally be discovered in footnotes, but more commonly you must get them by talking to other workers in the field. Here's a tip: Don't neglect Ph.D. theses; they often contain key experimental specifications that never find their way into journal publications.

2. *Unexamined assumptions.* The purpose of research is to learn something, and you learn things in just two ways: Either you do an experiment and observe the results, or someone else does an experiment and tells you the results. You don't learn anything from what you think ought to be true. Identify your assumptions and test them—before you begin.

3. *Uncontrolled variables.* You run a series of experiments in order to relate effects to causes. But the results can easily be invalidated if a single relevant variable is left uncontrolled. If you're very lucky, this neglect causes inconsistent results in your experimental series, warning you that something is wrong; you'll merely have to do all the experiments over. If you're fairly lucky, you'll get consistently bad results that cause you to abandon a project or an approach that

would have actually been viable. But if you're unlucky, you'll get consistently good results in the lab—and fail in the plant.

A process for an expensive adhesive additive worked beautifully in the lab, and the customer approved the sample. On scale-up, the product came out yellow and was rejected as impure. The entire batch had to be scrapped, at a heavy loss. The explanation turned out to be simple: Purified solvent was used in the lab experiments, ordinary drum-grade material in the plant.

REM

4. *Incomplete experimental series.* You run experiments usually to get data points. When you try to get by on the cheap, you're asking for trouble. It's surprising how often the curve takes a jog just where you decided to skip a point to save time; your interpolation can be dangerously invalid. Extrapolation is even worse—often strange phenomena lurk at the edges of your data set, and in the plant accident or mistake may move conditions into that uncharted area. Skimpy data sets are vulnerable not only to random error but to systematic error, especially if you skipped running "blanks" or control experiments.

Getting a complete study across the entire range of parameters is especially critical in process research. You're looking for a graph where the figure of merit shows a broad hump rather than a sharp peak. In the former case, a variation of the process parameters from the optimum will result in only a small degradation in results; you'll have a "robust" process. If your system shows a sharp peak, however, a minor mistake in the plant—and the plant usually can't control process parameters as tightly as the lab can—will result in serious problems.

Incomplete studies have consequences much more expensive than the cost of the skipped experiments. Ironically, though, skimping on experiments is usually motivated not by economy but by boredom.

5. *Unfinished or sloppy experiments.* It's tempting to abandon an experiment that "isn't working right." That's a mistake. Such experiments can be immensely informative if you take the time and trouble to investigate *why* they are not working right. When an experiment does not produce the "expected" results, Mother Nature is trying to tell you something! Maybe your experimental technique is not good enough. Maybe your theory is wrong. But maybe what you tripped over will turn out to be, if you take the trouble to look at it closely, a lump of gold. The rewards of serendipity come only to those who respond to a problem with an urgent need to find out what went wrong.

Thoroughness should be planned into your experiments from the start. Experiments that produce no information are a total waste. The "quick-and-dirty" experiment tells you nothing if it fails; did it "really" fail, or did it fail because the experiment was quick-and-dirty? What if it succeeds? Then you're really in trouble. You're half a kilometer down a blind alley before you realize that what you thought was a positive result was actually an artifact caused by one of the uncontrolled variables you didn't want to take time to deal with.

6. *Incomplete records*. Most scientists pride themselves on their notebooks, and most of them . . . shouldn't. This is one area where older scientists have the edge over the young whippersnappers. Once you've written a dozen or so research reports, and screamed at yourself "Why didn't I write that down?" a couple of hundred times, you begin to write it down. This isn't just for lab scientists, either; computer programmers are notorious for carelessness in documenting their work.

7. *Unorganized data*. What good are data if you can't find them? Even in a young company it's amazing how often effort gets duplicated in R&D because it wasn't properly recorded, preserved, organized so it could be found, or communicated.

We were beating our brains out over a tough process problem. One day a chemist came to me with an old report she'd run across. It described a solution to our problem that had been worked out ten years before—filed and forgotten.

REM

ENCOURAGING INNOVATION

As we've said, proficiency at basic R&D skills should get more of your attention than highfalutin notions of "nurturing creativity" and other buzzwords. Even so, you do need to attend to global aspects.

Most companies, in spite of good intentions, are poor at fostering innovation. Mostly this results from too much attention to pop psychology and too little to setting up simple control procedures.

The proper approach is to treat an idea like a child. When it first appears, handle it like an infant—very protectively. Avoid killer phrases like "We tried that once" or "Would it be cost effective?" Don't require the creator to justify or defend her idea. Instead, encourage her to expand it, amplify it, explore it, and elaborate on it. In a strong R&D organization it is very easy to get approval to start a new project. The major criterion is simply the inventor's commitment to her own idea. Is she willing to work on it, study it thoroughly, follow it through? If she is, give her the go-ahead.

But as the innovation matures it should, like a growing child, be exposed to increasing challenge. The swaddling appropriate for the infant spoils the adolescent. Similarly, as a research project progresses it should be required to meet increasingly strict criteria—technical, financial, and marketing—to qualify for continued funding.

Most organizations have it backward. They come down on infant ideas like Herod slaughtering the Innocents. Every suggestion must run the gantlet just to get a chance at initial funding. The more original an innovation, the less chance it has of passing the intimidating checklist of requirements.

But once a project gets started, it tends to be overprotected. The older it gets, the less it is challenged. Large companies often pour millions into such projects, years after it has become clear that the idea isn't ever going to work in the lab, let alone in the marketplace. Partly this is due to reluctance to write off a bad investment: "We've sunk so much into this we can't afford to quit now." But usually the major factor is managerial ego. Too many important people have signed on and now refuse to lose face by admitting they were wrong.

Don't kid yourself that this sort of behavior occurs only in big, bureaucratic companies. It happens all the time in small companies too, including some highly innovative high-tech start-ups. Trilogy, for instance, burned up over $50 million in venture capital trying to accomplish wafer-scale integration. If you don't watch out, it will happen in *your* company.

You must find the right balance between commitment and caution. The company that is too conservative and timid in R&D—that abandons a project as soon as difficulties appear—seldom accomplishes innovation. But the company that stubbornly insists on beating its head against a brick wall until it runs out of capital will do even worse.

> They said it couldn't be done.
> With a smile, he went right to it.
> He tackled the thing that "couldn't be done"
> And couldn't do it.

Ultimately, as so often in management, the solution lies in the kind of objectivity and judgment that comes only with experience. But there are some policy methods that can help.

It's instructive here to compare how American and Japanese research policies differ. The stereotype of Japan as a nation of imitators is now obsolete. Although still trailing the United States in innovation, Japan is coming up fast and is already a force to be reckoned with. How are they operating?

One important difference between Japanese and American R&D managers is their attitudes toward developing personnel. U.S. managers want to recruit scientists and engineers on a ready-to-work basis. Indeed, American companies in general have an obsession with instantaneous gratification on hiring that appalls foreign managers. Japanese companies, on the other hand, take promising youngsters and patiently train them.

But the greatest distinction between U.S. and Japanese companies is their attitudes toward technological risk. American corporations are far more conservative. Standard procedure is to generate a lot of ideas and flow them through an increasingly strict series of "filters," eliminating all but a few, which are finally carried to market. This tentative and timid behavior puzzles our Japanese competitors. They are ready to take large, though calculated, risks on new technologies, picking major innovations and committing themselves to bring them to market. Determination in following through on such commitments and a refusal to "cut one's losses" when the project meets setbacks are considered management virtues in Japan.

How do you avoid undercommitment? When a project is floundering, behind schedule and over budget, how do you decide whether it still makes sense to hang on? The key, once again, is to focus on *information.* Accept for the moment that the project is not meeting its commercial goals (such as readying a new product for market). Look past that and ask, is the project still producing useful information? Ask the project leader what he has learned, and what he is learning right now, and what he is going to learn in the coming weeks. If he convinces you that the work is generating real, tangible know-how, continue the program. As long as valuable data are coming out, the odds are good that something profitable will appear, though it may not be what you originally had in mind. But if the project is mired in confusion and information is not being produced, better pull the plug.

The decision to cancel a major research project is seldom easy or popular. A small company cannot afford an unfocused or undisciplined research operation, but neither can it afford to stifle the creativity of its innovators. The best way to prevent falling into a financial black hole while preserving the morale of your R&D team is to use some sort of objective criteria for these decisions. One valuable technique involves attaching a "stop-loss" flag to every project.

At each stage, when a project is initiated, continued, or expanded, ask the chief investigator to set objectives for the coming phase. He is, of course, likely to be overoptimistic. There's no need to curb his enthusiasm, but he should be required to suggest a stop-loss flag for the project. Ask: "What results—or failure—would convince *you* that this project should be abandoned?" You may need to negotiate the exact terms, but get it in writing right from the start and hold him to it. This can prevent those drawn-out disasters in which advocates of a hopeless project keep clinging to your knees, pleading for "just one more chance." Incidentally, the same trick in reverse can be used to pry a new product loose from a perfectionist designer. Make her agree in writing in advance on the product specs; then use the agreement when she tries to delay introduction to add a few "important improvements."

PROTECTING YOUR INNOVATION

To patent or not to patent—that is a question that has been heavily debated. There is no single answer. However, it cannot be emphasized too strongly that a patent is a hunting license and nothing more. It gives you the privilege of suing infringers, but there's a big difference between suing and winning. Judges know nothing about science or engineering, and juries less, so the odds of getting justice in a patent suit are lower than for any other kind of case except product liability. And if the infringer of your patent is a large corporation, your hunting license may be about as valuable as a license to hunt elephants with a peashooter. Keep in mind also that the U.S. Government has been known to rip off patent holders, and that many foreign countries refuse to recognize or enforce patents of certain types.

On the other hand, due to recent reforms, U.S. courts are much more inclined to uphold the validity of patents and to assess damages against infringers. This may work for you—or against you if another company is in a position to claim a dominating patent in your field. Recently, for instance, people in the computer industry were shocked to learn that a court had awarded a basic microprocessor patent to an obscure inventor.

Another good reason to apply for a patent, even if you have no realistic hope of enforcing it: Investors like patents.

There is a wide variation in the effectiveness of various types of patents. A "composition of matter" patent is relatively easy to obtain and to defend. (However, most foreign governments do not recognize this form of patent.) Device patents are less reliable. A process patent may be almost unenforceable, even for a large company.

Before you apply for a patent, consider your alternatives; maintaining your invention as a trade secret is one obvious option. But what about a design patent, copyright, or even trademark protection? Just exactly what do you want to protect, and what is the most effective way to do so? If you do patent, who is likely to infringe? How much would it cost you to sue them? How long would it take? Be sure you consider these questions at an early stage.

Perhaps the most significant factor is your objective in applying for a patent. Specifically, do you want to maintain complete exclusivity in using your invention, or are you willing (perhaps eager) to license it? If you really want to maintain exclusivity, getting a patent is risky. You're telling the world how to do it by getting the patent, and enforcement can be very difficult. If, however, you're willing to license, a patent becomes much more attractive. Even the brutal behemoths will usually pay royalties rather than infringe *if* you give them the option. Infringement is most likely to occur when a license is unavailable or unaffordable.

Whatever approach you take to protect your invention, you must institute policies to define and control your proprietary information. There are well-known guidelines for laboratory record-keeping to establish patentability. You may not be aware that maintaining a trade secret also imposes certain legal requirements. Indeed, since the law doesn't really approve of trade secrets—the government would prefer that you publish your invention, that's why patents exist—you have to be especially careful. Without going into detail, we simply point out that to enforce secrecy you must define what you consider to be proprietary; take reasonable precautions to protect it; and be prepared to prove that your employees and anyone else with access to it knew it was a trade secret.

Make a careful decision, but don't take too long. If you do decide to patent, file early. Be aware that any commercial activity—advertising your new product, negotiating with customers, setting up beta-test sites—can bar you from seeking a patent. There is a one-year grace period, but it's best to be very conservative, to ensure that you don't inadvertently blow your patent rights.

CONSULTING AS AN ENTRY POINT

It is common for high-technology businesses to start out as consulting or contract-engineering operations and later make a transition into manufacturing. This has a number of obvious advantages; in particular, the fees received often effectively finance the initial product development.

However, the technical types who typically found such companies frequently fail to realize how very difficult it is to move from custom services to proprietary manufacturing. These two types of business are pretty close to being completely orthogonal, and many high-tech companies crash and burn in the attempt to switch from one to the other.

If you plan to go this route, be especially careful. Give thorough consideration to your career objectives. If you really enjoy doing contract research, you probably will detest running a manufacturing operation. Of course, the latter is much more likely to make you rich. Is that enough incentive? If you decide to go ahead, don't underestimate the changes you will have to make. Seriously consider setting up a brand-new company to do the manufacturing—instead of, or better yet in addition to, the contract R&D firm. That allows you to build in management policies appropriate to the new operation without disrupting the old, and to bring in new key personnel (especially a manufacturing guru!). Also, if the manufacturing company fails, you still have the existing contract R&D firm to fall back on.

WORKING WITH OTHER MANAGEMENT

The R&D director must establish a productive working relationship with both Marketing and Production. The success of a technology-based company depends on cooperative effort among these three units. No one can be allowed to dominate. If Production is in control, the company will devote too much energy to cash cows and lose the future; within a few years, you'll have a beautiful plant optimized to make an obsolete product with very high efficiency. If Marketing dominates, you'll play it safe; then one day, a more innovative competitor will come out with a breakthrough product and jerk the rug right out from under you. But a company where R&D has unrestricted power may never get its brilliant innovations to market. A system of checks and balances is needed.

You can do much to forge such a system by establishing a policy of job rotation. No scientist or engineer should be promoted into R&D management until she has served a tour in Quality Control or handled some troubleshooting assignments in the plant—*and* put in time doing market research or a similar job involving customer contact. In the same way, Production's management candidates should get rotated into the marketing and sales side (Complaints & Returns is a good place for this) and also get some experience in product development. And yes, Marketing's bright young stars should be invited to put on their grubbies and spend some time getting themselves all dirty in the lab and the plant as part of their preparation for that corner office.

THE LOSS-LEADER TRAP

One of the most insidious traps for young companies is the R&D loss leader. One day your struggling start-up is approached by a really big potential customer. They are very interested in buying large quantities, and buying them from you—only, it's a product you haven't developed. Here are the specs; would you be interested in looking into it and giving them a quote on developmental quantities? Sure you would—this is your big chance. So all of your talent, not to mention your meager cash reserves, goes into R&D on this project. Naturally you gave Mr. Big a very low bid. This is your big chance and you don't want him to take it elsewhere. And of course you wouldn't be so insolent as to ask him to pay you anything up front—net 30 after you get into production is fine with you. So you turn in a proposal, and it's accepted, and you work day and night, and you turn in progress reports, and one day Mr. Big sends you a letter which very apologetically tells you that the project's been cancelled, or postponed, or they've decided to do it in-house. . . . And as your attorney is explaining to you the provisions of Chapter Seven bankruptcy you suddenly realize that you gave Mr. Big thousands of dollars' worth of R&D and didn't charge him a cent for it.

The marketing guys are frequently going to be on your case, trying to get you to do free R&D for your customers. If you're in a technology business, that's to be expected, and it's often a very good thing to do. But insist on approaching these projects in the same rational manner you use to evaluate in-house ideas. Make the marketing wallahs specify what the payback is to be, what the risks are, how the project can be justified, and how it fits in with the company's priorities. And make them specify a stop-loss flag.

A small company has very limited R&D resources. It is the responsibility of the R&D manager to see that they are allocated effectively. It is inexcusable to run a project just because he has a whim to look into the question. It is equally inexcusable to run a project because his fellow managers have a gut feeling that they can sell a million of 'em.

CAUTIONARY TALE
Cold Confusion

Although I'm by no means a technical type, I got caught up in one of the most contentious scientific controversies of the century. At a dinner at the Harvard Club one night I happened to sit next to another alumnus, Chase Peterson, who at that time was President of the University of Utah. Doctors Pons and Fleischmann had just come out with their amazing "cold fusion" claims, and there was immense interest in the subject worldwide. Of course, the scientific implications alone were enormous. But what was attracting intense interest within the university was the profit potential. If this technology really worked, and became commercial, it would put the University of Utah on the map in a big way, not only intellectually but financially. The university's endowment is not large, so of course visions of sugarplums were dancing in the heads of its trustees.

At that time, though, the problem was to get financing to develop the technology, prove it out, and turn it into something that could make money. Since raising money for new ventures is a big part of what I do for a living these days, naturally I volunteered. The university retained me to raise $15 million in nongovernment money for the Cold Fusion Institute.

Of course it would be helpful, in working on this project, to have some grasp of the technological issues myself. I needed not only a scientific evaluation of the results, but an estimate of the economic consequences—assuming the technology worked. Fortunately, one of my favorite nerds was already following the cold fusion saga closely. Ron and I happened to be talking around this time, and he offered to give me a summary. Here's some of what he told me.

×   ×   ×   ×

Fusion, the source of the sun's energy, is a nuclear reaction in which two light nuclei (such as hydrogen) are forced together to make a heavier nucleus (such as helium). This is very hard to do, and generally requires the kind of immense pressure and temperature found at the center of the sun, or in the explosion of an atomic bomb. Attempts to achieve "controlled fusion" in extremely hot plasma reactors have built a record of over thirty years of failure.

So when Pons and Fleischmann (call 'em "P&F" for short) claimed they could achieve fusion simply by running electricity into "heavy water" (deuterium oxide) with a palladium electrode, it caused quite a stir. For one thing, it violated the long-accepted scientific doctrine that—contrary to the claims of the alchemists—no element can be changed into another by *chemical* means. There was also a political aspect. The "hot fusion" research establishment, which has spent billions of dollars with nothing practical to show for it, would be highly embarrassed if a couple of lowly chemists built a working fusion reactor with a hundred dollars' worth of materials.

I had been following the cold-fusion controversy on the BIX computer conference, which tracked all the latest results. There was vigorous argument over whether the "excess heat" claimed by P&F was real. To my mind, most of this debate missed the point. The key to the whole thing—scientifically and economically—was just arithmetic.

On the scientific side, P&F were claiming their "excess heat" came from fusion of deuterium. Now, there are only three fusion reactions that deuterium can undergo, and the energy produced by each is well known. Two of the three produce radioactive products; one does not, it produces ordinary helium ("helium-4"). A simple calculation—just arithmetic—shows that *if* the heat came from either of the first two reactions, so much radioactivity would be produced that it would be unmistakable; in fact, it would kill the experimenters. Therefore, *if* the heat came from fusion, *then* helium-4 was being formed.

So detection of helium-4 was the crucial experiment that would settle the question of cold fusion one way or the other. Had P&F done this experiment? They had not. This was on a par with their track record of somehow avoiding publication of any data that could solidly establish or refute their claims. Month after month they failed to publish basic experimental details, offering a series of weak excuses—patent applications, negotiations with corporations, everything short of "the dog ate my lab notebook." As a result, their scientific credibility, which initially had been excellent, quickly eroded.

Simple arithmetic also gave me a good feel for the economic consequences of cold fusion, on the assumption that it really did work. Everyone was focused on the unlimited *quantity* of energy available from cold fusion. Deuterium is present in extremely small amounts in ordinary water—but there's a lot of water in the ocean! What struck me, though, was the question of the *rate* at which you could produce that energy. The limiting factor was not deuterium but palladium. This is a semiprecious metal, fairly expensive and fairly rare.

So I took P&F's most optimistic numbers for power density and did some more arithmetic. It turned out that to build one medium-size power reactor—1,000 MW, enough to supply a city with a population of a million or so—you would need around 100 tons of palladium. As it happens, that number is pretty close to the world's *total* annual production of palladium.

Of course, one could argue that with further development higher power densities could be obtained. And maybe palladium wouldn't be essential; some labs claimed to get positive results with titanium, an abundant metal. Nonetheless, it didn't do much for the credibility of the cold-fusion advocates that they hadn't looked into these elementary considerations.

In short, P&F lost credibility not just because they couldn't come up with the answers, but because they weren't even asking the right questions. So what I had to tell Harry was that if the University of Utah wanted to get backing for this investigation, they'd have to persuade P&F to pull their socks up.

× × × ×

Armed with this information from Ron (he provided a lot more detail, including analyses of how cold fusion, if successful, would affect specific industries), I went out to the first cold-fusion conference. There were all sorts of people there, from science, business, and of course the media. Some were believers, some were skeptics, some were agnostic, but all of them were serious, competent people. When Pons failed to show up for the meeting, the effect was disastrous.

P&F had handled the media badly from the very beginning. They were wildly premature in their first announcement, calling a press conference before publishing in scientific media. This, I gathered from Ron, is a no-no for scientists, but the rule is often violated without generating more than some nasty frowns. Unfortunately, P&F continued to get publicity of a sort that seemed to the scientific community a brazen defiance of professional standards. And since they had not the slightest conception of how to handle the media, this was worse than a crime—it was a blunder.

The media, of course, played up the cold-fusion controversy heavily—it made the cover of *Newsweek*, which was quite an accomplishment for a topic that didn't involve killing anyone, blowing anything up, or having sex. *The Wall Street Journal* had excellent coverage with, as is their wont, careful balance of viewpoints. *The New York Times* weighed in on the skeptical side. When P&F held their next press conference, the *Times* was pointedly not invited. This is not the way one gets a hostile media outlet to reconsider its position.

The tide of opinion was beginning to turn against cold fusion, and Chase Peterson was in trouble with his faculty. He stuck to his guns, however. The primary duty of a university president is fund-raising; Chase had been highly successful in getting money for the university, and he couldn't pass up the chance of cold-fusion royalties. He appointed an independent committee to evaluate P&F's results, battened down the hatches, and held on.

Meanwhile I was getting ready to raise some money for the Cold Fusion Institute. I figured the best approach would be private investments from super-rich individuals, who are accustomed to contributing to universities and research institutes. Unfortunately, just as I got started, the storm burst in Utah. Scientific opinion crystallized in decisive opposition to Pons and Fleischmann. The university's faculty revolted, government officials decided a Cold Fusion Institute looked like a boondoggle, and I was told to forget the whole thing.

This was not the end for cold fusion, which still generates rumors and even scientific papers as this is written. But it was the final blow for Chase Peterson. The faculty senate voted to request his resignation, and he submitted it. Failure, as they say, is an orphan. To my mind, Chase Peterson is the real hero of the cold-fusion saga. He had a lot to lose, but he chose to make a commitment.

The whole fiasco was an object lesson in how not to get credibility for your technology. Pons and Fleischmann faced problems not of their making; their claims conflicted with established doctrine, and they faced opposition from the establishment for political reasons. But ultimately they blew it themselves. They failed to play by the rules set by their peers and thus forfeited the immense advantage of endorsement by the scientific community. They mishandled the press and offended people they needed. And above all, they promised great things and then failed to deliver.

HDS

Ten

FINANCIAL PLANNING

Happiness is positive cash flow.

Fred Adler

An indispensable ingredient of any business plan is a set of financial projections (frequently called, incorrectly, *pro forma*s). Nothing gives the entrepreneur more trouble than developing financial projections; nothing seems more unrealistic and useless. What's more, although investors insist on seeing a complete set of detailed projections, nothing will satisfy them. If you make your projections conservative, you'll be told, "This company clearly isn't going to have enough growth and profitability to justify the risk of the investment." If you avoid this complaint, your plan will be rejected because "Your sales and profit projections are wildly unrealistic."

THE PURPOSE OF PROJECTIONS

Forget about satisfying investors for the moment. Why do *you* need financial projections? Does anyone really believe that you can predict future results of your venture in a quantitative way?

No. Not at all. The purpose of financial projections is not to *predict* but to *prepare*.

There's no such thing as a generic business. Every business is unique. And every business therefore has its own distinct financial structure, and behaves in a distinctive way. By doing financial projections, you begin to get a feel for the peculiar nature of your company. How does it respond to changes in the market and other environmental or management factors? By playing around with the numbers you learn a lot about your business—including some things that may surprise you.

Just what is involved in constructing financial projections? First, you must identify your *assumptions* about the financial and operating characteristics of your start-up. Second, you must develop *sales and budget projections*. Third, you must assemble these into a *P&L projection*. Fourth, you must then translate this into a *cash-flow projection*. Fifth, you must check your results by projecting your *balance sheet*. And finally, you should do *ratio analysis* to compare your company's projected behavior with that of similar companies.

As you do this, you will become aware of certain considerations that had previously escaped you. You will begin to see how your decisions regarding marketing, production, R&D, and so on affect the profitability and liquidity of your company.

In order to show you how projections are done, and illustrate some of the issues involved, we are going to walk you through the process, using our hypothetical start-up, Incandescent Fungoid Cutters, Inc., as an example. WARNING! We have greatly simplified the process for this example. In doing so, *we have left out a number of factors that most certainly would have to be considered in doing a real set of projections*. We will alert you to some of the major omissions, but there are likely to be factors specific to your business that should be taken into account when you do your own projections.

In the sample projections shown here, we show figures on a monthly basis for the first year of the company's operations. This is sufficient to illustrate the points we want to make. However, for a real-life business plan, financial results are commonly projected in monthly figures for the first two years, quarterly for years three and four, and annually out to the fifth year or further.

SPECIFYING YOUR ASSUMPTIONS

Let's go over the assumptions for Incandescent Fungoid Cutters.

1. We assume a unit price of $10,000. Note that for simplicity in building the spreadsheet we've allowed sales to grow in fractional units. However, if you are selling a very high-priced product, you'd do well to base sales projections on unit sales.

2. We take a direct production cost of $6,000 per unit—that is,

gross margin is 40 percent. Note that we have assumed that this number is independent of sales volume. In reality, costs for materials may actually vary with production level, since you can usually get a better price on larger lots. Labor costs are also oversimplified. Even for a very large business, labor costs do not vary smoothly with production levels—it's just not that easy to lay people off when production declines, or to hire and train them when it increases suddenly. For a small business, labor often is effectively a fixed cost.

3. We sell through reps, who get a 10 percent commission (payable when product is shipped), and there are no other marketing expenses. Of course, in real life, farm equipment is much more likely to be sold through distributors than through reps. Also, a 10 percent commission is rather optimistic. Even if reps are used, there are still costs for advertising, brochures, sales training, travel, and so on.

4. Taxes in this model are 46 percent of profits. This income tax model is *grossly* oversimplified (that cash refund in January would have them rolling on the floor at the IRS); to develop an accurate model you'll need expert help from your accountant. Don't forget that in real life you'll have to take into account state and local taxes, real-estate taxes, franchise taxes, sales and use taxes, inventory taxes, and so on *ad infinitum*.

5. We use straight-line depreciation with a five-year lifetime of the production equipment in this model. Your accountant will probably want you to use a more complicated method. The strange and mystical variations of depreciation methods, like the distinction between *homoousian* and *homoiousian,* are not to be appreciated by mere laypeople. Suffice it to say that there are several ways of depreciating capital costs; that the method chosen can drastically affect a company's profits and therefore its taxes; that it does not at all affect the company's cash flow; and that fiddling with depreciation can be a very effective way to frustrate the IRS, bamboozle investors, and get yourself so confused that you don't have the vaguest idea whether you're actually making money or not. See your accountant.

6. We assume a very optimistic sales cycle for this little example. We ship one month after receiving the order, and get paid within sixty days of shipment. If you think you should be able to collect your receivables in less than sixty days, wait till you get on the phone with dilatory customers and try it. Another tricky point is the implied assumption that we're paying for materials on net 30 days. A start-up may well have to pay C.O.D. or even pay in advance; it can take months or even years to develop credit. We are also assuming that we can project sales perfectly so as to order exactly the right amount of

materials for next month's production. *This is a lot easier to do on a projection than it is in reality!*

7. Let's assume that our initial capitalization is $500,000. We'll use $100,000 to buy plant and equipment and reserve the rest as working capital. We'll simply ignore all sorts of minor start-up expenses—incorporation fees, legal expenses, and so on.

8. We assume we get 12 percent interest on our cash. At the time this is written, that would be a very good return indeed; by the time you read this, who knows? Anyway, 1 percent a month is convenient for simplicity.

Projected Revenues and Budgets.

The basic assumptions made above provide a framework for our model. Now we have to fill it in. The root numbers come from our sales projections.

For this example, we made up some numbers. We assume that sales begin immediately. This is not exactly realistic—we've left out the entire development period during which the product is designed and debugged. We've also assumed that sales will grow at 10 percent a month. This is a bit optimistic, to say the least—it's equivalent to about 150 percent per year—but it's the sort of growth venture capitalists say they want to see. In the rare cases when this kind of growth rate is actually achieved, it never comes as a steady, month-by-month increase but as big, irregular jumps, and these sudden surges hit your cash flow like a karate chop in the kidneys. And here's another neglected factor: Would we not expect the market for an item of farm equipment to be highly seasonal?

All these complications are being neglected for this simplified example. For your business plan, sales projections should be based on market research, as discussed in Chapter Four, and should take these complexities into account. Above all, sales projections should be calculated as a function of sales effort and customer responsiveness, not just assumed. Do as we say, don't do as we do!

The projections in most business plans I see, particularly the ones written by engineers, have meticulous, detailed, and thoroughly justified calculations of expenses. But the sales numbers, which of course determine whether the venture will make money, are pulled out of thin air. One might almost say that an engineer is someone who knows the cost of everything and the profitability of nothing.

REM

Sales projections give you your top line. Then you have to budget your costs. As with sales estimates, this is not a matter of plugging in some more or less arbitrary numbers. You should be able to estimate your costs *as a function of sales*. As discussed above, cost of goods sold can be based on manufacturing-cost estimates.

There will also be selling costs. For this ultra-simplified model, we just use 10 percent of sales. You'll want to make a realistic estimate based on your market research. How many sales calls will it take, on the average, to make a sale? How many sales calls can a salesperson make per day? From numbers such as these you can calculate how many salespeople you will need to employ to achieve a given level of monthly sales.

In our model, R&D expense is treated as a constant, but in reality it too should be tied to sales projections. Thus, if we project starting sales of the Mark II Lasermatic Fungaslicer in Year 3, we should budget money for the R&D that will be necessary to develop the Mark II. Administrative expense we again assume to be constant for our model. In reality, much administrative cost is proportional to sales, and this should be taken into account.

In all these calculations, you'll be putting in numbers for wages and salaries. Don't forget to add the "wedge"—payroll costs over the base salary, including Social Security and other taxes, benefits, and so on. These days the wedge generally runs around 30–35 percent of base payroll, so it is a significant factor.

The Income-Statement Projection.

In Exhibit 5 we show the projected income statement (or "P&L") for the first year of Incandescent Fungoid Cutters. We constructed this as follows.

The "sales" line comes from our sales projections. Note that for purposes of the P&L, sales are recognized when the product is shipped and the invoice is sent out. (If your company is well run, these two events will occur on the same day.) Thus we show no sales for the first month, since the orders taken in January are not shipped until February.

"Cost of goods sold" is, by our assumptions, 60 percent of sales. Note that for the P&L, this is recognized as of the time of sale so that costs are attached to the product for which they were incurred.

"Gross profit" is simply the difference between sales and cost of goods sold.

Then we deduct the various expense items—Marketing and Sales, Research and Development, and General and Administrative—estimated in the manner we discussed above.

For these projections, we put in depreciation of our production equipment ($100,000 amortized on a straight-line basis over five years)

Exhibit 5. Incandescent Fungoid Cutters, Inc.—projected income statement ($000) (growth rate = 10%).

	Jan	Feb	Mar	Apr	May	Jun	Jul	Aug	Sep	Oct	Nov	Dec
Sales	0	100	110	121	133	146	161	177	195	214	236	259
Cost of goods sold	0	60	66	73	80	88	97	106	117	129	141	156
Gross profit	0	40	44	48	53	59	64	71	78	86	94	104
Marketing expense	0	10	11	12	13	15	16	18	19	21	24	26
R&D expense	5	5	5	5	5	5	5	5	5	5	5	5
Depreciation	2	2	2	2	2	2	2	2	2	2	2	2
G&A expense	5	5	5	5	5	5	5	5	5	5	5	5
Total expense	12	22	23	24	25	27	28	30	31	33	36	38
Operating profit	-12	18	21	24	28	32	36	41	46	52	59	66
Other	4	3	2	1	1	1	1	1	1	1	0	0
Net profit (pretax)	-8	21	23	26	29	33	37	42	47	53	59	66
Net profit (after tax)	-4	12	13	14	16	18	20	23	25	29	32	36

as part of expenses. This is not the way you'll see it done normally. Accountants insist that depreciation of manufacturing equipment should be put into the cost of goods sold. This is indeed the logical way to do things, but because fudging depreciation is so common, many investors prefer to see it broken out so they can keep an eye on the chicanery more conveniently. Also, putting depreciation into the expense line brings out its role as a more or less fixed cost. For a start-up, which is operating at a low fraction of capacity, putting deprecia-tion into cost of goods sold will often result in wild and confusing swings in calculated gross margins.

By summing up the expense rows and subtracting the total from the gross profit, we arrive at the "operating profit." (You'll sometimes see this called "EBIT"—earnings before interest and taxes.) This measures the fundamental performance of the company.

We then take into account other items. For a large corporation, this might include "extraordinary items" such as sale of a division or revelation of accumulated losses which had previously been swept under the rug. In our example, we have just the interest we collect on our cash. Incidentally, we've assumed that this company is financed solely with equity, so we have no debt on which to pay interest.

As you can see, our assumptions have resulted in a very nice projection. We are in the black by our second month of operation, and thereafter we make a substantial and continually increasing profit.

The Cash-Flow Projection. However, the income statement doesn't tell you everything. "Profit" is just a bookkeeping entry, and you can't pay your workers with bookkeeping entries; they demand real money. So we must now return to our assumptions and build a cash-flow projection (see Exhibit 6).

In the first line, we show the cash on hand at the start of each month. Recall that our initial capitalization was $500,000, of which we spent $100,000 on capital equipment, so we have $400,000 left to start with.

We then take into account the sources of cash. The second row shows revenues from sales. Since this is a cash-flow analysis, we don't recognize this revenue until it turns into cash—which, by our assump-tions, is two months after the sale is made.

Our only other source of revenue is interest on the cash we have on hand, which is shown in the third row. Summing this with the sales revenue we get, of course, the total revenue in cash.

We then must account for expenditures of cash. Our assumption is that manufacturing takes one month; so, in order to ship a unit in

Exhibit 6. Incandescent Fungoid Cutters, Inc.—projected cash flow statement ($000) (growth rate = 10%).

	Jan	Feb	Mar	Apr	May	Jun	Jul	Aug	Sep	Oct	Nov	Dec
Cash at start	400	338	245	143	131	118	103	88	71	53	34	12
Sales revenue	0	0	0	100	110	121	133	146	161	177	195	214
Interest revenue	4	3	2	1	1	1	1	1	1	1	0	0
Total revenue	4	3	2	101	111	122	134	147	162	178	195	214
Materials and labor	60	66	73	80	88	97	106	117	129	141	156	171
Other expense	10	20	21	22	23	25	26	28	29	31	34	36
Taxes	−4	10	11	12	13	15	17	19	22	24	27	30
Total outflow	66	96	104	114	125	136	150	164	180	197	216	237
Cash flow	−62	−92	−102	−12	−13	−14	−15	−17	−18	−20	−21	−23
Cash at end	338	245	143	131	118	103	88	71	53	34	12	−11

March, we must receive materials in January. During February we manufacture the unit, and in this month we must pay for the materials (on 30 days) and pay our laborers. So, given our simplified assumptions, we will be paying out the cash for materials and labor one month ahead of shipment.

Our other expenses, we assume, are paid in the month they are incurred, just as on the P&L. We omit, however, depreciation, which has no immediate effect on cash flow. (Of course, if we were to buy any capital equipment during the year, the cost would have to be taken into account.) We must allow for tax payments, too; as noted above, our tax model here is ridiculously oversimplified.

Subtracting total cash going out from total revenues we get net cash flow, and using this we can determine the cash balance at the end of the month.

You should realize that this kind of crude cash-flow statement is not the way accountants like to do it. They prefer a "Statement of Sources and Uses of Funds," which is obtained by analysis of balance-sheet changes. Roughly speaking, they take profits and compute cash flow by adding depreciation back in. (Hence their mysterious talk about how a change in depreciation methods will change cash flow.) Flow-of-funds can be very informative, but it takes a little more skill to read the statement.

Look at Exhibit 6 for a moment. Believe it or not, this is the same company as shown in Exhibit 5! Although Incandescent Fungoids is projecting terrific sales and excellent profits, by the end of its first year it will be broke.

THE PARADOX OF GROWTH

How can this be? How can a successful, growing, profitable company go bankrupt? It's easy.

Incandescent Fungoids, in our projection, is like many manufacturing companies in that money—cash—must be paid out well in advance of shipping the product on which it is expended, and money—cash—is not received in payment for the product very promptly. The first delay results in a significant cost for *carrying inventory* (in this case mostly work in progress); the second results in the need to *finance receivables*. The money needed to perform these two functions is called "working capital."

Every type of business has its own distinct working-capital needs.

> The working capital of a grocery store goes almost entirely for inventory, because sales are made for cash.

On the other hand, import-export sales brokers may carry no inventory, but must finance heavy receivables for their customers.

Some direct-marketing companies are able to get along with almost no working capital. They get their goods on consignment and are paid by their customers in cash. Nice work if you can get it.

If a company is doing about the same volume of business every year, it needs a roughly constant amount of working capital. One need only make sure, in planning such a business, that an adequate amount is allowed for. But a high-growth company presents a different situation; as we've seen, it needs increasing amounts of working capital to finance the growth.

What, as V. I. Lenin liked to say, is to be done? Perhaps we can get around the difficulty by increasing sales. If sales grow fast enough, the revenue coming in will eventually increase to the point where it can be used to make growth self-financing, right? Let's try it. We plug a 20 percent sales growth into the spreadsheet, instead of the 10 percent we previously assumed, and lo and behold—things get *worse!* The income statement (see Exhibit 7) indeed gets even better, but the cash-flow situation (see Exhibit 8) has become downright catastrophic.

The fact is, *high-growth businesses tend to have a tremendous appetite for cash.* Manufacturing companies are the worst offenders, but even service companies are not immune; any company that requires significant working capital will show this characteristic. The higher the growth, the heavier the appetite for cash. It is mature, stable businesses that throw off cash. This discovery comes as quite a shock to many entrepreneurs.

THE CRITICAL POINTS

The simplified example we've just worked through illustrates the importance, and value, of doing financial projections. Projections won't predict the future for you. What they will do is expose and analyze defects in your planning; that's what they're for. The invention of the spreadsheet computer program has made the development and testing of financial projections infinitely easier. In the old days, when we had to do it with paper and pencil, it was a hellish task to test the effect of a change in assumptions. Now it's just a matter of a few keystrokes.

Exhibit 7. Incandescent Fungoid Cutters, Inc.—projected income statement ($000) (growth rate = 20%).

	Jan	Feb	Mar	Apr	May	Jun	Jul	Aug	Sep	Oct	Nov	Dec
Sales	0	100	120	144	173	207	249	299	358	430	516	619
Cost of goods sold	0	60	72	86	104	124	149	179	215	258	310	372
Gross profit	0	40	48	58	69	83	100	119	143	172	206	248
Marketing expense	0	10	12	14	17	21	25	30	36	43	52	62
R&D expense	5	5	5	5	5	5	5	5	5	5	5	5
Depreciation	2	2	2	2	2	2	2	2	2	2	2	2
G&A expense	5	5	5	5	5	5	5	5	5	5	5	5
Total expense	12	22	24	26	29	33	37	42	48	55	64	74
Operating profit	−12	18	24	31	40	50	63	78	95	117	143	174
Other	4	3	2	1	1	0	0	−1	−2	−3	−4	−5
Net profit (pretax)	−8	21	26	32	41	51	62	77	94	114	139	168
Net profit (after tax)	−4	12	14	18	22	27	34	41	51	62	75	91

Exhibit 8. Incandescent Fungoid Cutters, Inc.—projected cash flow statement ($000) (growth rate = 20%).

	Jan	Feb	Mar	Apr	May	Jun	Jul	Aug	Sep	Oct	Nov	Dec
Cash at start	400	338	239	121	79	30	−29	−99	−183	−283	−402	−545
Sales revenue	0	0	0	100	120	144	173	207	249	299	358	430
Interest revenue	4	3	2	1	1	0	0	−1	−2	−3	−4	−5
Total revenue	4	3	2	101	121	144	173	206	247	296	354	425
Materials and labor	60	72	86	104	124	149	179	215	258	310	372	446
Other expense	10	20	22	24	27	31	35	40	46	53	62	72
Taxes	−4	10	12	15	19	23	29	35	43	53	64	77
Total outflow	66	102	121	143	170	203	243	290	347	415	497	595
Cash flow	−62	−98	−118	−42	−50	−59	−70	−84	−100	−119	−143	−171
Cash at end	338	239	121	79	30	−29	−99	−183	−283	−402	−545	−716

By experimenting with the effects of various assumptions on your financial projections, you can isolate the key factors in your business. Keep in mind that you as the CEO of a small business cannot keep track of everything. You are going to have to monitor and analyze the operation of your company using a very limited amount of information—far, far less than is used by the management of a big company. There are two reasons for this: First, to gather and organize information is costly—someone has to do it, and that someone must be paid for it. Second, even if you could get plentiful information, you will lack time to analyze all of it because you have too many other responsibilities. Harold Geneen could afford to spend almost his entire workday analyzing "the numbers" of ITT—you can't. This means that you must discover what the *key* numbers are—the truly critical factors that make the difference between success and failure—and watch them carefully. What are those key numbers in *your* business? You can find out by working with your financial projections.

In working with Vanguard Ventures, I set out once to finance a group of three retirement centers developed by a group in Alabama. The group sent us a set of financial projections indicating that it would require $1 million in equity funding to execute its marketing program and cover its working-capital needs. This assumed that it would take a year to fill up the units (to 95 percent, which is full occupancy in this business).

I looked at this assumption and felt extremely skeptical; I didn't think they could do it in a year. But did it matter—and if it did, how much did it matter? We put the numbers in our computer model and began to play various "what if" scenarios. What if it took a year and a half to fill up the units? Two years? Three? This is commonly referred to as "sensitivity analysis." You test how sensitive the results are to a particular kind of change in assumptions.

It turned out that the capital requirements changed dramatically, depending on the length of time required to get up to full occupancy. That number turned out to be the key factor for the business plan. If they didn't fill up within a year, $1 million wouldn't be nearly enough capital to see them through. We finally settled on $3.25 million.

HDS

Look again at the example of Incandescent Fungoid Cutters. Suppose we start up this company without doing projections. Around May or so, the rapid evaporation of our bank account is likely to result in some alarm. If we still do not analyze our financials, we may take the intuitive, obvious corrective action: Try to increase sales faster. But, as we've seen, if this strategy succeeds, it fails. Higher sales growth will actually make the cash-flow situation worse.

By financial analysis we learn that the critical factor is the length of the sales cycle. What's really killing us is putting out all that cash three months before we get paid for the product. Knowing this, we can start thinking about ways to take *effective* corrective action. Can we find a way to shorten the manufacturing process? Can we job out part or all of production? Can we get our suppliers to give us more generous credit terms? Above all, can we get our customers to pay us faster? Our attention is now focused on the factors that will really make a difference. There's no guarantee that we will find the answer, but at least we are asking the right question.

CHECKING YOUR WORK

Before you finish with your analysis you should generate one more spreadsheet to provide you with some additional information and serve as a means of checking your results. Build a balance sheet. This serves as a valuable check of your arithmetic; thanks to the miracle of double-entry bookkeeping, if you make a mistake in your calculations (or in your input to the computer) the balance sheet will not balance.

The balance sheet also gives you a picture of your future business from a different perspective, and this may help you to spot problem areas that are not obvious from the P&L or even the cash-flow projections.

Examine, for instance, the balance-sheet projection for Incandescent Fungoid Cutters, shown in Exhibit 9. The cash-flow projection told us that we had a problem; the balance-sheet projection gives us some very useful suggestions as to the nature and source of the problem. Examining the balance sheet, we of course observe the inexorable decline of cash; we also see the steady climb of receivables and inventory. With a little thought, we can see that the latter explains the former. (What we're doing here is in fact a primitive form of flow-of-funds analysis.)

AND DOUBLE-CHECKING

Consider what we've done so far: (1) identified the assumptions we have made about our start-up and its economics; (2) calculated the consequences of our assumptions; and (3) checked to make sure that our calculations were correctly done. This is all well and good, but we have one more task yet to accomplish: We should use our projections to test whether our assumptions are reasonable.

The technique we use is called "ratio analysis." The idea behind

Exhibit 9. Incandescent Fungoid Cutters, Inc.—projected balance sheet ($000) (growth rate = 10%).

	Jan	Feb	Mar	Apr	May	Jun	Jul	Aug	Sep	Oct	Nov	Dec
Cash	338	245	143	131	118	103	88	71	53	34	12	−11
Accounts receivable	0	100	210	231	254	280	307	338	372	409	450	495
Inventory	60	66	73	80	88	97	106	117	129	141	156	171
Fixed assets	100	100	100	100	100	100	100	100	100	100	100	100
less depreciation	−2	−4	−6	−8	−10	−12	−14	−16	−18	−20	−22	−24
Total assets	496	507	520	534	550	567	588	610	636	664	696	732
Common stock	500	500	500	500	500	500	500	500	500	500	500	500
Retained earnings	−4	7	20	34	50	67	88	110	136	164	196	232
Total liabilities	496	507	520	534	550	567	588	610	636	664	696	732

ratio analysis is that if there are a number of companies all engaged in the same line of business, and all are about the same size, their financial characteristics should be similar. Therefore, the ratios of various items in their financial statements should be similar.

What sort of ratios? Well, an obvious example is the ratio of profits to sales—"net margin." This ratio is razor-thin for some types of businesses, such as supermarkets, and very high for others. If you are proposing to open a supermarket and you project profits of 10 percent of sales, your investors are going to question it. You will have to explain why and how you are going to do so much better than everyone else in the industry. If you project a margin lower than the industry average, that too is likely to lower your credibility with investors.

There are literally dozens of ratios that can be calculated, some of them rather esoteric, some (like net margin) very fundamental indeed. Any sophisticated investor is going to look at your financial projections and do a few calculations to see how your ratios stack up against the averages for your industry. (These average or "standard" ratios are available from a book called *Annual Statement Studies*.) Then the investor is going to ask you to explain any discrepancies. So you'd better check out your ratios first.

Does this mean you should diddle your assumptions until the ratios come out right? Not necessarily. The important thing is that you must understand *why* your ratios deviate from the average. For instance, suppose your ratio of inventory to sales comes out much lower than the industry average. This is a signal to go back and look at your assumptions in that area. Have you been overoptimistic? Why is everybody else carrying so much inventory? Perhaps they know something about customer behavior you haven't yet grasped. On the other hand, perhaps you've developed a revolutionary new inventory-control system. That's good—just be ready to explain it to a skeptical investor.

CHECKLIST
Some Useful Financial Ratios

- ☐ Current assets/current liabilities ("current ratio")
- ☐ Cash + receivables/current liabilities ("acid-test ratio")
- ☐ Current liabilities/tangible net worth
- ☐ Net profit/net sales ("net margin")
- ☐ Net sales/working capital ("turnover of working capital")
- ☐ Net profits/tangible net worth ("return on investment")

☐ Accounts receivable/daily credit sales ("collection period" or "receivables age")
☐ Net sales/inventory ("inventory turnover")
☐ Total debt/tangible net worth ("debt-equity ratio")

SCENARIOS

At one time the fashion was to put three sets of projections into a business plan: worst-case, median, and optimistic. This went out of vogue, partly because in reality the scenarios turned out to be optimistic, very optimistic, and off-the-wall. Today the trend is to put in one good set of solid financials with some sort of factual base to them.

However, with the advent of computer spreadsheets, there's really no excuse for not testing the effect of variations in your assumptions. Investors inevitably are going to ask you "what if" questions, and it's a comforting feeling to have the answer in your pocket.

The traditional approach to scenarios works in terms of sales growth. These variations probe the effects of better- or worse-than-expected sales. Though such projections are certainly worth doing, they give you less than the complete story.

The point of checking out scenario projections is to be prepared for contingencies—to know what the effects would be if things don't work out exactly as planned. But the kinds of contingencies that tend to arise in real life are not the kinds that are normally assumed in business school calculations. "Sales growth equals 10 percent instead of 15 percent" just doesn't correspond to the way things happen in real businesses. Realistic contingencies tend to be sharp jerks, not a change in the growth rate of a smooth variable—and the variable in question is not always sales.

> A company with about half a dozen employees manufactured a gadget that monitored vending machines. Suddenly one day, PepsiCo called. Where would *your* company stand if a customer unexpectedly handed you a purchase order for a year's production, to be delivered immediately?

Our biggest customer—suddenly and without warning—disappeared. Letters were returned, phone calls got a recording saying that the phones had been removed, the principal could not be found. What would *your* options be if your sales were cut in half overnight?

REM

Here's one more thing you should take into account in your financial planning. In many industries. particulary electronics, the price of a newly introduced product tends to drop dramatically with time (think of calculators and personal computers). Start-ups frequently die because their financial projections assume that the price will remain steady.

CHECKLIST
Contingencies for Planning

- [ ] Sudden loss of a major customer
- [ ] Sudden acquisition of a major customer
- [ ] Serious QC problem in a major product
- [ ] Fire, earthquake, tornado, or the like destroys the plant (how's your business-interruption insurance?)
- [ ] Your product is found to be carcinogenic
- [ ] The raw material you use to make the product is found to be carcinogenic
- [ ] Government regulations change
- [ ] Tax law changes
- [ ] The area containing your facility is rezoned
- [ ] A key employee leaves suddenly—to join a competitor
- [ ] Interest rates double
- [ ] Inflation goes to double digits
- [ ] Supply of key raw materials from overseas is cut off by protectionists

THE REAL BOTTOM LINE

Financial projections are tedious, but they are *important*. They constitute the meat and potatoes of your business plan; investors are often "quants"—very interested in your numbers. What's more, financial projections are vital to your planning process. They give you the means to perform trial runs of your business. You can play the game on paper, without having to pay if you lose. Of course, this does not guarantee ultimate success, any more than playing the stock market on paper. When you're taking real risks with real money, it gets much harder to make the right decisions. But you can learn much about your business quickly and cheaply. Not everything; but the more you learn by poring over spreadsheets the less you have to learn later—when you must pay for your mistakes.

CAUTIONARY TALE
The Comeback Trail

This is a story of entrepreneurial reincarnation. A couple I'll call Mr. and Mrs. Stuart built over the years a very successful company in contract manufacturing of electronic components and computer assemblies in southern California. Their business was grossing around $50 million, and when a private investor offered them $20 million for it, they decided to cash out.

That may sound pretty good. However, businesses are seldom sold for cash on the barrelhead. Typically the buyer finances the purchase with a considerable amount of debt. This particular deal was done in the rococo period of the leveraged buyout era in the late 1980s. The buyer put up a sliver of equity and covered the rest of the $20 million with debt, almost entirely from the sellers. So the buyer, in effect, bought the company with the owners' own money, which was the sort of thing that frequently happened during that period.

The result was that the Stuarts got $200,000 for their company, which worked out to just one percent of the agreed-on price. What happened was that the buyer now owned a thriving company that no longer was so thriving, partly because it was carrying a big load of debt service from the buyout. It wasn't long before he took the logical next step and put the company into Chapter 11 bankruptcy. The idea of Chapter 11 is that a firm can keep operating while under court "protection" from its creditors. Stripped of euphemism, this particular buyer got to keep the company while stiffing the people who had financed his purchase of it, to wit, the Stuarts.

The Stuarts, who naturally felt a bit put upon, went to court. Unfortunately, their attorney had failed to write the necessary protections into the purchase contract, so this got them nothing but a lot of bills for legal fees. Finally they gave up and decided to start over. They went back into the same line of business under a new name.

They still had some money left, and their second venture got started on about $400,000 in equity. Most of that went for setup costs, leaving them with $100,000 in working capital. The Stuarts, being very experienced and successful in the business, did this start-up by the seat of their pants, not bothering with a business plan or financial projections.

The new company was extremely successful from the beginning. Short-run manufacturing is a tricky business. You're constantly shifting from product to product, dealing with new and unfamiliar items—not at all like stamp-it-out assembly-line manufacturing. The work is very labor-intensive and requires strong skills in handling people. So short-run manufacturing requires some very special management expertise. Not many U.S. companies are good at it (mostly it's done in the Far East). But the Stuarts are very good at it, and Mrs. Stuart is a genius at recruiting part-time people for low wages and keeping them not only productive but happy. These skills paid off just as they had before.

And that was the problem. The Stuarts had an outstanding reputation, and many loyal customers from their previous company came to them with orders. Within a few months the company was doing business at a rate of $8 million a year. Trouble was, that wimpy $100,000 in working capital couldn't support all those sales. Like any manufacturing company, they had to carry inventory—parts and labor that went into their products. And of course they had to carry receivables for their customers. So when the company reached a certain size, it simply choked and stalled out.

That's where I came in. They were referred to me by a venture capital firm they'd approached. I looked into raising equity capital. However, by this time the 1980s were over and money was not easy to find, at least on acceptable terms. This kind of company is not an ideal candidate for equity financing anyway. The business doesn't have enough sizzle to go public, so it's hard to offer investors a viable exit strategy.

Debt financing made more sense. What you like to do with this kind of company is set up a line of credit for financing accounts receivable. That way you can grow the financing sort of semi-automatically in line with the growth of sales. Of course you have to build up your equity base also to keep your debt-equity ratio from getting so high that the bank gets nervous. Even so, this requires far less equity investment than would be needed to finance all the receivables with equity, and much of it can come out of retained earnings.

So I started talks with a banker who had financed the Stuarts in their previous incarnation. He knew what they could do and had confidence in them. Unfortunately, they were so busy keeping the company alive one day at a time that they couldn't or wouldn't make time to meet with him. This is not as unreasonable as it sounds. Getting a significant line of credit from a bank is not like opening an account or putting a second mortgage on your house. It's not a matter of a one- or two-hour interview. It requires you to do some tedious work preparing and, in response to the bank's demands, revising financial statements and projections. You have to spend a lot of time in meetings to woo the lending officer, and then even more time in negotiations and filling out all the paperwork. I'm not saying it isn't worth it, but it can be difficult to find the time when your company is in crisis. Besides, I think the Stuarts still didn't really comprehend the problem; they seemed to think that if they could just push the product out the door a little faster they'd catch up and all would be well. Of course, the faster they grew, the worse things got.

In the end, the Stuarts' second venture failed. Did they quit? No, these are real entrepreneurs. They raised a bigger equity base, got some competent financial advisers, and started a third time.

At first glance, you might wonder how the Stuarts could get themselves into so much trouble so quickly. They had started a successful firm in the same line of business previously, and built it up to $50 million in sales. They were highly competent managers who knew the industry inside out. They were known quantities with a stellar track record and a superb reputation. They had customers breaking down their doors. What went wrong?

What went wrong was simply that they were too good. When they built their first company they started without all these advantages, and so it grew slowly over the years. Because it grew slowly, they never had much trouble financing its growth. The second time, on the other hand, they began with all those intangible but extremely valuable assets. It gave them a big head start and the company's growth rate was phenomenal. They had decades of industry experience; what they had no experience in was *running a high-growth company*.

Their big mistake was not running financial projections before they started. Would projections have predicted they were going to have sales at the rate of $8 million per year in Month 6? No. But projections would have told them how big they could get before running out of working capital. With this warning in hand, they could have gone out to line up financing before they got in trouble. Or they could have started out by seeking more favorable terms on their receivables. Or they could have taken other steps. A good set of financial projections would have shown them how the business they were starting had the potential to lead them into unfamiliar territory so that they could prepare themselves.

HDS

Eleven

MANAGEMENT SYSTEMS

A leader is best when people barely know he exists. Not so good when people obey and acclaim him. Worse when they despise him. But of a good leader, who talks little, when his work is done, his aim fulfilled, they will say: "We did it ourselves."

Lao-Tse, *Tao Te Ching*

A famous gangster, when invited to take that short walk from his cell to the electric chair, is said to have responded, "The thought is repugnant to me." Most entrepreneurs react in the same way to the idea of setting up management control systems. "After all, the reason I quit Monolithic Mushroom Machinery and started my own company was to get away from all that bureaucratic nonsense."

We hope to convince you that management control systems are not synonymous with bureaucracy. Their purpose is not to take up your time but to free up your time.

THE CLASSIC GROWTH MODEL

In the conventional wisdom, a new company starts out with essentially no management controls. The freewheeling entrepreneur manages by instinct, running the company out of his own head. As the company becomes larger and more complex, the founder can no longer run everything himself. In delegating tasks, he is forced to set up some control systems, since he cannot rely on his subordinates to make

228

decisions without guidance. Furthermore, the "family feeling" of the original tiny group dissipates with growth, and it now becomes necessary to police those who handle the money. Thus the growing company gradually accumulates rules, which grow into a rigid structure. Eventually the structure becomes an elaborate maze of red tape, and the company subsides into a safe but stultifying bureaucracy.

This model is depressingly accurate; most companies evolve exactly this way. The problem is that many theorists of business structure approve of this process, or think that it is natural and unavoidable even if not desirable. The traditional view is that it is impossible to run a small company with formal management controls—and that it is impossible to run a large company without a bureaucracy.

We'd like to suggest some ways in which you can make the routine functions of your company run themselves, freeing up your time for more challenging and interesting tasks. As a bonus, setting up effective control systems early can keep your company lean, efficient, and fast-moving even after it becomes large. A good control system unifies your company and supports your company culture. It focuses all your people, from top to bottom, on your objectives and encourages them to pull together to achieve common goals.

THE PURPOSE OF CONTROLS

Only a very small company can afford to be amorphous. To look like an amoeba is fine if you're microscopic in size, but if you're going to grow very large you need a skeleton. And, to continue the metaphor, to start out with a skeleton and let it grow along with you is a better strategy than to try to install it surgically in a shapeless blob that's grown too big to move.

As we pointed out in Chapter Three, employees will resist almost any major change in the rules. The older and bigger the company becomes, the stronger this resistance will be. You can establish controls any way you want at start-up; but if you wait, your people may evade them or even sabotage them. As Compaq cofounder John Gribi put it, "You have a clean slate, but you only get one shot at writing on it."*

We therefore recommend you set up a simple but effective management system right at start-up. As your company grows, gradually add more controls—but if you've done it right at the beginning, you'll

Fortune magazine, May 23, 1988, p. 32.

find that you'll never need to establish a bureaucracy. Red tape is characteristic not of planned systems but of those that "just grew."

Most management control systems, however, do "just grow." Consequently they are real junk. It is this sort of random mess that most of us are familiar with from experience and want to avoid in our own companies. A truly effective management control system should do the following things for you:

1. *Make operations conform to company objectives.* Obvious though this may seem, it is very difficult to put into practice. Often the hard part is defining company objectives. Of course good top-management teams clearly define and enforce these objectives—until they become too busy with operating responsibilities. Then the company's objectives gradually drift out of focus. How is this to be avoided?

Some theorists rely on exhortation: Top management, they say, should simply avoid being caught up in operating work and concentrate on strategy. However, few executives have the ability to hold themselves aloof in this way—and even if they could, should they? Others recommend that a separate strategic planning staff be set up. Nice work if you can get it, but not very practical for a small company.

There's no magic solution, but a few simple tricks can help a lot. For one thing, make your company's objectives *explicit;* if everyone knows where you're heading, you're more likely to stay on track. Get objective feedback; as we've previously advocated, a good board of directors can be invaluable. When you're mounting the latest alligator you killed as a trophy, they'll say, "Very nice. But tell me, how are you coming along on your swamp-draining project?"

2. *Motivate employees to accomplish company objectives.* Perhaps the major fallacy of the bureaucratic mentality is the belief that people do things simply because they are ordered to. Human beings just do not behave that way. People don't do what you tell them to do, they do what you motivate them to do. In most companies, these are not the same thing. In order for your management control system to work effectively, you must set things up so that your people are rewarded for doing what needs to be done, and punished for doing things that hinder achieving the company's goals.

Anyone who's worked for a large company has probably seen the classic example of poorly designed controls: end-of-year budget bulge. A department is given a certain budget for the year. If an unexpected contingency comes up and the budget is exceeded, the department manager will be punished. So she "pads" her budget to establish a protective reserve. But then if no emergency comes up, she'll have excess funds at the end of the fiscal year, which will result in a big cut in her budget for the next period. So just before the end of the year, she spends money like mad on anything remotely justifiable, in order to make the numbers come out right.

All this is very bad for the company. Valuable capital is tied up unnecessarily, then spent wastefully. Even worse, the department manager and her subordinates become cynical and resentful. Worse yet, they have learned that they must lie to get along in the system, a lesson they may apply when faced with other ethical dilemmas.

Note that all this results from the contradiction between what the company says and what it does. Managers who run their operations efficiently and cut costs, as they were told to do, get punished by having their budgets cut. Managers who inflate their costs and corrupt the system are rewarded.

3. *Run without continual attention.* All the procedures involved should be as simple as possible and designed to be self-enforcing. A system that requires constant top-management attention to make it work is a bad system. Not only does it waste the valuable time of executives, but its obtrusiveness irritates their subordinates and damages morale. What's more, when every routine decision depends on the boss's personal judgment, instead of explicit rules, employees soon begin to whisper about favoritism.

A well-designed system is, as they say in the computer business, "transparent to the user." You hardly notice the working of the system until an "error message" appears to demand top-management intervention. Such a system lets your top people devote their time to their real work, and their subordinates are guided almost without feeling the reins.

STRUCTURING YOUR MANAGEMENT CONTROL SYSTEM

Let's get down to specifics. A management control system is nothing more than a set of rules and procedures. It doesn't need to be fancy or complex; it does need to be logically structured and consistently followed.

Here is what you need. *First,* there must be procedures for setting company goals. No doubt you will set goals at the start-up, but you need an ongoing procedure to redefine your goals as the company grows and the market situation changes. *Second,* there must be provision for assigning the company's people the necessary tasks and objectives to accomplish the company's goals. *Third,* there must be a structure of rewards and punishments so that employees are motivated to accomplish their tasks and do them well. *Fourth,* there must be a reporting structure to provide information on the company's operations so that top management can monitor progress. *Fifth,* there must be some sort of enforcement to ensure that all this actually gets done.

Goal Setting.   We already discussed in Chapter Two the necessity of setting objectives for your company. Presumably, you have by now developed a set of goals for your start-up. But you must recognize that your company's objectives will inevitably change with time. Your company, your market, and the society in which you are embedded are all going to evolve over the years, and your original objectives will become at least partly obsolete. You must realize that (assuming you have not already started your company) you are in an unusually favorable position. You have the opportunity to think about your company's objectives and set them at leisure, undistracted by operating responsibilities. Once you are actually in business, it won't be so easy. There always seems to be some task more urgent than thinking out new objectives.

It seems almost impossible to convey to someone who hasn't yet been there how *distracting* it is to be an entrepreneur. A few months after I had started Reaction Design, the evidence began coming in that we were completely off the track. It was critical to rethink our entire approach and make major changes in our objectives and operations. Why couldn't I see this? Was I just stupid? Not really. There was just too much going on—too many important decisions to make, too many urgent problems to solve.

The last batch of naphthylalanine has hung up; what is poisoning the catalyst? That big check we've been waiting for has arrived—and bounced; how am I going to meet payroll next week? Aldrich is considering distributing some of our products, but wants them at a devastating discount; if we accept, will it make us—or break us? The HPLC is down, and that order *has* to ship next week . . . the last lot had only 96 percent purity—if we recrystallize, we'll lose at least a fifth of it and we'll have to run another batch to make up the order. . . . Martin wants a quote on grandlure right away. . . .

Believe me, it's not as easy as it seems to maintain an objective view of your business and revise your strategy as needed. I remember a scene from an old Western in which a cowboy is tied to a horse's tail and the horse ridden off

at a fast trot. The victim would run like mad for a few yards, then fall and be dragged along, then get back on his feet briefly. . . . That's what it's like being an entrepreneur.

REM

This is why you need a *system* for continued goal setting. Almost all big companies, and many small ones, pretend to have such a system—five-year plans, annual "strategy sessions," and so on. In reality, such procedures rapidly degrade into ratification of the previous course with only cosmetic changes. Most company "strategies" or "objectives" or "goals" or "principles" are actually nothing of the sort; they are merely words in the annual statement or the personnel manual. Top management may sincerely believe in them, but even if they do no action is taken to implement them, because they are detached from the management structure.

Begin by setting specific, measurable goals. A goal is of use only if you can determine whether or not you've met it! This doesn't necessarily mean that all objectives have to be numerical in form. But for every objective you set, develop a measurement of success.

Be wary of "long-term" goals, a hangover from the heyday of "strategic planning" in the 1950s. In our turbulent world, the market changes rapidly and sometimes radically. You can be selling military widgets to the Pentagon at the height of the Cold War, and five years later be negotiating a contract to convert a Russian missile factory to produce washing machines.

So you shouldn't plan? On the contrary, you must plan. But separate long-range planning from short-range. The short range is one to three years, a good planning cycle for a small business. Here is where you make objectives that have to do with external conditions, especially sales objectives. For long-range planning—three to seven years, say—focus on *internal* objectives, like strengthening your technological abilities.

Setting Your Standards. Once you have set goals, you must then translate them into standards in order to make them effective. For example, suppose you have set the goal: "We will manufacture the highest-quality widget in the industry." That's nice, but what do you mean by "quality"? Even more to the point, what do your customers mean by "quality"? You need to set some specific standard by which you are going to judge quality. For instance, "The MTBF [mean time before failure] for our widget will be longer than for any competitive offering." This assumes, of course, that MTBF is what your customers care about. You may want to use direct measures of customer satisfaction: "We will have fewer than 0.2 percent returns and fewer than 0.5 percent complaints."

All sorts of goals can be turned into objective, measurable standards. Sales: "$1 million next year." Profits: "20 percent before-tax ROI." Technological leadership: "50 percent of sales from products under three years old." Workplace quality: "Less than 5 percent annual turnover in personnel." Service: "No customer will wait in line more than ninety seconds." If it's a real objective, you will always be able to transform it into a standard against which you can evaluate your results. If you can't, maybe it's not an objective; maybe it's just a dream.

When you set standards for your company, don't get too entranced by the big, global targets. The standards that often make the crucial difference can be little, everyday things.

> A standard that has been critical to the success of McDonald's, and several other fast-food chains, is how long a hamburger is allowed to sit unsold in the rack: 15 minutes, then it goes to the pigs.
>
> Disneyland has standards for all the details, from sweeping the streets (a task made easier by the simple standard that no gum will be sold in the park) to how many times a day the restrooms must be cleaned (more often for the Ladies' than for the Gentlemen's, it turns out).

It's the little things that build your company culture. These everyday standards—"this is the way we do things around here"—set the tone for your company. Especially in today's economy, it pays to distinguish your company as one that has high standards of quality, of service, of ethics. If your management system emphasizes attention to those important details—cleanliness, courtesy, exactness—the company culture will be molded accordingly.

The result will be a class company. The effect on customers (and financiers) will definitely pay off. And you may be surprised how even seemingly unpromising employees will respond. As they begin to visualize themselves as members, however humble, of an elite organization, they'll find themselves exceeding their own expectations, let alone yours. Like graduates of a tough military training course, they develop a pride and an esprit de corps that give your company a base on which to build for the big goals.

Japanese department stores do not have autom
tors. The elevator operators are generally hired
of high school. Before they even begin to lear
operate an elevator, they get two weeks of trainn
must learn all about the store's history and culture, where
all the various departments are, how the merchandise is
processed, how to wear their uniforms, and many other
things. In this way they are indoctrinated into the store's
standards of courtesy and service, and equipped to handle, say, a customer's inquiries about where to find the
camera department. But more significant, they, and all
their colleagues at the store (who go through equally
rigorous training), absorb the lesson that they are working for a first-rate company and that their jobs are *important*.

Using Motivators. Now we come to the key part. No goal
however noble, no standard however ambitious, is of any use at all
unless your system is set up to *motivate* your people to meet the
standard and accomplish the goal. Your most difficult, and most
rewarding, task is to build a process that will tie rewards and punishments to your company's basic objectives.

As we pointed out previously, you must be very careful to ensure
that your system is motivating people to do what you really want them
to do. For the horrifying truth is that most of the time people *will* do
what you reward them for doing. Better be very exact in how you
disburse your rewards.

Take for example the common system under which every worker
gets a $100 bonus if the plant goes, say, three months without a lost-
time accident. It seems like a good way to promote safety, but if you
don't watch out you'll find that workers will try to cover up accidents
when they occur. Injured employees may be pressured by their colleagues to conceal their condition and keep working. Commonly management tries to prevent this snitching of the carrot by wielding the
stick, with threats of draconian penalties for hiding accidents. Of
course this requires a system of surveillance and enforcement, and
complications multiply.

This illustrates a common pitfall of motivational systems. You
may think you're paying people not to have accidents, but actually
you're paying them not to report accidents. Whenever you motivate
your employees on the basis of some measurement or indicator,
consider whether they might fudge the indicator.

It's also crucial to set the *right* standards for motivation.

When I worked as a salesman for Alcan, each district sales office was judged on the basis of how many sales calls were made, as measured by the number of "call reports." But sales statistics showed that the best sales figures came from districts that produced the *lowest* number of call reports. Taking time to close the sale produced much better results than rushing off to try to maximize the number of sales calls.

HDS

And remember that employees may be more motivated by their boss's attitudes than by formal rules—or even laws and regulations.

In a pharmaceutical manufacturing operation, the production manager was to a great extent evaluated on the consistency of results. When a batch came out with a bad yield, top management got very upset. When another had a very good yield, they expected every subsequent batch to excel also and became unsatisfied with average results. Unfortunately, the complex process had a large inherent variation in yield from batch to batch. So the manager secretly hoarded product from good batches to make up deficiencies in bad ones. Of course all the records had to be falsified to cover up this manipulation. This sort of thing is frowned upon by the FDA.

So how do you design motivation-control systems that work? Here are some principles developed over the years by managers, military leaders, and Montessori teachers.

1. Tie motivators to results of real value to the company, not arbitrary numbers.
2. Reward or punish employees only for results that are within their control.
3. Provide immediate feedback; reward or punish promptly after the behavior occurs.
4. Reward or punish on the basis of measurements that are objective and hard to falsify.
5. Try to make the job rewarding in itself.

Once you decide what behavior you want to reward, how do you reward it? You have three major classes of reward you can use to motivate your employees: money, status, and recognition.

Money. *Money* is a simple and objective reward, relatively easy to handle. At the beginning of each year, when you set objectives and define standards, develop a bonus schedule for each of your employees. Decide (in consultation with the person in question, if at all possible) what the employee's contribution to the company should be during the coming year; set up a compensation schedule of the type we discussed in Chapter Three. This is the backbone of your motivation system. Remember, though you set these goals at the beginning of the year, don't wait till the end of the year to pay the bonuses—pay them immediately upon accomplishment of the tasks.

Note how this approach ties in your management system and makes it effective; if you've selected the right goals and standards, you will be paying people to do what needs to be done, rather than just show up for work. The promise of a bonus check, like the threat of being hanged, concentrates the mind wonderfully. Your people will definitely belive that you are serious about achieving the objectives set because your financial commitment is very convincing. What's more, the fact that you have this system in place forces you to set objectives and standards, and applies a powerful reality check on them too; if they aren't realistic, some people will get absurd bonuses.

Status. *Status* is another powerful motivating factor. As Napoleon remarked, men who would take very little risk for money will get themselves killed for a bit of colored ribbon. If you wish to build a growth company, attracting, keeping, and above all developing good people are crucial. The best people are driven more by the desire for responsibility and authority than by greed for money.

If you promote haphazardly, your personnel development will be randomized. Promotion policies should be built into your management system. You should decide what talents your company needs, and will need in the future, and offer promotion to your employees in return for developing those talents.

Recognition. All of us know that *recognition* is a powerful motivator, but almost all of us use praise on an occasional and random basis rather than systematically. Cold-blooded though it may sound, recognition can be made a regular, controlled part of your motivational management system.

One of the major factors in the early rise of IBM was Thomas Watson Sr.'s shrewd use of systematic recognition, particularly for salespeople. The Hundred Percent Club, the Golden Circle, awards banquets—all were put on a standardized, formal basis. The company *made sure* that the employee who performed was rewarded with recognition by making it policy.

So much for rewards; what about punishments? The conventional wisdom says that the carrot works better than the stick; and the conventional wisdom, for once, is quite correct. Demerit systems and similar weapons from the arsenal of punitive measures will not enhance relations with your employees.

Negative motivators should be, ideally, simply the consequences of the action in question. If an employee makes a mistake, she cleans up the mess herself—whether it's mopping up cookie batter from the floor or apologizing to an angry customer. One who consistently fails to perform will be transferred, or if necessary demoted, to a job commensurate with his demonstrated ability or lack thereof. An employee who does not come up to the company's ethical standards will be given a pink slip and a letter of recommendation to Malignant Enterprises, where she will feel more at home. One who violates the law will be personally escorted by the CEO to the reception area for his meeting with the sheriff.

You should punish reluctantly but systematically. Especially in the current litigious environment, you must be very careful to base disciplinary action on predefined rules, consistently applied.

Effective motivators don't have to be in-your-face obvious. My favorite example of a subtle and highly effective motivator is the mall store that was losing business because it had become popular as a hang-out for some not-very-nice teenagers. Attempts to get security to move them along had resulted in some unpleasant confrontations. Solution: Play classical music on the store's sound system. The loiterers evaporated immediately.

REM

Establishing a Reporting Structure. The fourth element of your management control system is a reporting structure. You must have some sort of feedback mechanism to let you know how you are doing and whether your people are performing. One nice thing about setting up a motivating payments system is that it automatically requires you to develop a reporting structure so that you will know how to distribute the rewards.

You won't want to burden your company with a complex edifice of reports. Ask yourself: What is the minimum amount of information I need to control the company? What are the key numbers that define the really important information? What do I need to know today? What do I need to know on a monthly basis? What do I need to know for an annual review of results?

CHECKLIST
Some Useful Indicators

☐ Cash flow. You should have this report at least weekly.

☐ Accounts receivable. Demand frequent reports, broken down by age, with particular attention to overdue accounts.

☐ Inquiries. If you want to know what sales will be in the future, look at how many inquiries you're getting now. If inquiries drop off, better jump on the sales and marketing people at once.

☐ Conversion ratio. Divide purchase orders by inquiries to get this number. If it starts to drop, ask your VP Sales why sales aren't being closed as effectively.

☐ Backlog. If you have too many unfilled orders, you are probably developing some irritated customers.

☐ Sales cycle. Break it down into sales time, turnaround time (required to fill the order), and receivables age (already discussed). These numbers will give you indications of selling or manufacturing problems.

☐ Sales per employee. This is a key ratio for tracking productivity. For retailers, sales per square foot of selling space should be tracked and compared to industry standards.

☐ Project slippage. If you're in a high-tech business, better monitor progress on key R&D or engineering projects at least monthly; weekly is better.

You'll find that your accountant can be your best assistant—or your biggest obstacle—in setting up an effective reporting structure. The accounting system for your company is its basic information-gathering mechanism, and if structured properly it can be used to carry not only the standard financial information but most of the other information you need.

For a very tiny company, it proved quite satisfactory to handle the entire accounting system by hand, using the traditional handwritten journals and ledgers. I set up the bookkeeping so that the original records contained extra information. For instance, the sales journal contained, in addition to the normal entries, the customer's purchase order number, our invoice number, and notations of all actions related to the transaction. This centralized the information and made it very convenient to deal with inquiries or overdue receivables.

REM

The whole science of accounting consists of the development of reporting structures and methods of analyzing the data they produce, so your accountant will be very pleased to be invited to perform this task for your company. However, you will have to work with her actively to get the system you need.

Accountants are expected to organize systems with the aim of preventing (or at least exposing) any hanky-panky in the books of the client company. To facilitate this objective, strict rules are set down with inhibit innovation. (Note that "creative accounting" is a synonym for suspicious, if not criminal, reporting.) As a result, small companies and innovative companies often find that the rules obstruct development of an accurate model of the business. Of course one can't blame the accountants alone for this; IRS and FASB (Financial Accounting Standards Board) regulations mandate a great many ridiculous procedures.

Laziness is also a factor. Many accountants rely heavily on "canned" computer programs to generate financial statements. They hand you a chart of accounts, tell you how to make entries, then just feed the data in and print out the reports. Unfortunately, such standardized programs generally assume that you have a "typical" business; often the software can't be adapted to your company's idiosyncracies, or if it can the accountant doesn't want to take the trouble to make it adapt.

Your monthly financial statements will generally come out nicely organized in the format specified by the IRS, so that the numbers can be conveniently transferred to your tax returns. Unfortunately, this format carries very little of the information that's really important to you in running your business, so you'll have to insist on customized reports.

Finally, many accountants suffer from a chronic inability to understand that there is a cost associated with gathering information, and that management would prefer receiving only an approximate account of the source of its profit to getting the exact information at such cost as to result in a loss.

We tend to neglect the details of the accounting system when we start a business; though necessary it seems a dry and rather unimportant task. It can, however, be critical; and you would do well to give it your full attention. Sit down with your accountant for a couple of days and thrash it out thoroughly. Also, budget time for revisions during the first year; you'll find you need a considerable shakedown period before the system operates efficiently.

What should you aim at? You will of course want the traditional three statements every month: income statement ("P&L"), balance sheet, and cash flow statement ("Sources and Use of Cash"). But instead of, or in addition to, the IRS-oriented format, ask for statements broken down to give you a clearer picture of operations. You should also get a supplementary statement, on at least a monthly basis, that provides key parameters for your business, such as those we've listed above. Just what items to include depends on your business.

Keeping 'Em Honest. It is our experience that, contrary to their usual image, entrepreneurs are too trusting of their employees, too forgiving of those who fail that trust. Often an honest person, on being cheated, is reluctant to make a fuss. But this toleration sets a bad example, encourages further offenses—and may even be misinterpreted as complicity by onlookers who do not know all the facts. One need not pursue a vendetta against dishonest associates, but it is wise to make one's position clear even if one chooses to turn the other cheek.

A good management control system should embody enforcement mechanisms to ensure that the rules you've so carefully designed really are obeyed. Double-entry bookkeeping contains, as an integral part of its design, safeguards that make it difficult, complicated, and perilous to falsify records. The use of regular, or better yet irregular, audits augments these controls substantially. But people's ingenuity can find a way around even the best of bureaucratic controls.

Your motivational reward system is a source of temptation, but also a means of control. You will obviously need to take precautions to ensure that those whose rewards depend on a certain indicator are not in a position to manipulate its readings. Fortunately, it is frequently the case that attempts to inflate one indicator depress others, and those whose bonuses would thereby be decreased will act as your police force to prevent such fraud.

Enforcement, like the other functions of your control system, functions only if people are motivated to make it work. When your company is very small, you can be the sheriff and keep an eye on everything. As it grows, the day will come when you have to rely on your people to let you know when there is a problem. If you drift into the natural policy of shooting the messenger who brings bad news, your people will get the message and give you the well-known mushroom treatment. So it's better to make it clear that your attitude is: "Whatever I do to you if you tell me about the mess you made, I'll do it to you twice as bad if you try to hide it." You should state officially that concealing trouble from top management is an unforgivable sin— then act accordingly.

This allows you to use the "problem flag" as a valuable method of saving management time. Simply define the key factors in your operations and "flag" exceptions. For instance, your production people might be instructed: "Notify me at once if the yield on step 4 drops below 90 percent." This might be a long-term, permanent flag; one can also set up temporary flags: "Notify me at once if the big order for IBM falls behind schedule." It's important to understand that flag conditions should never be defined as a disaster—presumably you'll find out anyway if something really catastrophic happens. The good flag condition is the small cloud no bigger than a man's hand that presages disaster in advance; that way you get told in time to take effective action.

The key to making a flag system operate is twofold. First, make it clear that you mean it and that heads will roll if a flag doesn't go up when it should. Second, once you've got it set up, forget about it until a flag does go up. The whole point of this system is to free up your time. If you constantly look over your people's shoulders to make sure they're keeping you posted, they won't take the system seriously. Make it clear that you're relying on them and they'll generally live up to it.

These are a few ways in which you can enforce your policies. But ultimately there is no substitute for a company culture that is based on strict honesty. Employees who are encouraged, or even just permitted, to enhance their company's profits by sharp practice with customers will invariably feel free to cheat their employer if they think they can get away with it.

COMPUTERIZATION

It used to be that no company would consider computerizing until it could afford to buy a mainframe and hire a data-processing department. With the advent of the cheap microcomputer, it seems only a matter of time until your daughter's lemonade stand does its accounting by computer. We're not computer gurus and can't give you specific hardware recommendations, but we do have some principles you can apply from a management point of view.

First, when it comes to computerization, *do it early*. There is a tremendous amount of hassle, inconvenience, and confusion associated with putting your company's procedures on the computer. The larger and more complicated your management and accounting systems, the longer it will take and the more it will cost to adapt them to the computer. Now that personal computers are so cheap, even very frugal start-ups can afford to own one from day one. If you're already a sizable company and haven't computerized, do it today before you get any larger.

The president of a very successful mail-order operation once confided to me that computerization had given him some scary moments. His company developed an integrated system that combined sales and order entry with automatic inventory control. It proved immensely valuable once it was running. However, the cost of setting it up vastly exceeded estimates. Much worse, the firm experienced devastating foul-ups during the transition period, when neither the manual nor the computer systems were working properly.

REM

Another good reason to computerize early is that all your written data will at some point have to be put into the computer. Somebody has to sit down at the keyboard and type in all those records. The older your company is, and the bigger, the more time it will take.

Start today—but once started, don't rush. If you have any but the simplest of systems, *practice on paper first*. If there is a "canned" commercial program available that will do what you want, great. Test it out carefully, then put it into use. But anything that requires customized software will be difficult and expensive to debug, and even more of a hassle to revise. So work out your system by hand first and implement it with old-fashioned paper forms. Run it a few months to see how it works, and fix problems as they arise. Then have whoever is doing your programming simply translate the system as is to the computer. That way you know the system is good, and all you have to debug is the software itself. Also, your programming costs will be dramatically lowered.

If you expect your company to grow, better *allow for expansion*. Switching from one type of computer system to another is almost as difficult as switching from manual to computer. If you're going to buy a microcomputer, plan for when you buy two or three more; how you will eventually tie them together into a network; and beyond that, how you might make the transition to a minicomputer. Standards and compatibility matter. This applies not just to hardware but, even more, to software. That el cheapo desktop publishing program may look attractive now, but when your customers force you to upgrade and your files can't be translated, you may be in for some pain.

Finally, *put it all on the machine*. You will anyway, in the long run. The great value of the computer is its ability to quickly find, collate, and analyze information. So try to get as much of your information as possible off of paper and onto disk. Integrate systems as much as possible—for instance, tie your inventory records into the accounting system directly.

CAUTIONARY TALE
Sunken Timbers

Some years ago I became involved with a company called Inter-Allied Resources. This was a small public corporation, but the securities didn't trade. It was what is referred to as a nonreporting public company, with a couple of hundred shareholders and one operating subsidiary.

To understand why this business was interesting, you need to realize that for a company to go public is a very difficult and expensive proposition. For most young companies it is possible only during exceptionally good bull markets, and the SEC requirements and other regulatory hassles make going public a very complicated process. But being public has some very substantial advantages, particularly in the ability to raise capital by selling stock. So just being a public company is an asset with a tangible value, and even if the company has no other assets and no ongoing business, it may be kept in existence as a "public shell" that can usefully be merged with a real, operating company. You can see ads for these shells in *The Wall Street Journal* sometimes.

My partners, who were active in another business but were very deal-oriented people, saw this as an opportunity to pick up a public shell, turn around its operating subsidiary, refinance it, and then enter or acquire other businesses. If a history of success could be established, a larger public offering could take place further down the road.

The operating subsidiary was a distributor of industrial fasteners—nuts and bolts, in other words. It bought fasteners in Japan and other parts of the Far East and sold them to manufacturers up and down the East Coast through direct solicitation, telephone salesmen, and a string of reps. It wasn't doing too well. I took over the operation as CEO and went to work on turning it around.

We had a sixth-floor walk-up loft in a building on Leonard Street in Lower Manhattan, where we paid some modest rent to the previous owner of the company. The personnel had a rather vague idea of where the products were. There were thousands and thousands of nuts and bolts of many sizes and head shapes and threads and so on. But there was no clear inventory-control system, so the place was a real mess. The first thing I did was to bring in a major accounting firm to set up a control system. It was a manual system, but even without a computer, within six months we had a handle on the system. We now knew what our inventory was, what we had, what we needed to buy, and—very important—how long it took to buy. When you order heavy metal from the Far East, it comes on a slow boat from China, so you must plan on a four- or five-month delivery cycle. To run this new system, we hired a person who had worked with Abraham & Straus as a systems control manager, and we really got the nuts-and-bolts company running like a well-oiled clock.

My partners and I went out and got some long-term contracts from major industrial concerns for some new products. We brought the products in; there were significant margins; and we began to really make money. Within a year we were doing $4 million or $5 million in sales. The Chase Manhattan Bank was the company's major lender; it had been very nervous before we came in and now was very pleased because we had developed a substantial net worth. They increased our line of credit. We had a going business; we were meeting our debt service; and there was general satisfaction all around. I'm happy to say that I was blamed for all this success, although, needless to say, a lot of other people played important roles.

By this time we felt ready and mature enough to go into another business. There was inadequate room for expansion in fasteners. We had demonstrated our ability to function well in a trading business, so we wanted to set up another distributor of some sort. I looked throughout the economy and came up with the idea of becoming a distributor of railroad ties and other forest products—grade lumber, specialty logs, and so on. My partners were active in the railroad industry, so this seemed like a logical approach. At that time the larger American railroads were upgrading their roadbeds—which hadn't been done in a major way since the Korean War—so it looked like an opportune time to enter the business.

The concept was this. There were a number of small sawmills in the concentrated hardwoods area of the Southeast—Tennessee, Kentucky, and Alabama mostly—that needed help with distribution. They were too small to generate enough wood to justify the cost of direct marketing. So we planned to establish so-called concentration yards at various key points. We would buy from the small mills, and sell in quantity—ties to the railroads, grade lumber to furniture manufacturers, high-quality logs to German interests who made veneer out of them.

We started out by getting a very substantial order from the Chessie System for railroad ties, and that was the backbone of the whole operation. Against that order, the Chase lent us a significant amount of money. We got another order from Burlington Northern, we ran the financing up to a couple of million dollars, and we started buying railroad ties as if they were going out of style.

I was flushed with my recent success in fasteners, the board of directors was totally supportive, the banks were enthusiastic—and somehow I became more interested in building volume than in the quality of the results. Of course, I fully intended to put in management controls. But I had no idea of the various quality differences of railroad ties or lumber. I didn't understand the lumber business, and I failed to hire people who could make up for my deficiencies in this area.

The disaster really began when we decided we could get an edge on the competition by going around to the small mills, buying ties on the spot, and paying cash. As a means of maximizing the flow of lumber into our concentration yards, this was a truly brilliant innovation. Every mill operator in the Southeast was tripping over his own feet in his haste to get to us before we changed our minds. But from the point of view of financial controls, we were calling in artillery strikes on our own position. Our agents, of course, were equipped with checkbooks to make these payments, and we didn't know how much they'd spent till they got back from a trip and turned in the stubs. It was like the problems of a husband-wife joint checking account but a thousand times worse. We never knew how much we had in the bank and our accountants were going bonkers.

All this while we were accumulating a *lot* of railroad ties. Now our agents, in going around to the various mills, were buying stacks of ties. They could see what the ties looked like on the outside, but the quality of the ties in the interior of the stack was anybody's guess until we sent them to the railroads and they got inspected. The idea was that this was no problem because our agents knew the various mills and their reputations and would buy only from people who could be trusted. But could our agents be trusted? We had no *system* to monitor the people and enforce the rules, so things tended to follow the line of least resistance.

Pretty soon we had $2 million worth of railroad ties—or rather, ties for which we had paid $2 million, in cash. Chessie and Burlington then inspected them and let us know what they actually were worth, and—surprise—it turned out to be quite a bit less than $2 million. As the quality reports came in, I suddenly realized that water was pouring over the gunwales. In just five months we had gone from success story to disaster.

I scrambled to keep us from sinking. The first priority was to plug the leak; I instantly stopped the purchasing program. Then I located a fellow who had run a huge concentration yard for ITT's forest-products subsidiary and who really did know the business. He straightened things out quickly, changing the operation so that ties were delivered to our yards, where they were inspected by qualified people, using a monstrous moving table.

Unfortunately, I had caught on too late. We had shipped too much water, and even the buoyancy of the nuts and bolts couldn't keep us afloat. Some of the people who a few months before had been chanting, "There is no god but Mammon and Sedgwick is his Prophet," now looked upon me, shall we say, somewhat less favorably. I stepped aside as CEO, though I remained on the board.

There was nothing for it but to take our bath, so we liquidated the company. However, we maintained the public shell. A few years later we merged it into a successful West Coast company that supplies plastic parts to high-tech companies in Silicon Valley. We as investors were of course heavily diluted in this operation, but the stock is up, and if the company continues to do well we may yet get our heads above water.

Not one of my greatest accomplishments. The nuts-and-bolts operation succeeded because it was right under my eye and I made sure that management control systems were operating. But when we went into lumber, the operation was spread out over half the country. I couldn't personally watch over it, so it was crucial to set up a *system* to monitor our employees and our suppliers. We needed rules to control our disbursements, rewards to ensure the rules were followed, and reports so we'd immediately know what was happening. Failure to properly attend to these boring details was sufficient to destroy a thriving business in a matter of months.

HDS

Twelve

THE BUSINESS PLAN

The planning is more important than the plan.

General Dwight D. Eisenhower

You've come a long way, Baby. We can remember the days when entrepreneurs used to ask, "Uh, what's a business plan?" Today, just about everyone knows what a business plan is, and intends to write one. The business plan has become a universal element of entrepreneurship.

One of my hobbies is watching Japanese soap operas on a Los Angeles TV channel. The plot of one show concerned a woman who divorced her abusive husband and, to support herself, started a telephone message service. As she went through the start-up process, I found the scenes amazingly familiar. Our Japanese heroine went through all the typical stages: getting advice from experienced entrepreneurs, finding partners, scrounging around for capital— and writing a business plan. Even in Japan, where customs are frequently so different from ours as to seem more extraterrestrial than simply foreign, start-ups are based on business plans.

REM

What can we say about business plans that's fresh? The shelves groan under guides to writing business plans, many of them quite good. If you don't want to pay for one, just walk into a Big Six accounting firm's local office and they'll probably give you one free. There are audiotape courses, and videotapes, and even computer programs that will do a lot of the work for you.

So instead of providing you with YABPO (yet another business plan outline), we'd like to talk about the realities of building and using

247

a business plan. With our chapter epigraph as a starting point, we'd like to emphasize that the planning is much more important than the writing and should be your primary concern. Let's begin by absorbing some lessons from a couple of other generals.

ROMMEL VS. MONTGOMERY

Planning, like many other human activities, comes in styles. We call it the Rommel vs. Montgomery alternative, after the two famous World War II desert generals.

Rommel was a brillant improvisor. Whenever he thought he might catch the enemy off balance he would start an attack and see what happened. Relying on surprise, rapidly shifting troops wherever he found a weak point, Rommel simply started mixing it up and seized any opportunity he could find.

Montgomery, on the other hand, insisted on careful preparation. Resisting pressure from his superiors for quick action, he slowly accumulated his forces and meticulously trained his men. Not until he had all his ducks—or rather tanks—in a row would he go on the offensive.

We see these same contrasting styles among entrepreneurs. Some are like Rommel: They aim to get into the market early; to start selling something fast. Once they're in business, they adapt themselves to circumstances, refining their product on the fly in response to market feedback, raising money as they go.

Others resemble Montgomery. They take their time, work hard on preliminary studies, write a thorough business plan, and raise all the capital they need before they make their first move.

Which is the right way? Either. It's really a matter of style. Rommel was by no means averse to planning; he simply was so expert that he could develop a plan quickly in his head and modify it on the spot if conditions changed. He had a clear and simple objective—the Suez Canal—which he never lost sight of. On the other hand, Montgomery was by no means a paper-pushing strategic planner. He had a keen appreciation of the importance of intelligence and understood the vital necessity of taking into account the realities, not just the theory, of desert combat.

You'll have to decide for yourself which style better fits your personality. But we do have a couple of recommendations. If you're new to the business world, or if you're entering an unfamiliar industry, you might do well to lean toward the Montgomery style. On the other hand, in really fast-moving growth industries there's a lot to be said for adopting the Rommel approach. If you're getting heavy financial backing for a major venture, the Montgomery style will probably be mandatory; the investors will insist on it. Again, if you aren't quite sure of your business idea, try doing a small shoestring start-up and experiment in the style of Rommel.

In this post–Cold War era we are probably pushing our luck, but bear with us for one more military analogy. In warfare, as in business, a commander must often make a plan quickly to deal with a constantly changing challenge. To facilitate this on-the-fly planning, leaders are taught to use a standard format, such as the U.S. Army's "five-paragraph field order." It's simple and fast, loose enough to allow for flexibility, and structured enough to ensure that key elements don't get overlooked.

Using this same method, an experienced entrepreneur can slap together a quick preliminary business plan in a couple of days. You can learn to do the same thing. It's a useful skill. Writing a full-up, industrial-strength business plan can take months of full-time work. Often you need to cobble together something quickly to show to a seed-money investor or a prospective cofounder. Following start-up, you might find you need to change course. That's when an ability to quickly whip up a short revised plan can be very useful. For, to paraphrase Karl von Clausewitz (the nineteenth-century Prussian military strategist and author of *On War*): No business plan ever survives the first contact with the market.

THE FIVE-PARAGRAPH BUSINESS PLAN

This sort of skeleton or summary business plan is especially helpful if you are looking at a number of possibilities, trying to decide on your business concept. Sit down and do one of these short-form plans for each possibililty; you'll quickly see what their strengths and weaknesses are.

Just write a short paragraph—a couple of sentences or so—on each of the following five factors.

1. *The need in the market.* A business plan should always begin with a succinct explanation of the *need* for the product. Every successful business is born of human frustration. People want something, and they can't get it, and the entrepreneur finds a way to make it available to them—at a price, of course. By beginning your pitch with a description of the need you propose to fill you avoid a major financing pitfall: the stigma attached to "a solution looking for a problem."

Who has the need? (This is what defines your market.) Do they know they need it? Why do they need it? These and related questions lead naturally into the issues we discussed in Chapter Four, which your market research has answered, or will answer.

2. *The product and the strategy.* Now you turn to your product. But don't overdo the product description. Most entrepreneurs, especially inventors, are prone to describing their widget in stultifying detail. The real issue is customer satisfaction.

How are the features of your product going to translate into benefits for the customer? How and where are you going to sell the product? How will you price it? As you can see, this part of your plan summarizes your market strategy, and must deal with the considerations we discussed in Chapters Five and Six.

One business plan that crossed my desk concerned a venture to make imaging chemicals for use with CAT scanners. Page after page was devoted to the superior technological features of the product. Completely omitted was: What's in it for the *customer*? No reason was given why the customer needed this product or would prefer it over competitive offerings.

Another plan I examined dealt with a novelty product that was to be sold by direct marketing. The inventor had been ripped off by the company that had initially distributed the product and now resolved to do it herself. I advised her to procure, by hook or by crook, the sales figures of the company that had cheated her. Those figures would provide tangible proof that this product would sell.

REM

3. *The team and its qualifications.* Now the focus shifts to: *Who* is the business? If you are going to seek venture capital or other professional financing, the qualifications of your team is the most important single factor in whether or not you get the money. You need to establish that you and your cofounders know what you're doing. More, you must put this in a market context against the competition. In business, it's not enough to be good; you've got to be better than the other guys.

So ask: Who are the people on your team? Are they qualified to manage the kind of business you envision? Do they have experience in this specific industry? You should also go into your production and R&D plans; have you got what you need to get the product functional and out into the market at a viable cost? And of course, you must survey the competition and come up with some sort of proposal for a competitive edge. In short, what have you got that the other guys ain't got?

4. *The financial plan.* At this point you're ready to consider whether the numbers make sense. Often even a quick-and-dirty spreadsheet will show up a business concept as fundamentally unattractive. If, on the other hand, it looks like it ought to be a winner, you can quickly get a rough fix on key parameters.

The P&L projection tells you how profitable you can expect the venture to be. From the cash flow, you can quickly determine how much investment should be needed to get to positive cash flow. A look at the balance sheet tells you what your options are for debt financing. And a little paper-and-pencil work with the first crude numbers will determine whether the key ratios are in line with industry experience, and thus give you a check on whether your plans are realistic.

5. *The deal.* By the time you've done this much, you have the information you need to propose a structure for the deal. You can sketch out the possibilities and decide whether it's attractive enough to get financed—and, if it is, whether it can get financed on terms that will be attractive to *you.*

How much money will you need? What will it be used for, and when? How much of it will have to be equity? What valuation can you reasonably put on the company? Should you finance in stages, and if so, at what stages? What exit will you make available for the investors to cash out?

FROM THE SHORT FORM TO THE REAL THING

Once you've put together a short-form plan that looks interesting, take it around for some expert advice. In addition to the usual friends and relatives, show your two- or three-page document to a few people who know something about the subject. Talk to experienced entrepreneurs, people within the industry you want to enter, a lawyer, an accountant, and of course a customer or two. Ask them to look it over and do their best to shoot it down. Often they'll pick up on subtle weaknesses that you would otherwise overlook until, too late, you discovered them by experience. Looking at the positive side, they will equally often point out opportunities you've missed.

If it still looks worthwhile, now you can go ahead and begin on the real business plan. You have a structure already; all you need to do is flesh it out with more data, answering questions in more detail.

A business start-up can be an intricate dance that requires careful choreography in the business plan. Recently I worked with Terra Aerospace Maintenance and Engineering. This start-up planned to build a facility on Puerto Rico to service

commercial and military jets. The island's government was ready to guarantee $40 million in tax-free bonds; Terra need only put up $2 million in equity. This made it an extremely attractive deal.

Of course, a project this big and complex required a very detailed business plan. As we were working on the plan one day, something leaped out at me. In order to get the $40 million, we had to specify exactly the buildings and equipment and so on that we would spend the money on. To do that, we had to get fixed-cost construction bids. To do that, we would need final drawings, in excruciating detail, for the construction companies to bid on. And to get those drawings prepared, we would need—*up front*—at least $800,000.

But that would change the whole complexion of the deal. We had planned to go to the equity sources with the approach: "Give us a commitment for $2 million contingent on the $40 million in bonds. If it goes through, we draw down the $2 million; if not, you're in the clear." This would be a very easy sale. Now we realized we'd have to say: "We need $800,000 on spec, and if the bonds don't come through your money is gone." The financing wasn't out of the question even on these less favorable terms. But if we hadn't caught this point during the planning stages, we would have had to face the financial backers with a revised plan when the problem came up during start-up—and that's an excellent way to kill a deal.

HDS

HOW TO BLOW IT

There are certain business-plan clichés that are almost universal. If you can avoid them your business plan will really stand out. Here are some of the worst:

- *Chinese-Glove Theory*. We heard this one from Barry Unger of the MIT Enterprise Forum in Cambridge, Massachusetts: "There are 800 million Chinese, that's 1.6 billion hands. Now, assuming we got one percent of the market . . ." This is the typical top-down market-research approach, and venture capitalists react to it as to fingernails scraping a blackboard. If you do real, talk-to-customers-type market research, you're ahead of the pack right at the start.

- *Humongous-Market Theory*. "The market for household appliances is umpty-zillion dollars worldwide and we . . ." Define your market tightly; it's much better to project a strong market share (anywhere from a fourth to three-fourths) of a medium-size market.

- *"Up like a rocket . . ."* Entering a strong growth market can make up for a multitude of management sins, but its efficacy must not be overestimated. A forecast of 50 percent growth rates from market experts is not a panacea. The fact is, if you're entering a market that is starting to experience that kind of growth, you're probably getting in too late. Everybody else is looking at the forecasts too, so you're going to have a *lot* of competition. The people who get rich in high-growth industries are generally the ones who entered the business back when everybody was pooh-poohing it and saying it would never amount to anything.

- *Hockey-Stick Theory.* You generally see this one in the plan of the company that's been around a couple of years and hasn't shown much for sales. But its projections show a sudden dramatic jump in sales to appear soon—when a new product is launched, or that big customer is landed, or something. These "hockey-stick" sales charts have been peddled so often that they are a joke among investors.

- *Hundred-Year Theory.* "Management has over 100 years of combined experience in the electronic fuzzmagoo business . . ." Translation: "My partners and I have been not-too-successful middle managers at big companies. We're getting on in years, and we figured it would be nice to start a company and get rich before we retire."

- *What? Me take a risk?* Claiming that your venture is risk-free is an excellent way to destroy your credibility with sophisticated investors, and to set yourself up for a lawsuit if you manage to get the money from unsophisticated investors. Much better to identify the risks, estimate how serious they are, and explain how you will minimize them.

- *Competition? What's that?* Contemptuous dismissal of the competition does not enhance your credibility; rather it undermines the reader's belief in your objectivity.

I just saw a plan that confidently claimed that the venture had "no effective competition." Existing market size for the product was estimated at $500 million. My response: "Your competition is selling $500 million a year; that sounds pretty 'effective' to me!"

REM

- *Speedy Gonzales.* How is your tiny little start-up going to compete successfully with much larger, established companies? Well, because you're smaller, you can move much faster, right? You're going to zip into the market, slurp up the cream, and move on before IBM even notices your existence. Yup. Any professional investor has heard this one more often than why the chicken crossed the road. It may be true, but it isn't *automatically* true. What *evidence* do you have that the competition will be slow to respond? Assuming that you *are* first, what evidence do you have that you'll really gain all that much advantage from it? And what *specifically* are you going to do to get the jump on the big guys?

- *The Headless Horseman.* What we hardly ever see in a business plan: a real board of directors. The top box on the organization chart is almost always empty. Recruit two or three strong outside directors, and put their resumés in your plan. Here's another way to stand out from the crowd.

- *Business Utopia Theory.* Most entrepreneurs have strong ideals and see their businesses as vehicles for implementing them. We all want to demonstrate how one really *should* treat employees or the local community or the environment. But beware of inserting a lot of rhetoric about your business philosophy in your plan. A list of lofty ideals is a turn-off, especially if the investor you're approaching has different ideals. And the term "mission statement" evokes the image of head-in-the-clouds bureaucratic types. If you must push moral or political goals, be very explicit on how you are going to implement your ideals in practice, and how this is going to result in greater profits for your investors.

- *Spam in the Can.* Beware of the people who offer to write your plan for you. Usually their products, derisively known as "canned plans," aren't very good. In any case, investors want to know whether *you*, the entrepreneur, are any good at planning.

I once received one of these commercial plans that was really spectacular. It was literally a book, bound in leather, with four-color photos used liberally. Unfortunately, it didn't offer much specific or useful information about the business. How could it? Real-life business plans are constantly under revision as new data come in. Can't do that with a bound book.

REM

COSMETIC FACTORS

Investors do judge your book—your business plan—by its cover. If your plan is reproduced with a cheap photocopier on low-grade newsprint and held together with a rusty paper clip, it doesn't give your company the image of a class act. If you take so little care with your business plan, you must not have much regard for its value; why should the investor value it any more highly?

On the other hand, an ostentatious binding and extravagant materials are going to arouse suspicion. Are you trying to impress the investor? If you spend your own money recklessly just to make your business plan a triumph of rococo, will you waste the investor's money on a sumptuous office and a company Porsche?

The best policy is to reproduce your plan cleanly using good-quality paper and binder. Use a letter-quality printer (nobody uses typewriters any more) if not desktop publishing. Have every member of your team proofread it; a typo or misspelling can ruin your image. Check the grammar and usage too; the investor who reads it may be one of those eccentric characters who know that "presently" does not mean "at present" and understand the distinction between "disinterested" and "uninterested."

> Merrill's Law of Proofreading: The average number of typos per double-spaced page equals the reciprocal of the number of *different* people who have proofread the manuscript.

The first thing in your plan should be an Executive Summary. Every business plan should have one; most investors won't bother to read a plan if they have to search through the whole thing to get the key points. They also use it as a screening device, on the basis that if you can't sum up the major factors of your plan in a page or two you don't have a clear idea of your business. A good Executive Summary should cover all five of the key factors we discussed above, and the length should be held under 500 words—well, 750 tops. Be sure the key information is provided by the Summary; don't try to tease the reader.

Speaking of length, what about the plan itself? Contrary to what some business-plan guides tell you, there is no fixed rule. It depends on the business; obviously a complicated start-up takes more space to explain than a hot dog stand. It depends on the investor; Silicon Valley venture capitalists like shorter plans than their Route 128 cousins, for instance. It depends on fashion; in the 1970s the vogue was for huge tomes; later there was a reaction in favor of short plans, and as this is written professional investors seem to like a medium-size plan. We recommend that the plan itself occupy around twenty pages. You should then attach supporting material, which gives more detail, as appendices.

Show respect for your plan by restricting its circulation. If you run off a hundred copies and trawl them through the financial community, you're not likely to get many bites. Don't be paranoid about security, but exercise some discretion. Every copy of your plan should be numbered and tracked; treat your plan as something valuable, though not necessarily priceless. Send low-numbered copies to investors. If an investor is reading copy number 17, he's likely to wonder which competing venture firms have copies 1 through 16.

CHECKLIST
Common Business Plan Deficiencies

- ☐ Hype or exaggeration of any sort
- ☐ No Table of Contents
- ☐ No Executive Summary
- ☐ Executive Summary too long (more than two pages is too long)
- ☐ Executive Summary doesn't summarize
- ☐ Plan doesn't say what's in it for the customer
- ☐ Plan doesn't say what's in it for the investor
- ☐ No market research
- ☐ Entrepreneur has not talked to customers
- ☐ No description of specific market strategy
- ☐ No market share data
- ☐ No analysis of competition
- ☐ Competitors airily dismissed
- ☐ Excessive fixation on product (more than two pages of product description is excessive fixation)
- ☐ No consideration of production costs
- ☐ Management resumés absent or skimpy (put at least half a page per person in the plan, and three or four pages on each founder in the supporting material)
- ☐ No historical financials (if company has a history)
- ☐ No financial projections
- ☐ Financial projections incomplete (for instance, no cash flow)
- ☐ Financial projections skimpy (for example, broken down only by year, or lacking detailed expense breakdown)
- ☐ Sales projections drawn from thin air
- ☐ Projections not congruent with, or not supported by, specific assumptions made (for instance, sales assumed without commissions for salespeople)
- ☐ No consideration of possible problems
- ☐ Projections incompatible with standard ratios for the industry, and no explanation given for the deviation
- ☐ Plan does not present specifics of proposed deal (what does the investor put in, and what does he get for it?)
- ☐ No discussion, or vague discussion, of proposed use of funds
- ☐ Company is grossly overvalued for deal

☐ No mention of when and how investor can cash in
☐ Present stock distribution and debt situation of company not described
☐ Plan has too many typos or sloppy grammar
☐ Plan is shoddy in appearance—or excessively luxurious
☐ Plan is out of date

CAUTIONARY TALE
"Most Likely to Succeed"

I have a huge personal deal flow. For years now I've worked with all sorts of entrepreneurs to help them organize or reorganize their businesses, usually with some kind of financing involved. I can't count how many business plans I've peddled to venture capitalists, bankers, and other financiers. Of course all these financial types are very picky and critical about the plans submitted to them. So I watched with interest when a financier acquaintance of mine came out from behind the desk, wrote his own business plan, and became an entrepreneur.

Paul Gruenberg was not a literal "venture capitalist," but his credentials in the money-moving business were solid: a Yale MBA and experience at one of the top merchant-banking firms. He was (and is) smart, tough, and meticulous. And he had the guts to go out into the real world and do it himself, which is greatly to his credit.

He called his company Video Yearbooks Inc., and the name speaks for itself. School yearbooks have been around a long time and producing them is a steady business. Gruenberg's idea was to make yearbooks on videotape, which schools could sell; these would be produced instead of, or in addition to, the traditional yearbook with still photos. The students' senior year would be captured on tape—football games, the senior prom, interviews with the Most Likely to Succeed, and so on.

Gruenberg wrote, as might be expected, an exemplary business plan. He had, of course, no experience in the business. However, he had thought through the issues very carefully. He did market research and some testing. He found that the concept went over very well with high schools. Universities were much less receptive, but the smaller junior colleges and prep schools were good markets. In view of his background in finance, it's no surprise that his cost analyses and financial projections were first-rate.

There was just one little detail . . .

Video Yearbooks' product concept made a point of involving the ultimate customers. Most schools these days have media classes, so the idea was to have the students taking media courses do the actual videotaping during the school year, under the guidance of their instructor, of course. Then Video Yearbooks would take the raw tape, have it edited by professionals, add music, and so on to create the finished product. This method cleverly killed two birds with one stone. On the one hand, it created an automatic constituency for the product within the student body; on the other, it resulted in an immense reduction in production costs.

Just one problem: The product wouldn't sell. The material produced by the students was so bad that not even first-rate professional video experts could edit it up to an acceptable quality. As anybody who has endured his relatives' interminable home videos can testify, making an interesting video takes real professional skills behind the camcorder. Amateur hour just doesn't sell to today's generation, who were brought up on television and have high standards as video consumers.

So Video Yearbooks' first commencement was somewhat less than successful. The company quickly ran out of money and Gruenberg had to scramble, in the best entrepreneurial style, to retrieve the situation. The only way he could produce a product that would sell reliably was to have the entire production done by professionals. Of course, this more than doubled the cost of making a video yearbook, but the concept was so strong that he could still sell even at the much higher prices required to cover the increased costs. The only difficulty was raising more money to provide the extra working capital needed.

Fortunately, this problem played to his strong point. He went out, applied his financing skills, and raised another million dollars or so from private investors. With this additional money he implemented his revised business plan. The venture succeeded in the market, and was eventually sold to Reader's Digest at a profit that made everyone happy.

This case makes an interesting companion piece to the story of the Stuarts, told in Chapter Ten. The Stuarts knew their business intimately from experience, so they thought they could get away with skimping on planning. Gruenberg, by contrast, took painstaking care with his planning, but he was almost tripped up by underestimating the impact of his lack of practical experience.

                                                                    HDS

Thirteen

FINDING CAPITAL

"Your insight is clear and unbiased," said the Sovereign. "But however entrancing it may be to wander unchecked through a garden of bright images, are we not enticing your mind from another subject of almost equal importance? . . . in the trivial matter of mere earthly enrichment—"

"Truly," agreed the other. "There is, then, a whisper in the province that the floor of the Imperial Treasury is almost visible."

"The rumour, as usual, exaggerates the facts grossly," replied the Greatest. "The floor of the Imperial Treasury is quite visible."

Ernest Bramah, *Kai Lung's Golden Hours*

Young and growing companies have an astounding appetite for cash, so chances are the floor of your company's treasury will be alarmingly visible throughout its early years. Therefore you need to first master the elements of raising capital.

We've got some bad news and some good news. The bad news is that you probably underestimate how much money raising you have to do. The good news is that you probably overestimate how hard it is to raise money.

HOW MUCH DO YOU NEED?

Financing should accomplish one of two things. If possible, it should get you to cash-flow break-even. If it doesn't do this, it must get you to a position from which you can successfully do another financing—a "milestone," such as making a profit or completing product development, that will enhance your credibility and attract more money.

A financing that does not focus on one of these two goals is a classic danger sign of a dying company. When you start raising money just to keep going a little longer, with the idea that when this infusion runs out "somehow" you'll get another, chances are you're doomed.

From your financial projections you should be able to estimate how much money you need. You will require money for fixed capital (such as manufacturing equipment), working capital (including carrying inventory and accounts receivable), and—very important—a reserve for contingencies.

We recommend that you provide for a reserve equal to 50 percent of your calculated needs—and this assumes that your estimates are honest and conservative. There is a trade-off, as always. Some experts recommend that you seek the minimum you can get by with in your initial financing. The reasoning is that as your company matures and grows, it will be worth more; you will thus give up less of your company over the long run by financing as little and as late as possible. This is quite valid as far as it goes. If you can get sufficient financing by giving up only 40 percent of the equity in your company, why surrender 60 percent in order to get that reserve?

But—what if things don't go according to plan and you find out you're underfinanced? You'll have to go out into the capital markets at a time not of your choosing and try to make a deal when your company is not looking good and you're under pressure to make your next payroll. If you can get funding at all in these circumstances, you can bet the investors will really stick it to you.

You're going to need more than you think you're going to need. Raise it while you can and give yourself a good cushion. After you've raised it, guard it. Be stingy, be a tightwad, conserve every precious penny.

FINANCING STAGES

Your initial financing probably will not be your last safari into the financial jungle. The more successful you are, the more money you will need to raise. A typical growth business will go through about five financings in its early years. It begins with *seed money,* which pays for developing the product prototype, market research, and other preliminary work. Then comes the *first-round financing.* This provides the money needed to actually get the business started. After the company has established a track record and shown good growth potential, it will usually look for *second-round financing*. This money is used to get on a high-growth track, by leapfrogging the need to accumulate working capital and funds for expansion out of retained earnings. The next step might be *third-round,* or *mezzanine financing.* Usually this is aimed at expanding or consolidating the company's position, getting it ready for the final step: *going public.* Access to public equity markets poises the company for growth into a big business.

CONTROL: 51 PERCENT VS. REALITY

The entrepreneur's objective through all this is to get the money while giving up a minimum of equity. There are two reasons you want to retain equity. First, it's worth money. Other things being equal, the more equity in your company you retain, the richer you will get. The operative phrase here is, "other things being equal." It's a truism that it's better to own 10 percent of a billion-dollar company than 100 percent of a million-dollar company. As far as strictly financial motives are concerned, it's in your interest to sell equity if the funds received for it will increase the value of your company by more than the proportion you gave up. But of course very few entrepreneurs are driven only by financial considerations. Most of us are in business primarily in order to get our destiny into our own hands; getting rich is a secondary consideration. The second value of equity is that it provides control. But what *is* control? It is not simply a matter of holding 51 percent of the common stock.

> Three engineers fresh out of MIT started their own company and developed an extraordinarily successful electronic testing gadget. Soon they were doing a million a year in sales. They wanted to maintain complete control, so they sold no stock, instead financing expansion with bank loans. Then they blew it; they spent too much money on R&D and found themselves in a cash-flow crisis. Now they were technically in default on their bank loan. The bank was forbearing; it wouldn't push them into bankruptcy—as long as the entrepreneurs did exactly what they were told. They still had 100 percent of the stock; did they have control?

Control of a company is a subtle phenomenon. There is no such thing as absolute control; if nothing else, you are subject to the "control" of the market. Your customers are your bosses; they can fire you by not buying your product. So the ultimate source of control is success in the marketplace. With it, you need little else to maintain control of your company. Without it, no amount of stock, no majority on the board, no agreements, bylaws, or influence will do you any good.

In the early days of your start-up you will probably have control simply because there would be no company without you. As the key founder, you are more or less essential to the enterprise, and all you need to maintain control is the threat to walk away from it all if you don't get your way. Of course, the threat won't be credible unless you have the guts to face the financial losses, the stigma of failure, and possibly some nasty lawsuits. And in any case, as the company matures and develops a full management team, this source of power will become much less effective.

Another factor, of course, is voting stock. If you hold a majority, or if you can muster a majority with the help of your cofounders or sympathetic investors, you're obviously in a strong position. Keep in mind that a majority of the stock need not necessarily translate into a majority of the board of directors. You may be able to use preferred stock or other techniques to maintain effective control in spite of a minority equity position.

Even when successive financings have diluted your equity holding to the point where it has little influence, you can try to hold control the way management does in big companies: by contract. If you are shrewd enough to look ahead and negotiate terms early—while you still have "indispensability power"—you may be able to get an employment contract that will protect you later.

Entrepreneurs commonly are too obsessed with control, and you should keep a rein on yourself. But just because you're paranoid it doesn't mean they're not out to get you. Venture capitalists, for instance, admit when questioned that, in over half of the companies they invest in, they expel the founding CEO at some point. Fortunately, if you're doing a good job, it's unlikely that your investors will want to remove you. On the other hand, if the company is flaming out, they'll either find a way to eject you in spite of all your precautions, or arrange to bail out and leave you spinning down alone, in full "control" of the burning wreckage.

FINANCING ALTERNATIVES: FROM THE WORST TO THE BEST

Let's start by considering some of the major ways of raising money for a start-up. Not all money is the same; its usefulness to your venture may depend on where you get it.

The most obvious, easiest, and worst way to raise money for your venture is to put it up yourself. Let's face it, it is really reckless, indeed downright irresponsible, to put your own hard-earned funds into some hare-brained high-risk venture.

Of course we're kidding, but only a little. Most entrepreneurs are not rich, nor anywhere near it. A business start-up is inherently risky. If your company crashes and burns, you will need savings to tide you over till you can get a job or start another company. If it doesn't, it may still take a lot longer to get into the black than you expected, and you may have to go months, or even years, with little or no salary; you'll need savings to live on. So you should not be eager to pour your own money into the start-up.

There is also an insidious trap in funding your own venture. If you get your funding from outside investors, they'll screen your venture. They'll be picky. They'll look for flaws. They'll be very negative. They'll drive you crazy, and that's just what you want—if you're smart. If a top venture capitalist turns you down, what has happened? You've just had one of the best brains in the business go over your venture with a fine-tooth comb and find that you missed something essential, and he didn't charge you a dime for the service. Be grateful. If you are the lucky possessor of a thick personal wad and you use it to pay your own way, you miss out on this objective evaluation. History is littered with inventors who blew their personal fortunes on ideas that never had a chance. If they'd gone outside for investment, they might have learned something.

So hang on to your own money if you can. Of course, investors prefer—indeed, they usually insist—that you put up some of the money yourself. But don't volunteer too readily. Your job is to build the company; their job is to put up the money.

Family Troubles. The next-to-worst source of funds is your nearest and dearest. Your relatives and friends who believe in you and trust you can be a very fertile source of money. But if your venture goes down the tubes and their life savings go with it, telling them what happened will be somewhat less than the most pleasant task of your life. A lot of successful ventures have relied on seed money of this type; before you go this route, though, be sure you're ready for the consequences.

When you mix business considerations with family or social bonds you inevitably create some tension in the relationship. Different opinions on how the business should be conducted can cause strain even when things are going well. If the business fails, the financial troubles of the parties involved may be dwarfed by the emotional consequences, which can range from broken friendships to vicious family feuds.

Nonetheless, many of the most successful companies would never have been created if it had not been for this sort of financing. If you're going to use it, you can avoid many pitfalls by treating the investment as seriously as you would one from a less personal source. Be sure all the paperwork is in order. Sure, she's your sister, she trusts you—but what if you drop dead from a stress-induced heart attack, or get ejected from the company in a takeover? The new management may demand to see the documents when she makes her claim. If all she has is your handshake, she won't collect. Keep everything as businesslike as possible. Avoid zero-interest loans, loans with no due date, vague promises of equity, and so on. Not only can they lead to family friction, they can attract unwelcome attention from the IRS.

The Invisible Empire.   Private investors are the invisible empire of venture financing. Venture capitalists get the publicity, but it is the amateurs who put up most of the money—especially seed money and other high-risk investments.

Contrary to the popular image, private investors number relatively few doctors and lawyers. Mostly they are successful executives or entrepreneurs. They're not easy to find. Your best bet is to look around among people who are familiar with your industry or your technology.

The private investor is like the little girl with the little curl. When they're good, they're practically ideal investors—knowledgeable, able to contribute advice and connections along with money, not overly greedy. When they're bad, they're horrid—calling you up every day to ask why you're not doing better, insisting that you hire their unemployed relatives, and going into a panic every time you have a bad quarter.

Before you accept an investment from a private investor, *check him out!* Try to talk to founders of other companies he's invested in. And be sure he meets the legal requirements of your state's blue-sky laws, or you could be in deep yogurt.

Private investors are often flexible on the structure of the deal, but it's best to keep it simple. They usually take straight equity or debt with an equity kicker. A less common but attractive alternative is the sales royalty: In return for capital, you commit to pay a percentage of sales to the investor. This allows you to retain equity and keep a clean balance sheet, while giving the investor immediate returns and an opportunity to clean up if the business takes off. But you should have a cap or time limit on the royalty, or else a buy-out provision.

One more thing: Generally speaking, private and professional don't mix. If you plan to get venture capital funding for your second round, keep in mind that professional investors don't like having amateurs in the deal.

Tapping the Pros. The next step up then is professional investors of various sorts. Venture capital funds are most prominent, but if the stock market is presenting one of its IPO "windows" you may even encounter investment bankers who want to take you public.

The professionals represent the elite of financiers, and they fund only a tiny percentage of new ventures. They can give your start-up credibility in the market, as well as expert advice. On the other hand, these folks have a nasty habit of making you give up mucho equity in your company, and they aren't shy about demanding effective control.

The Venture Capitalist. The most prominent form of professional investor is the venture capitalist. Let's look at venture capital in some detail; the realities may surprise you.

Venture capital comes in funds. The firm raises money from various sources—large corporations, pension funds, insurance companies—to create the fund. A small fund these days may be around $20 million, a large one around $100 million. Then the venture capitalists invest the money, over a period of a few years. After a few more years, the investments are cashed in; the bulk of the money goes to the originial investors, and the partners in the venture capital firm take a cut. If the fund is successful, the firm can raise a new fund.

How do venture capitalists behave? The business is really very simple: *Venture capitalists make short-term equity investments in small, high-growth companies.* If this is not what you're looking for, don't bother seeking venture capital.

Venture capitalists take equity in your company. These days it isn't often a simple common-stock deal. They prefer preferred stock, or heads-they-win-tails-you-lose convertible instruments. This way if the company succeeds, they get stock and capital gains; if it doesn't, they have a loan equivalent and a place at the head of the line when you're liquidated. But under all the fine print, the reality is that venture capitalists are looking for a big slice of your company's equity, and they will also seek effective control. Not that they want to manage the company, but if you seem to be running it into the ground they want the power to replace you.

Venture capitalists are only interested in high-growth ventures. They want you to grow by a factor of ten in five years, or thereabouts.

If you're looking to have a nice, profitable but stable business, forget it. What's more, they need size; a small venture capital deal these days will be around $2 million. (Typically this will be split among two or three firms to spread the risk.) If you need a smaller amount—three-fourths of new companies start on less than $100,000 (according to a BDO Seidman survey*)—venture capitalists may not be interested.

Above all, venture capitalists make short-term investments. If you're looking for a permanent partner who will buy and hold your stock for decades, forget it. The venture capitalist will insist on an "exit strategy"—either going public or selling out your company to a larger corporation. And you'd better figure on being ready to exit by one of these two routes within five to seven years. Remember, the venture firm has to make its investment in your company liquid so that it can pay back the people who put up the money in the first place.

Is venture capital for you? If you have a credible shot at becoming a major success story, yes. Otherwise, you're wasting your time.

How do you get venture capital? Here are few tips. *First,* you must have a complete management team of strong people; credentials are very important. People are as important to venture capitalists as "bricks and mortar" are to bankers. *Second,* be sure everything about your venture is out of the top drawer; use a Big Six accounting firm, be sure you have a first-rate business plan, and make every effort to convey that you are a class act. *Third,* approach a fund that specializes in your industry. *Fourth,* make the approach via an intermediary who has worked with that fund (lawyers and accountants are common network nodes); don't just mail in your plan.

THE DEBT OPTION

How about another alternative? There's always your friendly banker. She probably won't be so friendly if you ask her for a loan for a start-up. You may wonder if you've developed bad breath or leprosy, but the actual explanation is simple: Above all, the bank is concerned with how you are going to pay back the loan. If you have a good job the bank will lend you money, even if you admit you intend to spend it on something frivolous. Your banker doesn't care if you're going to buy a Volcano X-15 Speedster. Your salary gives you the means to pay the loan back, and that's her only concern. But if she invests in your start-up, the money has to be repaid out of cash flow—a very iffy proposition. However, under certain circumstances she may cough up some

*Inc. magazine, January 1991.

funds—particularly if you have good collateral and are willing to co-sign the loan on a personal basis.

> You're most likely to get a loan if you have some very tangible evidence that it can be paid back. One start-up entrepreneur, for instance, walked into the bank when his company was only a few months old carrying a big purchase order from a solid customer. He asked for money to buy some equipment and raw materials so he could fill the order—and got it. The loan was paid back, as promised, when the customer paid him.

Don't, in short, expect much credit from a bank during the early days of your business. Even so, pick your bank carefully. Look for one that has a track record of working with small businesses. Ask if they have customers who are in the same line of business that you're in. You want to deal with bankers who understand something about your industry. This, incidentally, is a principle of general validity: *Approach investors who understand your market, your industry, your business; they are much more likely to be receptive.*

When we started Reaction Design we began by looking for people we knew who had money. We wasted a lot of time trying to get financing from an acquaintance of my partner who'd made a bundle in real estate. We got nowhere; he didn't understand high-tech and wasn't comfortable with it. We financed successfully only when we shifted focus to locating scientists who happened to have money.

REM

Investors who don't understand the business can sometimes be brought in with an indirect approach. Some years ago I worked on the financing of a squid-fishing venture. (Believe it or not, the world market for squid is over a billion dollars.) We were trying to get a $6 million bank loan to build a highly specialized ship for processing the squid on board. Now, banks that understand the squid business are very rare. So I went to a marine insurance company, people who understood ships and fishing and so on very well. We paid them a $350,000 fee up front, and they in turn guaranteed the loan to the bank—that is, they promised to buy the ship if we defaulted on the loan. That did the trick and the bank came through.

HDS

Make a point of building a relationship with the *person* at the bank who handles your account. Note that banks hand out vice-presidencies very liberally, so don't be impressed by a title; find out where the person actually is in the organization chart. It's desirable to deal with the home office rather than a branch; usually the officers at a branch office have very little authority and everything must be referred back to the home office for decision anyway.

Of course debt has its drawbacks. Debt service can put a considerable drag on your cash flow. It doesn't take much in the way of loans to unbalance your balance sheet and leave you with very little financial freedom of action.

Some entrepreneurs prefer debt financing to selling equity because they believe it maintains control. This may not be the case. A bank loan, for instance, invariably comes with "restrictive covenants"—acres of fine print specifying what you may or may not do and providing that you are automatically in default and must repay the loan on demand if anything whatsoever goes wrong. In practice, the bank will be reluctant to take over and run your business unless the situation becomes desperate indeed—but it probably won't hesitate to give you some gentle hints with an unspoken "or else." Debt results in "leverage" in both directions. When things go well, it allows you to multiply your profits. When things go badly, debt will often fatally complicate your problems.

HITTING UP THE GOVERNMENT

If you're looking for a loan, don't forget that there are other lenders—SBICs, MESBICs, the SBA, and many other governmental and quasi-governmental sources. You may also qualify for an outright grant; the federal government's SBIR program backs R&D by small businesses, for instance. Check out the state and city where you intend to locate; these days many of them have seed capital funds, "business incubators," or other assistance.

When seeking government money, keep in mind that decisions will be motivated much more by politics than by economics. Fill out the forms with great care; bureaucrats pay a lot of attention to this, because they are graded for complete and correct paperwork, not for how successful their investments are. In your application, emphasize political considerations rather than profit prospects. If you have female or minority founders, are hiring in a depressed area or helping to clean up the environment, that will count much more heavily than business experience or a strong market. It certainly doesn't hurt if you can get your representative or some other bigwig to put in a good word for you, though you should avoid heavy-handed pressure tactics. Make it clear that you're a Democrat, even if it is a Republican administration at the time. You have nothing but good to say about affirmative action, regulatory agencies, and unionized labor.

LEASE OR BORROW?

If you need expensive capital equipment, look into leasing. It very definitely is not the cheapest way to get equipment, but a lease is often much easier to obtain than a loan for a start-up. Another nice thing about leasing is that it is "off-balance-sheet" financing, which doesn't clobber your financial statements the way big loans do. Of course your accountant may make you put in one of those nasty little footnotes.

The big commercial leasing companies are not too receptive to start-ups. They prefer to finance only items of general use: IBM computers, standard-brand office equipment, the most commonly encountered plant equipment. Try approaching the vendor, especially if it's specialized equipment. They may be willing to carry the lease themselves, or to refer you to a receptive leasing company with whom they've worked before.

Another possibility is to set up a lease with a private investor or a family member. They buy the equipment and lease it to your company. This can have a tax advantage, especially for an investor who's nearing retirement age. The basic idea is to strip off the deduction for depreciation, which your loss-making start-up can't use, and give it to the investor, who has income against which to deduct it.

THE CORPORATE PARTNER

What is "corporate partnering"? This buzzword describes just about any kind of cooperation between companies. When it comes to practical venture financing, what you need is an arrangement with a larger firm in which they provide direct or indirect financial backing to you because your company's product complements theirs. For instance, you may have software that runs on their hardware and enhances their appeal to customers. They may then back you so that your product can be marketed along with theirs.

What do you need to know about corporate partnering? Three things:

1. Corporate partnering is the most complex and time-consuming financing avenue that has yet been invented. It requires a major effort to set up, and constant attention to maintain.

2. The key to making a corporate partnership a success is the personal connection between the entrepreneur and the contact person in the larger company. If this person departs or gets transferred, or the relationship breaks down, the partnering arrangement is in big trouble.

3. In spite of all the publicity they get, true corporate-partnering arrangements are very rare. If you run across an opportunity, great; but be wary of spending a lot of time looking for this kind of deal.

SUPPLIES FROM SUPPLIERS

Can we find a better way? Sure we can. How about hitting up your vendors? Many vendors will give you, almost for the asking, a short-term loan to buy their products. It's called "net 30." Interest-free too. Can't ask for much better than that, right? Wrong. If they'll give you thirty days, ask for ninety days. Settle for sixty. If it's a big-ticket item, ask them to finance it for you, or find someone to lease it to you. When you think you've wrung a vendor dry and there's nothing more to be had—start talking about making them your sole source and see what happens. Don't be shy; you're a customer. If you hit it big, you'll become a very lucrative customer. This is their chance to get in on the ground floor. But of course, this source of funding is limited to the amount you're buying from your vendors, right? Wrong. If you're willing to sell equity in your company, maybe you can do it on good terms to one or more of your vendors. Raise the possibility. Don't stop yet—be creative. Need some printing done? Before you go to the print shop and (ugh) pay for it, ask one of your larger suppliers if they have an in-house printing operation (many large companies do) and would they mind running off 5,000 copies of this brochure for you, just this once? Need some technical expertise to get your production line running? Don't spring for that thousand-dollar-a-day consultant till you've checked whether the company that sold you the equipment will send over one of their experts to help you out.

Study the possibilities thoroughly and select your vendors carefully. Then—not to put too fine a point on it—exploit the hell out of them. Never, repeat never, put out hard cash for anything if you can manage to wheedle it out of one of your suppliers.

But also: Though you pay them as little as possible, pay it on time and cheerfully and never try to welsh. Thank them effusively. Praise them to the skies to anyone who will listen, especially other prospective customers for them. And when you join the Fortune 500, remember who helped you in those tough early days.

THE ULTIMATE FINANCING SOURCE

When you get into full-blown vendor financing you're starting to think like a pro, but you don't get your certificate until you've mastered the best financing of all: customer financing.

The entrepreneurial amateur tends to be very timid with customers. This results from a very natural lack of self-confidence. When you're inexperienced and unsure of yourself, it's easy to get the feeling that your product is not really that valuable and that the customer is doing you a favor by buying it.

Well, maybe that feeling is quite correct; unfortunately, it often is. But if it is, the earlier you find out the better! You should go out and peddle your wares as soon as you possibly can—well before the formal start-up of your company if at all possible. That way, if customers show a lack of enthusiasm, you can modify or even drop your venture before you have too much time and money invested in it. On the other hand, if customers are really turned on by what you're selling, you can use them as a significant financing source.

This is a crucial reason why customer financing is best. As we pointed out before, a financing can be a source, not just of money, but of information. When you put up the money out of your own pocket, it doesn't tell you *anything* about whether your venture is a good idea. If you approach professional investors, you'll get an expert opinion. But when you use customer financing, you get the best possible information about your company's viability in the market.

Try to get three things from your customers:

1. *Get them to buy your widget or whatever.* Buy it right now too—"Yes, it's true that we only have a prototype now and production won't begin till next year, but remember we'll have only limited capacity. If you order right now you'll be at the head of the waiting list . . ." Also, try to get them to buy a lot—"Better order at least a year's supply—you don't want to get caught short when demand explodes. In fact, two years would be better . . ."

2. *Get the best possible price.* In many start-ups, we see an inexorable drop in the proposed product price before the roll-out. The founders, as actual contact with the market approaches, becomes more and more nervous and repeatedly cut the price in hopes that if the

product is made sufficiently cheap then customers will deign to consider it. This preemptive commercial self-abasement slashes profit margins and puts a tourniquet on your cash flow. Worse, it is often counterproductive; the low price gives your product a cheap, low-quality image and actually reduces sales. Don't be afraid to ask for full value from the customer.

3. *Get the money up front!* Step right up and ask the customer to pay in advance—and the further in advance the better. Do you find the prospect of making such a radical request embarrassing or unnerving? Then consider this: Getting paid in advance has an absolutely extraordinary effect on your cash flow. A company that sells on net 30 may need $1 million in venture capital to get to positive cash flow, for which the founders will probably have to give up most of the equity. The same company, if customers pay 30 days in advance, may require no venture capital and the founders get to keep *all* of the equity. Does that make you feel motivated to persuade those customers?

When I was running Reaction Design, I got an inquiry from Syntex about a chemical they needed for an important project. I really wanted the order, which was pretty sizable by our standards, enough to keep us going for months. We had the technology to make the product; unfortunately, we were close to broke and couldn't afford to buy the raw materials. So, in sheer desperation, I worked up the nerve to ask Syntex if they'd pay half the money in advance. And they said, to my utter astonishment, "Sure, no problem."

REM

Of course, you also hit up your customers for everything else you can. See if they'll recruit other customers for you. (This is called "bird-dogging.") Ask them to pay your R&D costs. In fact, ask them to pay for shipping, inspection, your long-distance phone calls to them, and anything else you can plausibly hit them with.

And, once again, cultivate a good memory. Work like hell to give your customers a good product, to solve their problems, and to make their lives easier. Don't wait to be asked—*you* ask *them* what you can do to give them good publicity, to help them get their own customers. And when your dreams come true and your widgets are selling like hotcakes, be sure your old friends are at the top of the allocation list.

SPOTTING THE FLAKY INVESTOR

When you're eagerly, not to say desperately, seeking money to finance your venture, anybody who says he's interested in investing looks like

EXERCISE
Your Financing Plan

A. Working with your financial projections, decide how much money you will need and when.

Needed to reach cash-flow break-even: _____

Plus reserve for contingencies: _____

Total financing needed: _____

You may decide to finance in stages. If so, decide on the milestones that mark the stages, when you plan to reach them, and how much you need to raise at each stage.

B. Now break down the financing into types of money.

Sale of common stock: _____

Preferred or other equity: _____

Debt financing: _____

Leasing or other off-balance-sheet: _____

You should then feed these assumptions back into your financial projections to see how the numbers come out. For instance, after doing a debt financing, will your debt-equity ratios remain acceptable?

C. Finally, decide what types of financing sources to approach for each of these segments of the financing. Then investigate specific financiers. Make a list of investors or companies who (a) do the kind of deals you want to do, and (b) know your industry.

---

a real godsend. You may be stunned to find out later that he never had the slightest intention of investing; in fact, he may never have had the money to invest at all. "Negotiating" with these people can seriously damage your venture. You can lose time, miss a market opportunity, and damage your credibility with serious investors.

Why would somebody pretend to be an investor? There are a few outright crooks out there who find posing as an investor useful cam-

ouflage. Others are freelance deal makers ("five-percenters") who try
to line up an investor for you, then collect part of the money for their
services. The less ethical among these may pretend to be real investors
themselves in order to enhance their credibility. But the most common
motive is simply ego. There are all sorts of moderately prosperous
people—doctors, lawyers, Indian chiefs—who like to brag at cocktail
parties about their venture capital activities and explain the fascinating
deals they are considering but who never actually put up a dime.

How can you spot the flaky investor? Here are a few telltale signs.

▪ *He wants money from you.* If he tells you he needs for you to
put up "good-faith" money—or any payment under any excuse to him
or any other outsider—turn around and run.

▪ *He's a braggart.* If he's continually telling you that "money is
no problem" and letting you know how rich he is—he isn't. If he lets
you know what valuable political connections he has—he hasn't.

▪ *He's mysterious about his money.* Legitimate investors, amateur
or professional, are not reluctant to tell you their source of funds.
Anyone who tantalizes you with dark hints about Arab money or other
unspecified sources of wealth should be discounted heavily.

▪ *He doesn't ask serious questions.* Real investors want to know
about your market, your team, and your product. They want to see
your business plan, dig into your facts and figures, and understand the
business. If instead the prospective "investor" spends a lot of time
talking about how rich you're all going to get, forget him.

▪ *He's arrogant.* You may meet someone who starts giving you a
lengthy lecture on how to run your business. He lays down the law
with such confidence that you are inclined to think he must be a really
shrewd venture capital expert and you are privileged to sit at the feet
of this Gamaliel. Well, he may teach you something but you won't get
a check. He's on an ego trip. If a real investor thinks you're so ignorant
that you need to be taught your business, he won't waste time educat-
ing you; he just won't invest.

▪ *He reduces the proposed investment.* Real investors frequently
propose to give you more money than you ask for. Experience has
taught them that entrepreneurs commonly underestimate how much
capital they need to get to positive cash flow. The flake entices you by
offering big sums at the start, but as negotiations proceed he cuts the
amount he's willing to commit. He tends to get cold feet as the moment
of truth approaches—and often he doesn't even have the money he
"offered" at the opening.

▪ *He's ignorant of the business and the industry.* Real investors put their money into things they understand. Venture capital firms specialize and won't touch a deal, no matter how attractive, in an industry where they don't know the ropes. If the investor clearly shows he doesn't understand what you are trying to do and what your industry is like, you probably will get no money from him—and if you do, you'll regret taking it.

AND WHAT ABOUT FINDERS?

You may be approached by a "finder"—someone who offers to introduce you to investors in return for a percentage of the investment. These people sometimes call themselves brokers or advisers or even investment bankers. The cynical call them "five-percenters."

To the naive, this looks like a good deal. You get "expert" help with the daunting task of finding and dealing with investors; and after all, the fee is contingent—no investment, no pay, so what have you got to lose? But turn it around for a moment and look at it from the point of view of the investor. He knows that if he makes a $1 million investment in your company, $50,000 immediately goes to the finder. Does this make the investment more attractive to him? What it amounts to is that the finder performs a service for you but is paid by the investor, who is likely to ask, "Why should *I* give this chap $50,000?"

If you're going for venture capital, don't use a finder; it's an almost certain deal killer with professional financiers. A finder *may* be useful in locating private investors. Before you sign on with him, though, check him out thoroughly. Get his resumé; ask for references; talk to some well-connected people and see what they know about him. *Never* give a finder cash up front until you've done a meticulous background check.

> Incidentally, this may be a good place to mention a rule that applies not just to finders but to investors, employees, or anyone else you meet in business. If someone tells you how honest he is, put your hand on your wallet. If he assures you that you can trust him, resolve to sign nothing.

TIMING

In planning your financing effort, you should take into account the state of the economy. There are times when investment money practically rains down from Wall Street on the deserving and the undeserving alike. Then again, when there's a credit crunch, you should avoid wearing out shoe leather going around to the banks for a loan. You need to adapt your strategy to the environment.

How can you achieve good timing in your effort? Nobody can predict the business cycle with perfect accuracy. But if you can be objective, you can do surprisingly well. Read the business press; watch leading indicators; and be *willing* to believe them.

When a business expansion matures, this is your signal to get hopping and finish your business plan. You're now entering the ideal time to raise money. Many investors have cashed in their gains from the rising stock market and are looking for new worlds to conquer. The boom is at its height and optimism is king. Recession is inconceivable. The only worry is inflation—and to beat inflation, investors naturally think of venture capital. Normally staid, gray-suit types are in a feeding frenzy, buying stock in anything that claims to be a "growth company."

Eventually leading indicators will start to fall. The rule of thumb is that three declines in a row signal a recession. The third consecutive decline invariably brings articles in the business press pointing out that "after all, leading indicators have predicted nine out of the last five recessions." By now you should have your financing done and the money in the bank.

And what do you do as the economy crashes and crumbles? Wait—until the economy touches bottom. You are now in that ideal situation where great fortunes are founded: at the bottom of a recession, with cash and a cool head. Now, when there's gloom everywhere and people are convinced the country is entering another Great Depression—*now* you start operations.

Why? Because before you start selling, you'll have to buy. You need to lease premises for your business. In a recession, there's plenty of empty space and desperate landlords will give you terrific terms. You need to buy equipment and furniture. Go around to auctions and bankruptcy sales, and you'll find some astounding bargains. You need to line up vendors for raw materials. With customers rare, they'll give you a good price—and that's not all. You won't have to worry about shortages or long lead times; service will be excellent; and vendors will be surprisingly liberal about credit terms. You need to hire workers; in a recession, plenty of good people are available, and their salary expectations will be quite reasonable. We guarantee you'll be pleasantly surprised what cash in the bank can accomplish in a recession.

But what about sales? Well, chances are your first few months, maybe your first year, will be lousy no matter how you time it. Your production process will take longer to get running than you think. Your advertising will be misdirected. Your sales presentations will be ineffective. Your instruction manual will have to be rewritten from scratch. A million things will go wrong and sales will roll in far more slowly than you expected. (This is the way it will be if you've done your homework very carefully. If you haven't, it will be a hundred times worse!) If you start during a recession, you'll have time to iron out all these problems before the economy picks up. Meanwhile, you won't be missing much. If you start during a boom, on the other hand, you'll probably get your act together just about the time the next recession begins.

We can't always have what we want. It's nice to time your start-up perfectly to meet the business cycle. But the really essential factor in timing is *readiness*. Don't go out for capital until you are prepared. Of course you shouldn't dawdle during your planning phase, but never skip essential tasks—like market research—because you're in a hurry and fear an investor or a market will get away from you.

MAKING THE APPROACH

Once you decide how you want to finance your venture, you have to make the approach. There are four rules to follow in dealing with just about any sort of investor.

1. *Approach the right sort of investor for the deal. Money has tastes.* A deal may be very appealing to a venture capitalist but horrify a banker—and vice versa. Each general type of investor specializes in certain sorts of deals, and within investor types, individual investors may further specialize. A deal that one bank would jump at might be unacceptable to another bank. Before you approach an investor, find out what sort of deals he does.

2. *Understand the investor's objectives.* A surprising number of entrepreneurs regard investors simply as passive but generous money-bags, whose function in life is to hand out currency to deserving ventures. Fact is, most investors have a terribly crass attitude and a distressing tendency to ask, "What's in it for *me?*" It is essential to understand not only that the investor wants a return on his investment but also that he will have very specific ideas about what sort of return is acceptable, how long-term the commitment of funds should be, how much risk is acceptable, and how much oversight he will exercise. If you make it a point to determine what his objectives are and structure

the deal to satisfy them, you have good odds of getting a check. If you rush blindly ahead without bothering to find out what he wants, you don't.

3. *Approach the investor properly.* Most people who have money to invest have a lot of applicants and find it necessary to set up procedures, formal or informal, to screen them. You may find his rules arbitrary, but it's his football and if you want to play with him . . .

4. *Evaluate the investor carefully.* There's a tendency to assume that anyone who has money is the answer to your prayers. But your relationship doesn't end when you pick up the check. You're going to be living with this person a long time, and a nervous or hostile investor is like a rusty nail in your knee. Not everyone who has a lot of money is nice. Check him out thoroughly before you even approach him—and this applies whether you're approaching an individual investor, a bank, or a venture capital firm. What is the investor's history? Look especially at his previous investments, and talk to the entrepreneurs who received them. How did he behave? Was he constantly interfering with management? Did he act as a gadfly? Did he welsh on commitments for additional funding? Was he a nervous type, always calling up the CEO to demand reassurance? If you're expecting him to sit on your board, or give advice, or provide contacts with customers, how did he perform for previous investees?

THE PRESENTATION

Your first meeting with a prospective investor will make or break your chances with her. Treat this as a formal sales presentation, because that is exactly what it is. Prepare your pitch very carefully and rehearse it at home before you use it. Try to get an objective critique. (The MIT Enterprise Forum, and similar organizations, can give you extraordinarily valuable feedback.) Be sure your presentation focuses on the benefits to the investor, not on how much you could do with the money. Try to anticipate possible objections and have answers ready. Don't rely on your advertising (in this case, your business plan) to make the sale for you.

The probing may get quite personal, especially if you're dealing with professional investors. Venture capitalists, for instance, like to say that they make investment decisions primarily on the basis of the quality of the management team. The standard cliché is: "I'd rather see first-rate people with a second-rate idea than second-rate people with a first-rate idea." So the presentation will be regarded primarily as a chance to evaluate you and the rest of your team. Be prepared to field questions about your goals, your attitudes, your past failures and successes, and your character.

After you've made your presentation, you must decide whether the investor is serious or not. If he is, you don't want to be dealing with a lot of other prospects. But if he isn't, you certainly can't afford to sit idly by while he ponders the deal for months. How can you determine how serious an investor is?

Obviously, if he tells you your widget is the greatest invention since sliced bread and your management team is a bunch of geniuses, you should feel encouraged. On the other hand, *any* expression of a negative evaluation, no matter how mild, signals poor prospects.

Speed is a very good indicator of investor interest. Prospects who move quickly, who want to see your business plan right away, set up an appointment next week—these are good prospects. The languid sort who don't seem particularly to care how long it takes to go through the process are more likely to be just playing with you. Silence means "no." A good rule of thumb is that three unreturned phone calls is a turn-down.

Look for the investor who is specific. If he says, "I like your plan, but you need more market research on the second product, and I think you should have more budgeted for advertising"—and especially if he goes on to say "Fix those and I'll be ready to talk terms"—he's a very hot prospect. Vague types, on the other hand, seldom come through with the check. If he "would like to think it over" or is "not sure about a couple of things"—if he's unwilling to make a commitment but has no specific objections to cite—don't waste time on him.

Finally, the good prospect is independent—she clearly makes the decisions herself. The minute you hear that the investor wants time to consult a committee, or a partner, or a friend, or an adviser, you can check her off your list.

THE NEGOTIATION

When the investor says yes, you'll be tempted to relax and heave a sigh of relief. Don't. Your troubles are just beginning. Now you have to negotiate the specifics of the deal, and it probably will not be easy.

Successful negotiating strategy is a whole subject in itself, and we cannot go into it deeply here. Let's just emphasize three principles that are especially important.

1. *Do not negotiate until you are in a strong position.* It's said of bankers that they are people "who loan you an umbrella when the sun

is shining and take it back when it rains." This attitude is characteristic of *all* investors. Nobody is willing to give you the money if you need it desperately. So seek funding only when you don't "need" it. It's best to have the foresight to borrow the umbrella when the sun is shining. But if you didn't, instead of going out for funding when you're in trouble or up against a deadline, try to muddle through with what you have. Concentrate on getting through the crisis, even if you have to take a few body blows in the process, and get to the point where the situation is stable. *Then* look for funds. You should not sit down at the table unless you are ready to get up and walk away if you don't like the results.

2. *Get your objectives on the table right at the start—and get the investor's objectives on the table also.* Many people think that you should hide your objectives from the "enemy." But this is neither necessary nor desirable if you've accepted the first point. If you know clearly what you want, are determined to get it, and are prepared to walk away if you don't, you have nothing to lose and everything to gain by making your position clear. Insist that the other side do likewise. If your goals and the investor's goals are incompatible, you'd better find it out at once, rather than thrash around interminably speaking at cross-purposes. If your objectives and theirs are compatible, getting the key requirements out into the open will greatly facilitate clearing up the details and reaching a quick agreement.

3. *Aim for a positive-sum deal.* You're going to be living with these investors for a long time. Don't worry about squeezing out the last drop of advantage in the negotiations. Look for the best results for everyone. You should feel that you really cleaned up on this deal, and the investors should feel exactly the same way. If it seems impossible for this to happen, maybe the deal shouldn't be made.

ISSUES IN STRUCTURING THE DEAL

Once you've decided on a structure for your company, the next question is the deal. What kind of offering will you make? There are hundreds of ways to structure an offering, most of them unnecessarily complicated. Try to keep your deal, like your company structure, as simple as possible. The more complex it is, the more chance for error; for misunderstanding that can cause friction; and for inadvertent violation of securities laws.

Please note that whenever you offer an investor something that is, or could be construed to be, a "security," you make yourself

subject to federal security laws, and also to state "blue-sky" laws.
Get a complete briefing from your lawyer before you start talking to
investors. This includes any investor, even (or especially) your brother-
in-law.

An investment deal must concern itself with three issues: valuation, risk, and control.

How Much Is the Company Worth?

If you are doing an equity
deal, the valuation of the company is crucial. (Even for a loan, the
company's value makes a big difference.) You are selling part of your
company. How much is that part worth? Obviously, that depends on
how much the whole company is worth.

This is where many entrepreneurs run into a little problem. Let's
say you've done your financial projections carefully and you have
determined that you need $500,000 to get you to positive cash flow.
You're building a service business—no bricks and mortar—so a loan
doesn't look viable; you'll have to seek equity. You decide to offer 20
percent of the company's stock for $500,000.

When you talk to your first prospective investor, he says: "Well,
let's see. If 20 percent of it is worth $500,000, you're valuing your
company at $2,500,000. You've got yourself and your two partners, a
business plan, and $132.19 in the company bank account. How is this
company worth $2,500,000?"

Your vision of a glorious future has limited value in the investment
market. Entrepreneurs tend to think of an investment as a *bet;* put
down your money, and if the venture goes as planned, you get back
your wager and a lot more. But most investors are outraged by the
idea of being regarded as gamblers. They see themselves as carefully
purchasing something of value, taking into account the prospect for
increased value in the future. Only the most naive investors will buy
stock as if it were a lottery ticket; sophisticated, and especially
professional investors, have a very strong focus on what your company
is worth on the hoof right now.

So, before you even start to seek money, ask yourself how you
can maximize the value of your company. Try to put some substance
behind it. Get the structure set up by incorporating (if you're going to),
have stationery printed, get all the cofounders committed and all the
paperwork done. Got a great idea? That and a dime will buy you a
piece of bubble gum—but if you patent it, or even submit an application, you have something tangible that you can claim has monetary
value. Build a prototype, or at least a mock-up, something solid that
investors can see and touch. Above all, get *customers.* Short of money

in the bank, there's nothing better than a stack of purchase orders just waiting to be filled to provide convincing evidence that your company has real value.

Who Is Going to Take the Risk? Once you've put a value on what you're selling, you need to deal with the issue of risk. Professional investors are expert at shoving maximum risk onto the entrepreneur. They want you to invest everything you own and everything you can borrow into the venture. They also like to use shrewdly designed financial instruments, such as convertible preferred, that maximize their equity if the company succeeds and minimize their contribution to the loss if it fails. Be prepared for some stiff negotiating.

There are some easy steps you can take to reduce investor risk, or at least its perception. Try to issue your stock under Section 1244 of the IRS code. This makes it "small-business" stock. Losses on 1244 stock can be deducted against ordinary income; normally investment losses can only be deducted against capital gains. Some restrictions apply, but they're not very onerous. The main requirement is that there be only one class of stock—you can't issue preferred or other types of stock with different voting rights.

Plan to issue a relatively small number of shares (say, a couple of thousand) with each share having a high value. This has the cosmetic advantage of giving your company a blue-chip image; a company whose shares are valued at $500 apiece must be pretty substantial, right? Anyway, limiting the number of shares simplifies stockholder relations paperwork. If you have a million shares and 500 stockholders, you're going to be spending a lot of time and money just keeping track of them all, recording transactions when they sell shares to one another, and so on.

Ultimately you have to deal with the significant risks as perceived by the investor. There's market risk. Will there be enough customers willing to pay the price? Will competitors beat you in the market? There's management risk. Do you and your cofounders know what you're doing? Are you motivated to make this venture succeed? Are you honest and reliable? And there may be other risks: technology risk (can you really make this miracle widget work?), regulatory risk (will the government ban your product?), legal risk (could this lead to a bunch of liability suits?), and so on. You can improve your bargaining position by being ready to demonstrate that you have considered these risks; that you have thought out the possibilities; and that you have a realistic idea of the odds.

Who Gets to Run the Show? The final element of the deal is the settlement of control issues. Investors try to reduce risk by maintaining control. To some extent this is a psychological issue. We all feel better taking risks over which we have control, regardless of whether we can improve the mathematical odds; that's human nature, and investors aren't immune.

As we've discussed at the beginning of this chapter, control of the company will inevitably be an issue, and many factors can be involved in getting effective control. As you structure the deal, you should keep an eye on the following points.

Obviously *distribution of voting stock* will be a major factor. Investors, particularly venture capitalists, are likely to insist that founder stock be vested gradually as the company develops. In other words, you don't get all your stock at once; you receive it in installments.

Investors will probably also insist on some control over *future issues of stock*. They can't allow you to just issue more stock whenever you please and sell it to anyone you like at any price you choose. This would dilute their holdings. On the other hand, you'll probably need to do more financings in the future. The usual solution is a restriction on how much stock may be issued in later financings, and a minimum price for it. There is also likely to be a "preemptive rights" clause, which gives the original stockholders first crack at any later issues.

How will stockholdings translate into control? This will be determined by the corporate bylaws. Major investors may insist on having a seat on the *board of directors* guaranteed. If a struggle develops between the founders and the investors over control of the board, you may want to break the deadlock by suggesting a "neutral" board, with the balance of power being held by outside directors acceptable to both sides.

Finally, if you work with professional investors they will want you and your cofounders bound by *employment contracts*. Don't just shrug and sign. These agreements usually have very serious restrictions hidden in the boilerplate and can be used to quietly take back the "concessions" made by the investors on other issues. Take the employment contract to your lawyer—your *personal* lawyer, not the investor's lawyer!—and have her go over it with a fine-tooth comb. Then get ready to argue.

INVESTOR RELATIONS

We pointed out in our discussion of your presentation that financing your company is a sale. As in any other sale, the most frequently neglected step is follow-up. *Never neglect investor relations.* Even if you have firm "control" of the company in terms of stock ownership, a disgruntled investor can wreak havoc. She can call for special meetings, harass you unmercifully, demand reports or audits, sue you, sic the SEC or other regulatory agencies on you for real or imagined crimes—never underestimate the problems she can cause. And it's not enough just to avoid making enemies among your investors. You really want them to be happy. You may want to go back to them for more money. Even if you plan to seek elsewhere for further funding, you at least want your original backers to recommend the investment. And, from a simple moral point of view, these people took a heavy risk because they believed in you, and helped you in accomplishing your goals. You owe it to yourself to be good to them.

The primary principle of investor relations is openness. Keep investors informed—fully, frankly, and frequently. Of course you will provide them routinely with a detailed annual report. But it's well to give them something in writing more frequently. A quarterly report is about right. It's not so frequent as to be onerous to produce (it needn't be detailed; just a letter and a set of financials), but it gives them a good feel for the company's progress and prevents a lot of nasty surprises. Small business tends to move fast, and so much can happen between two annual reports that stockholders can sometimes get an unpleasant shock.

Unless you have a really unwieldy number of investors—something to avoid, by the way—it's a good idea to augment your written communications with occasional telephone conversations. Just put it on your calendar to call each investor at regular intervals—it may be once a week or once a year, depending on the situation and the person involved. Beware the temptation to hide when things are going badly. No matter how embarrassed you are, step up and take your medicine—it will be worse if you put it off. And when things go well, it's nice to thank your investors for their confidence in you and give them some of the credit for the company's success.

CAUTIONARY TALE
The Nerve of Those Fellows

Not being terribly scientifically inclined, I don't often get into high-tech ventures. But American Biointerface was too interesting to pass up.

It started in 1985 with some experimental work on nerve repair. The human body is capable of repairing most types of damage; wounds to skin and muscle heal, broken bones knit, even the heart can rebuild tissue destroyed by a coronary. The big exception is nerve tissue; any damage to the brain or nervous system is likely to be permanent, because nerves, when damaged, almost never regrow. So it would be a major contribution to medicine if one could stimulate nerve repair, and this is what these scientists found out how to do.

I won't try to explain the technology. The basic approach is to put a "cuff" around the damaged area of the nerve and charge it up with a direct-current electrical field supplied by a battery. If you do this just right (the devil, as always, is in the details) the nerve can repair itself, at least partially.

In contrast to the cold-fusion scientists (see Chapter Nine), these guys took the right approach from the start. They worked very carefully to achieve scientific credibility. They ran tightly controlled experiments on rats and other unsuspecting furry friends, and published fifteen or twenty papers in very reputable scientific journals. They used outside testing labs to establish objective evaluation of their results. They assembled a scientific advisory board with two Nobelists on it. Even when they achieved partial restoration of motor function in animals with severed spinal cords—a spectacular accomplishment—they heroically refrained from calling in the news media.

When they came to me they were ready to take the next step. You must understand that taking any kind of new medical treatment to the market is a *very* slow, difficult, and expensive proposition. You can't just jump out and start peddling it to doctors. The FDA makes you do extensive testing in animals, then in people, and assemble immense tomes of data on the results. This is not the kind of business that can be financed on a shoestring.

What has to be done in this business is staged financing. You take it one step at a time: Raise some money; use it to meet a major milestone in the FDA approval process; and, with that achievement to point to, go out to raise more money for the next step.

We began by raising $200,000 to do a study in dogs. In keeping with the principle of approaching informed investors, I looked for this money from orthopedic surgeons. They see a lot of nerve injuries, appreciate more than anyone the need in the market, and are able to understand the technology.

Meanwhile, the founders, Mike and Phil, tapped into government grant money, from the National Institutes of Health and New York State. Altogether this brought in about $350,000 with which to do research.

They also recruited a third cofounder, whom I'll call Thaddeus. He had a background doing regulatory-affairs work in the pharmaceutical industry, which seemed likely to be helpful. Unfortunately, the partnership arrangements were handled very informally, and this planted the seeds of future trouble.

I was turning my attention to getting professional financing. Each time we passed another milestone in the lab, it created a need for even more money to work on the next, more expensive milestone. So I started working the deal with venture capitalists. It turned out to be a tough sale.

A lot of venture firms had burned their fingers on ill-advised investments in the early 1980s and were leery of high-tech ventures. They worried about hassles with the FDA. Of course, if this had been biotech . . . but it wasn't.

Venture capitalists are ungulates, and get very nervous about straying far from the herd.

A further problem with the venture people was that American Biointerface's founders didn't have heavyweight credentials. All they had were results. We were handicapped by the previous history of electrically stimulated nerve repair. The basic idea isn't new at all, but early, crude attempts had raised false hopes and then failed.

There was nothing we could do but plug along and keep improving our scientific credibility. Gradually acceptance came. The people out there in the universities began to get enthusiastic about our work. Our experiments in animals were so successful that the FDA authorized clinical trials in humans. The Mayo clinic became one site for testing our method, and the top nerve-repair expert in Japan approached us with an offer to do clinical trials in that country.

Meanwhile, trouble was brewing at home. Thaddeus was becoming a problem. He didn't make much of a technological contribution; worse, we found him to have a negative, distrustful personality. He came across very poorly with the venture capitalists.

This kind of personality mismatch is not uncommon in founder teams. Often you have to seek an amicable parting of the ways when somebody doesn't work out. That's tricky at best, and much worse when it's never been made quite clear who owns what. Mike and Phil had understood that Thaddeus was to get 15 percent of the initial equity. Thaddeus thought he merited a larger cut; when he complained, Mike, who had his mind on other, pressing concerns, incautiously muttered something along the lines of, "Don't worry, we'll take care of you."

When we realized that Thaddeus had to depart if the company was to progress, and broached the subject to him, all these mutual misconceptions surfaced. There were various claims and counterclaims about verbal promises. The one thing that was sure was that unanimous consent of the partners was required to do anything important—like sell stock or make changes on the board of directors. So Thaddeus was in a position to paralyze the venture.

If only we could have put a nerve cuff on the founding team. As it was, it took five weeks of practically full-time negotiation, and $20,000 the company couldn't spare, to change the bylaws and settle accounts with Thaddeus. His departure put us in a position to get moving again.

Our current focus is on generating interest in the big pharmaceutical companies. They have the money to back the research and, more important, they have the marketing channels to get the product out to the medical community when it finally gets FDA approval. Whether we'll succeed or not, I don't know. But when you have something that meets an important need in the market, you have to believe in it. That's entrepreneurship.

HDS

APPENDIX

ASSORTED UNAVOIDABLE TOPICS

Nobody but a lawyer can tell legal from illegal, and the lawyers can't tell right from wrong anymore.

Larry Niven and Jerry Pournelle, *Oath of Fealty*

Here we offer some advice on various technical and legal issues that come up in building a new company. These topics range from the boring to the unpleasant, but this book wouldn't be complete if we skipped them.

STRUCTURING THE COMPANY

There are five simple ways to structure a company, and many more-complicated structures. Because corporate and tax law are in constant flux, you should consult your attorney and accountant before committing yourself.

The Sole Proprietorship. The sole proprietorship is the oldest and simplest form of business organization. You simply run the business out of your own pocket. You are the sole owner; at any time you can transfer funds freely into or out of the business from your personal assets. Setting up legally is very simple; usually it's a matter of getting a DBA ("doing business as") or similar form from the state. Its simplicity and convenience make this the usual form for the micro-business. But if you're planning to expand much, the sole proprietor-ship can lead to problems. Because there is no solid distinction between the assets of the business and your personal assets, liabilities of the business are your personal liabilities. Creditors can attach your house, car, or bank account if the company's funds are inadequate to pay them. Since you, as the owner, are personally subject to unlimited liability for the company's obligations, you will probably want to use this structure only if you intend to run very conservatively, with little or no debt.

The Partnership. The ordinary partnership simply combines the assets of two or more individuals in the business. You and your partner(s) can define your relationship pretty much any way you wish; just write the partnership agreement to specify how much capital is contributed by each partner, the assignment of duties, and distribution of the profits. Note, however, that the partnership is similar to the proprietorship in that each partner has unlimited liability for the company's obligations. What's worse, each partner remains liable even if debts are incurred by another partner without authorization. Because of the high risk resulting from this rule, partnerships, which were very common a century ago, now are limited mostly to legal, accounting, and other professional firms that have special reasons for using this form of organization. If you decide to go into partnership, you had better select someone you've known for a long time and be *very* confident of your partner's integrity. There's an old joke: "We went into partnership on the basis that I would supply the money and he would supply the experience. Sure enough, six months later he had the money and I had the experience."

The Limited Partnership. In a limited partnership, some of the partners are "limited"—that is, their liability for the company's obli-gations is limited to the amount they invested. There must be at least one "general" partner, however, who is fully exposed. The limited partners are forbidden to participate in the company's management. Limited partnerships used to be popular because they offered certain tax advantages; changes in tax law abolished most of their tax-shelter capabilities, so they are not seen so often now.

The Corporation. The simple corporation should be regarded as the default for company organization; this is the form to use should you have no good reason to do otherwise. A corporation, as the word implies (derived from *corpus,* the Latin word for "body"), is an artificial person with a separate existence for legal, tax, and economic purposes. Thus investors lose no more than they invest; they have limited liability. (Hence the British "Ltd.," or "Limited.")

A corporation is not hard to set up. Cheap do-it-yourself kits are available, but you'd better spend a few hundred bucks and have a lawyer take care of it. (If that's a lot of money for your company, you're probably too small to incorporate; try a sole proprietorship instead.) There are some formalities—generally you have to have a board of directors, even if it's only yourself, and hold meetings for the record. Be sure to follow the rules or you may have tax troubles or other legal problems.

There is one important point that is not as commonly understood as it should be. The limited liability conferred on investors by the corporate form applies only to conventional business debts. If the corporation goes bankrupt, the creditors cannot take their pound of flesh out of the personal assets of the stockholders. But the limited liability does *not* cover criminal or improper actions. The corporate form does not automatically protect the management of the company from lawsuits directed against them personally.

The S Corporation.

Because a corporation has the privileges of a separate existence, it also has the responsibilities—in particular, it must pay taxes on its income, that is, its profits. This means that the return of the investors is taxed twice—once as profits of the corporation, and once as dividends to them. The S corporation allows small businesses, under certain circumstances, to avoid this double taxation. The corporate form remains, with its limited liability, but the profits are treated directly as income to the stockholders for tax purposes and are free of the corporate income tax. There are certain restrictions, and some states do not recognize S corporation status for state income taxes. Talk it over with your attorney and accountant. The S corporation can be a valuable expedient for the small but established and steadily profitable company, allowing the cash cow to be milked with minimal losses to Uncle Sam. For growth companies, this structure is usually inadvisable.

In some states there's a form called the "limited liability company," which is similar to the S corporation but more flexible. However, this form is new and many legal and tax issues haven't been decided yet.

❖ ❖ ❖ ❖

Before you decide on a form for your business get together with your lawyer and go over your plans very carefully. Remember, keep it simple. Usually one of the five forms above will do. The paperwork, meetings, and negotiations required by more complex organizations can seriously drain you of your energy and your time, as will legal and accounting fees of your money. Be wary of advice that a more complicated approach will offer big tax advantages.

> One start-up was organized as a limited partnership, of which the general partner was a corporation. Stock in the corporation was held by the founders and by another corporation, the stock of which was sold to employees. The alleged tax benefits of this structure never came to fruition because the company never made a profit. Perhaps it would have, if setting up and maintaining all this apparatus hadn't used up so much management time.
>
> Another Enterprise Forum presenter, with less than $1 million in sales, had issued common stock, warrants, and three classes of preferred stock—in addition to setting up an R&D limited partnership. This mess was a serious handicap in raising new capital.

IF YOU INCORPORATE

If you incorporate, your lawyer will probably suggest you use a set of standard, "canned" bylaws. Don't do it. Bylaws can be revised later, but it's a rather tricky proposition—and may require the cooperation of the directors or stockholders who are the problem that made you want the revision in the first place. Before you approve a set of bylaws, try to foresee problems that may come up. Often an entrepreneur prefers bylaws that give the controlling stockholder—himself—almost unrestricted power; this is feasible in some states. Sometimes, after his holdings have been diluted by later financings, he is ejected and finds "his" bylaws now work against him. It's best to have rules that protect the interests of minority stockholders—you may be one someday. Besides, prospective investors are likely to insist on such protection anyway. Find a balance between restrictions so tight that flexibility is lost and looseness that results in vagueness and conflict.

Try to set the size of your board of directors at five or seven. A small company seldom needs a larger board. Some states will let you get away with two, or even one. But be careful—what if you desperately need extra members in the future?

Make provision for the removal of directors. The time may come when it is crucial to get rid of a dissident without waiting for the next annual meeting.

Officers should be specified carefully and their duties taken seriously. *These are legally meaningful titles.* The people who hold them are responsible for the assigned duties and can be sued if they fail to perform them properly. If you make your spouse Secretary or Treasurer, you may not be doing him or her a favor!

Make absolutely sure the minutes of your board meetings are properly kept. They may figure in an IRS audit or a lawsuit.

HOW TO STAY OUT OF COURT

The first principle of business law is that invoking the law is to be avoided at almost any cost. Ambrose Bierce defined a lawsuit as a process that you go into as a pig and come out of as a sausage. And the legal system is much worse now than it was at the turn of the century. Anyone who lives in a large city is aware that the criminal justice system has pretty much broken down. You may not realize, however, that civil law is in just as bad a shape.

Lawyers used to tell their clients that justice was slow and uncertain. Now it's even slower, but more certain—more certain to produce an unjust outcome. Juries routinely decide cases on "Poor-Fellow Theory" (if the "little guy" gets hurt, *somebody* must pay, regardless of responsibility) and award damages on "Deep-Pockets Theory" (whoever has or seems to have a lot of money pays, whether at fault or not).

In response to the breakdown of the legal system, the business community has gradually developed an alternative: the use of negotiated settlements and arbitration. The threat of lawsuit is still used, but mostly in the way the threat of nuclear attack is used in international relations.

You can generally stay out of court by following a few simple rules.

1. *Deal with honest people.* As we mentioned in Chapter Three, Providence, which gave the rattlesnake its rattle to warn us of its poisonous fangs, has similarly equipped dishonest people with a danger sign. Crooks, no matter how hard they try to appear honest, invariably suggest some sort of shady or off-color transaction early in their acquaintance with you. They literally cannot help it.

When I was in graduate school, the chess club went to the Oregon State
Penitentiary for a match with the convicts' club. My opponent, when he got
into a bad position, tried to move a knight diagonally. It was inconceivable that
I would overlook the "error," but he just couldn't help himself. It was an
interesting lesson in criminal psychology.

REM

It really pays to investigate important business associates before
you make heavy commitments. Always check references for job applicants. Look into the backgrounds of your cofounders very carefully
before you accept them. Check out the history and credit record of a
customer before you ship that big order. You don't have to be a prig,
but do keep in mind that people whose overt behavior is just a little
off-color sometimes turn out to be really nasty on closer acquaintance.

2. *Get it in writing in advance.* This applies to contracts, sales
agreements, employee relations—anything that may have important
consequences. If you go into a court case relying on your memory of
a conversation you're dead meat. Even if a formal legal document is
not needed, get it down on paper; that way everyone knows exactly
what was decided.

It's a good habit to use an appointment book or a diary. Every
day jot down notes on what was said and done; never can tell when
you might need to prove an alibi.

3. *Always use an arbitration clause.* Before you sign a contract
or agreement, put in "Any disagreement between the parties shall be
settled by arbitration under the auspices of the American Arbitration
Association." This, as your attorney will inform you, is by no means
foolproof; but it helps—and if the other party resists, watch out!

4. *Don't put temptation in people's way.* Again and again, when
previously honest people are convicted of embezzlement, pilferage, or
other crimes, they say in court, "I never did anything like that before,
but when I saw how *easy* it would be . . ." Trust is nice. Trust the
other players—but always cut the cards.

5. *Don't let small problems become big ones.* Few lawsuits begin
with one big offensive tort coming out of the blue. More commonly a
misunderstanding becomes a disagreement, a disagreement an argument, an argument a feud. Pretty soon the writs and subpoenas are
flying. When a conflict arises, resolve it early.

6. *Don't rely too much on contracts.* There's ultimately no such
thing as an ironclad contract. If the terms become too onerous for the
other party, there's generally *some* way for it to wiggle out—legally or

not. In such a case, you're almost always better off renegotiating or settling than trying to force compliance.

DEALING WITH THE GOVERNMENT

Every year it gets more difficult to run a business. Laws are passed, regulations appear, court rulings are laid down. Today, almost anything you do in business involves legal hassles with the government. Zoning, building permits, fire department inspections, OSHA, sales tax collection, payroll deductions, workers compensation, business permits, licensing—for even the most simple and harmless business, the list is almost endless. If you are involved in a regulated industry—and more and more industries are becoming regulated—the restrictions and harassment are an order of magnitude worse. It is important to understand that all this is *intentional*. Small companies cause a lot of trouble for their large corporate competitors, and the purpose of government regulation is to restore the advantages of size.

The government is like a water buffalo. Testy, clumsy, and enormously powerful, it can do a lot of damage even on the rare occasions when its intentions are good. The best way to deal with government at all levels is to stay out of its way as much as possible. It's a shame to have to say this, because if businesspeople were more courageous and regularly stood up to the bureaucrats our nation would be a much healthier and wealthier place. However, what would be good for the nation would generally be fatal for the small business!

Where small businesses usually go wrong is in thinking that the government is sincere. Since the stated purpose of an agency is to promote workplace safety or reduce pollution, you may fall into the trap of assuming that since you run a safe or nonpolluting operation you will be okay, without the trouble of reading all those complex regulations. Wrong. The only thing that counts is being in compliance with the letter of the law. Watch out for some common pitfalls.

▪ *Tax violations.* When your business gets desperately short of cash, it can be awfully tempting to delay—just for a few days—your payroll-tax withholding payments. Forget it. The IRS is *mean*. It will wipe out your business without the slightest compunction. If it fails to collect from a corporation, it will come down on its managers, directors, stockholders, or the lady who stepped into your office to ask directions to the bus stop. Pay the IRS *first*. If you can't pay, run for it. It's said that Paraguay may be safe.

■ *Pollution*. One good thing about being a new company is that you can start with a clean slate. Some big companies have crud in their backyards that dates back a century or more, and now they have to try to clean it up. You, on the other hand, can start clean and stay clean. It won't be easy, but in view of the current paranoia about pollution, it's a good policy. Keep in mind that when you hire someone to come and haul away your waste, that does *not* end your responsibility. If she dumps it in the river and disappears, the EPA will come down on *you*. And note that strict regulations can apply to many things you may not think of as "chemicals"—copying machine toner, nail polish remover, salt, things like that.

■ *Safety*. A good record is no protection. You should be fanatical about the safety of your employees—because it's the right thing to do. But it will not excuse you from the paperwork requirements—from warning labels to formal training of workers to Material Safety Data Sheets.

And of course we haven't even mentioned the hassles you'll find yourself in dealing with antidiscrimination and affirmative action rules, pension plan rules, health insurance rules, workers compensation rules, and so on.

How can you minimize this sludge and stay out of trouble? Here are a few suggestions:

■ *Stay small*. Many—not all!—regulations have small-business exemptions. Typical cut-in points are fifteen or fifty employees. If you have high-growth ambitions, you won't want to stop, of course. But if you just want to grow a little bigger, you might consider jobbing out some operations to keep your head count low.

■ *Demonstrate intent to comply*. Never say you can't; never say you won't. The bureaucrats give top priority to scofflaws.

■ *Don't argue the standards*. Unless you can clearly demonstrate that the bureaucrat is violating the law, don't argue; even then, think twice. Most regulations give very great discretion to the regulators; the agency writes the regulations, interprets them, and enforces them. The agency is judge, jury, and executioner and the business seldom has any recourse.

DEALING WITH THE INSURANCE CRISIS

Closely related to regulatory problems is the issue of insurance. You need many different kinds of insurance for even a small company, ranging from workers compensation to liability. A good independent agent can simplify your life amazingly by handling all these needs. A small company usually has a special need for expert assistance in selecting insurers because of insurance redlining: refusal to insure certain kinds of companies, especially small ones.

I'll never forget an incident that occurred when I had just started Reaction Design Corporation. We wanted to buy liability insurance. I made an appointment with an agent from one of the nation's top business-insurance companies. He walked in the door and looked around the laboratory. His first words were, "This is a chemical company." I said, "That's right." He said, "We don't insure chemical companies." Then he turned on his heel and walked out.

REM

Small companies are at an inherent disadvantage in getting insurance because they represent small risk pools. Here are a few suggestions.

- *Analyze your risks.* Here's where a good independent insurance agent can make a real contribution. All insurance consists of playing the odds. It's much like playing poker—if you don't know the odds and the payoffs, you'll get fleeced.

- *Have a risk-control program.* Insurers are usually happy to help you reduce your exposure, and thus your premium. Locks, alarms, a sprinkler system and other fire protection—often a small investment in precautions can result in substantial savings on insurance. There are also steps you can take to reduce your liability exposure. Again, consult your agent. Ask the insurer to send a risk-control adviser to inspect your company.

- *Buy only the coverage you need.* Insurance policies are often loaded with special coverage items that sound good but actually represent minimal risk. Don't pay for coverage unless you see a real need for it from your risk analysis. Beware of impulse buying.

- *Use high deductibles.* Although insurance companies publicly bitch and moan about multimillion-dollar settlements, most of their payouts go for the myriad of smaller claims. You can often save a lot of money by taking the highest possible deductible. Remember, the purpose of insurance is not to pay for every loss but to cover the catastrophic loss.

- *Go naked until you have something to cover.* A small company with a chronic cash shortage is not a very attractive target. You probably don't need heavy liability coverage at this stage. In fact, if you pay a fortune for a big liability policy, you may just be painting a bull's-eye on your company.

READING LIST

ENTREPRENEURSHIP HOW-TO

Baty, Gordon W. *Entrepreneurship in the Nineties*. Reston, Va.: Reston, 1990. The bible of Route 128.

Morrison, Robert S. *Handbook for Manufacturing Entrepreneurs*. Cleveland, Ohio: Western Reserve Press, 1973. A heavy tome with detailed advice—from the horse's mouth.

Putt, William D., ed. *How to Start Your Own Business*. Cambridge, Mass.: MIT Press, 1974. A collection of essays on special topics in entrepreneurship.

Rich, Stanley R., and David Gumpert. *Business Plans That Win $$$*. New York: Harper & Row, 1985. Covers the entire start-up process, not just business plans; first-rate.

Schollhammer, Hans, and Arthur H. Kuriloff. *Entrepreneurship and Small Business Management*. New York: Wiley, 1979. A solid and useful textbook, though the style is a bit dry.

Vesper, Karl H. *New Venture Strategies*. Englewood Cliffs, N.J.: Prentice-Hall, 1980. One of very few books that discuss how entrepreneurs come up with venture ideas.

White, Richard M. *The Entrepreneur's Manual*. Radnor, Penn: Chilton, 1977. Very readable but now rather dated. Good sections on market analysis and stock-distribution plans.

TRUE STORIES OF BUSINESS

Dessauer, John H. *My Years With Xerox: The Billions Nobody Wanted*. New York: Manor Books, 1971.

Frieburger, Paul, and Michael Swaine. *Fire in the Valley*. Berkeley, Calif.: Osborne-McGraw-Hill, 1984.

Levy, Steven. *Hackers*. Garden City, N.Y.: Anchor Press, 1984.

Rogers, Everett M., and Judith K. Larsen. *Silicon Valley Fever*. New York: Basic Books, 1984.

GENERAL MANAGEMENT

Drucker, Peter F. *The Effective Executive*. New York: Harper & Row, 1966. Though intended for big-business executives, this book has much to teach the entrepreneur.

Drucker, Peter F. *Management: Tasks, Responsibilities, Practices*. New York: Harper & Row, 1974. Still a classic.

Grove, Andrew S. *High Output Management*. New York: Random House, 1983.

Holtz, Herman R. *Profit-Line Management*. New York: AMACOM, 1981. Management advice with a much stronger hands-on orientation than most books on the subject.

PERSONAL DEVELOPMENT

Bolles, Richard N. *The 1992 What Color Is Your Parachute?* Berkeley, Calif.: Ten Speed Press, 1992. This perennial best-seller is aimed at job hunters, but we recommend the self-analyses described here for prospective entrepreneurs too.

Lakein, Alan. *How to Get Control of Your Time and Your Life*. New York: Signet, 1973.

Molloy, John T. *Dress for Success*. New York: Warner Books, 1976. Also: *The Woman's Dress for Success Book*. Milwaukee: Follett, 1977. How to look your best when you go out to meet with investors—and, sometimes, customers.

Molloy, John T. *Molloy's Live for Success*. New York: William Morrow, 1981. Also: *How to Work the Competition Into the Ground and Have Fun Doing It*. New York: Warner Books, 1987. Good advice and fun reading too.

Pearson, Durk, and Sandy Shaw. *Life Extension: A Practical Scientific Approach*. New York: Warner Books, 1982. Also: *The Life Extension Companion*. New York: Warner Books, 1984. How to keep healthy when you're under stress, and a lot more.

Shimer, Porter. *Fitness Through Pleasure*. Emmaus, Penn.: Rodale Press, 1982.

SPECIAL TOPICS

Breen, George, and A. B. Blankenship. *Do-It-Yourself Marketing Research, Third Edition*. New York: McGraw-Hill, 1990.

Deming, W. Edwards. *Quality, Productivity, and Competitive Position*. Cambridge, Mass.: MIT Center for Advanced Engineering Study, 1982. Rambling, disorganized, and brilliant discourse by the father of modern quality control.

Drucker, Peter F. *Managing for Results*. New York: Harper & Row, 1964. Contains some excellent ideas on cost analysis.

Konold, William G. *What Every Engineer Should Know About Patents,* Second Edition. New York: Marcel Dekker, 1989.

Lesko, Matthew. *Lesko's New Tech Sourcebook*. New York: Harper & Row, 1986. If you are looking for technology-based opportunities (and maybe even if you're not) this book may stimulate some ideas. Information sources and key industry experts are listed, complete with names, addresses, and phone numbers.

Luther, William M. *How to Develop a Business Plan in 15 Days*. New York: AMACOM, 1987. Badly mistitled, this book emphasizes not speed but thoroughness. A good place to find all the intimate details of grinding out financial projections, statistical market analyses, and so on.

Merrill, Ronald E., and Gaylord E. Nichols. *Raising Money*. New York: AMACOM, 1990. Complete coverage of the financing process in detail, from writing the business plan to negotiating the deal.

Morris, Jane K., Susan Isenstein, and Anne Knowles, eds. *Pratt's Guide to Venture Capital Sources*. Needham, Mass.: Venture Economics, 1990. Basic reference book with names and addresses of financing sources, as well as essays on how to approach them and deal with them.

Robert Morris Associates. *Statement Studies*. (Annual). This basic reference provides values of various financial ratios for about 300 different lines of business.

Stone, Robert. *Successful Direct Marketing Methods,* Fourth Edition. Chicago: Crain Books, 1988. Essential if you plan to use direct marketing; even if you don't, it teaches you a lot about marketing.

Westwick, C. A. *How to Use Management Ratios,* Second Edition. Brookfield, Vt.: Gower Publishing Co., 1989.

ENTREPRENEURSHIP AND SOCIETY

Gevirtz, Don. *Business Plan for America*. New York: G. P. Putnam, 1984.

Gilder, George. *Wealth and Poverty*. New York: Basic Books, 1981. Also: *The Spirit of Enterprise*. New York: Simon and Schuster, 1984.

Sowell, Thomas. *Ethnic America*. New York: Basic Books, 1981.

INDEX

accountants
   production cost control and, 179–182
   report structure built by, 239–240
   selection of, 74–75
advertising
   big- and small-business, 106, 107
   help-wanted, 66
   market opportunities in, 29
   methods of, 138–140
airplane maintenance business, 251–252
Apple Computer, 39
arbitration, 292
attorneys, *see* lawyers

balance sheet, 220
bank financing, 266–267
board of directors, *see* directors
break-even analysis, 183–184
budget system, 230–231
business plan
   circulation of, 255–256
   cosmetics of, 254–255
   executive summary of, 255
   "five-paragraph," 249–251
   length of, 255
   mistakes in writing, 252–254, 256–257
buying a business, 30–32

cash flow
   breakeven of, 259–260
   growth and, 215–216
   payment terms and, 272
   projection, 208, 213–215
clinic, airport, 25–26
cofounders, 76–78

competition
   investigating, 89, 99–101
   "monopoly" needed against, 44–45
computerization, 242–244
consulting
   fee-setting for, 26
   manufacturing business derived from, 201–202
   naming business for, 141
contracts, 110, 292
control of business, 261–262, 283
corporate form, 288–289, 290–291
corporate partners, 269–270
cost-cutting, 182–183
craft businesses, 25, 54–55
culture, company, 78–80, 234–235
customers
   attitudes toward different purchases of, 116–117
   business judged by, 49
   entrepreneur's attitude toward, 10
   financing and market information from, 271–272

DBA ("doing business as"), 288
deal structure, 280–283
delegation, 56–57, 61, 228–229
Dell Computer, 39
depreciation, 209, 212–213
direct marketing, 119, 126–128
directors, 75–76, 283, 290–291
distribution, 125–134
distributors, 130–131
Dun & Bradstreet (D&B), 3, 99

employees
   advantages of not having, 36, 55, 294

employees *(continued)*
  compensation of, 72–73
  controlling hiring of, 61–62
  development of, 62
  hiring process for, 63–72
  honesty of, 241–242, 292
  motivation of, 69, 72–73, 230–231,
    235–238
employers, breaking with, 20–21
employment contracts, 21, 283
entertainment, selling of, 118
entrepreneurs
  academic model of, 4
  involuntary, 19–20
entrepreneurship
  advantages of, 4
  disadvantages of, 2–3
  entry into, 18–19
  qualities needed for, 5–7
  management and, 8
  preparation for (checklist), 21
equity
  company valuation and, 281–282
  control and, 261–262·
  debt vs., 268
  preservation of by customer fi-
    nancing, 272
experience
  employees', 65
  entrepreneur's need for, 42
  needed for production, 171–172
export-import business, 30

family problems, 17, 263–264
financial projections
  balance sheet, 220
  cash flow, 213–216
  income statement, 210–213
  purpose of, 207–208
  ratio analysis to check, 220–223
  scenarios for, 223–224
financial reserves, 260
financing a business, 39, 42
  customers as best source for, 271–
    272
  debt used for, 266–268
  government money for, 268–269

market assessment by means of,
    263
  plan for, 273
  stages in, 260–261
  suppliers' assistance in, 270–271
finders, 275
flag system for problems, 242
founders, *see* cofounders
franchises, 33–34

goals, 9, 12–14, 230, 232–233
growth companies, 59–60

health worries, as business opportu-
    nity, 30
hieroglyphics business, 25

IBM, 46
ideas for business, 24–30
income statement, 210–213
information, selling of, 118–119
initial public offering (IPO), 265
innovation, 197–198
insurance, 76, 294–295
international trade, 30
inventors, 25
investors
  approaching, 277–278
  flaky, 272–273
  judging prospects with, 279
  negotiating with, 279–283
  selection of, 267

Japan
  business plans in, 247
  elevator operators in, 235
  R&D management in, 198–199

lawyers, 287
  selection of, 73–74
learning curve, 136, 172–173
leasing equipment, 269
legal problems, 20, 291–293
loans, 266–268
location, 34, 45

magazine business, 119

management
  R&D, 190–191
  skills and character for, 43–44
  styles of, 54–61
"market-driven" business, 40
marketing
  big- vs. small-business, 105–107
market research
  "bottom-up," 86–87
  competitor intelligence from, 89, 99–101
  customer characterization from, 88–90
  sales projections from, 87–88
  surveys for, 93–94, 96–98
  test-marketing as best, 95–96
  "top-down," 84–86
markets
  growth of, 36–39, 108–114
  needed for success, 42–43
  opportunities in, 28–30

names, company and product, 140–143
negotiation, 279–280
nepotism, 62–63
newsletter business, 93

officers, corporate, 291
overhead
  cost accounting and, 180–182
  personal, 16–17

P&L, *see* income statement
partnership
  legal meaning of, 288
  limited, 288
  management by, 59
patents, 200–201, 281
PERT/CPM, 193
pheromones, 27–28
planning
  financial, purpose of, 207–208
  financing, 273
  long- and short-term, 233
  R&D project, 192–195
Predicasts, 85

pricing, 45, 134–139, 271–272
product
  market stages and, 108–114
  prototype, 95
  types of, 115–122
  unique, 44–45
production
  cost control of, 179–184
  experience important in, 171–172
  jobbing out of, 173–174
professions as businesses, 25–26
"pro formas," *see* financial projections

quality
  customer perception of, 177–178, 233–234
  market opportunities and, 29
  production methods for, 177–179

ratio analysis, 220–223
recessions as opportunities, 276–277
"reconstruction" of financial statements, 32–33
regulations, 36, 293–294
reports and controls, 238–241
reps, 129–130
retirement centers business, 86, 219
risk
  business failure, 2–3
  investor perception of, 282

safety, 235, 294
sales
  closes for, 158–161
  entrepreneur's attitude toward, 26–27, 147–149
  expense of, 131–134
  follow-up and service and, 161–163
  necessity of, 147–148
  objection handling for, 152–157
  planning for, 166–167
  presentations for, 157
  process of making, 150–163
sales cycle, 91–93, 209–210, 220
salespersons
  in-house, as sales channel, 128

salespersons *(continued)*
  managing and motivating, 163–166, 236
sales projections, 87–88, 210
sales reps, 129–130
SBA and SBICs, 268–269
S corporation, 289
service, 46
  business selling, 117–118
  friendliness isn't, 28–29
social satisfaction, selling of, 121
sole proprietorship, 287–288
startup
  timing of, 39, 42
status, selling of, 119–121
stock
  apportioning of, 77–78
  preemptive rights and, 283
  "Section 1244," 282
  vesting of, 283

taxes
  buying a business and, 32–33
  payroll, 211, 293
  projection of, 209
  R&D advantage for, 189–190
technology
  advantage from, 47
  ownership of, 20
"technology-driven" business, 40

unemployment, 19–20

valuation of company, 281–282
Velcro, market for, 90
venture capitalists, 265–266, 275, 278
vesting of stock, 283
voicemail, 163

wedge, payroll, 211
working capital, 215–216

Zabar's, 15